AF531784

REDESIGNING INCLUSIVE DEVELOPMENT

REDESIGNING INCLUSIVE DEVELOPMENT

Edited by
Mrs. S. Jyothi Lakshmi
M.Com., KSOU University
National Centre for Inclusive Growth &
Development Research
Mysore (India)
&
Dr. Sunitha V Ganiger
Assistant Professor
Dept. of Studies & Research in Sociology
Tumkur University
Karnataka (India)

DISCOVERY PUBLISHING HOUSE PVT. LTD.
NEW DELHI-110 002

Published by:
Tilak Wasan

DISCOVERY PUBLISHING HOUSE PVT. LTD.
4383/4B, Ansari Road, Darya Ganj
New Delhi-110 002 (India)
Phone : +91-11-23279245, 43596064-65
Fax : +91-11-23253475
E-mail : discoverypublishinghouse@gmail.com
sales@discoverypublishinggroup.com
parul.wasan@gmail.com
web : www.discoverypublishinggroup.com

***First Edition:* 2014**

ISBN: 978-93-5056-450-9

Redesigning Inclusive Development

In Association with

Printed at:
Aditi Fine Art Press
Delhi

Foreword

India is basically a rural dominated country. Agriculture is still remains a main occupation. This agricultural sector has huge potential for growth which needs a lot of continuous investments. However, still major portion of India formers are having only small lands. In the same way urban India has also major poverty ridden region. Recent report says more than 27 per cent of urban populations are living under poverty. Even though trickle-down theory effect of economic growth works in a long run experts have felt need to focus on rapid inclusive growth and development of the poor. Indian GDP is normally and basically depending on manufacturing and service sector. More demand for manufacturing and service sector is coming from the rural end only. A report says consumption expenditure is more in urban India than rural. Hence we have to take policy decision to increase the growth in agriculture, secondary and service sector in rural areas. If agriculture growth is rapid one; manufacturing price will be reduced and inflation will be under controlled. In the same way non-form sector also is a major potential sector which absorbs most of the labour force. However it requires infusion of modern technology, huge capital, and skilled man power. Also large scale investment is required on infrastructure, communication, roads, power, etc. One of the main hurdles in the rapid inclusive growth and development of the poor population is lacuna in their social and financial inclusion. It is know that Banks have a chief role in extending banking facilities to rural areas for inclusive growth and accessibility of financial facilities to common man across the country. Even Private Banks can play a major role in reaching the needy through various measures using newly available technologies. To cater the financial services and products to the poor people, emergences of micro finance institutions have done major impacts in reaching the needy. Micro-finance institutions have survived even in the unstable political, cultural and economic growth of the country. Also banks can do some wonder like banks shall recognise a place in the village for the Ultra Small Branch. More funds are required to undertake new research activities in upcoming financial and social inclusion process. In this regard an edited volume of Mrs. Jyothi Lakshmi is highly appreciated and commendable and I wish her a great success in her endeavor.

Dr. Nanjunda
Faculty Member
UGC-CSSEIP
Mysore University
(*India*)

Preface

India's government has made 'inclusive growth' a key element of their policy platform, stating as a goal: "Achieving a growth process in which people in different walks in life...feel that they too benefit significantly from the process". (Ahluwalia, 2007). As we are aware India is essentially a rural subjugated country. Agriculture no more remains a major livelihood. Today service sector has huge potential for growth which needs a lot of continuous investments. However, still major portion of India are social and financial excluded. Recent Human Development report (2011-Provisonal) indicates India has showed mere performance in case of health, nutrition and education and social development. Even in the last Fifteen years in the state budget Government has not fixed sufficient amount of money for the holistic social development Many Government offices are running in rented buildings. Human development report (2005) also indicates poor infrastructure development in northern states. Gender and educational disparity is quite wide in many northern states. High quality education also plays a vital role in the regional development. Studies have shown that income inequality is very much linked to regional disparities. They reinforce each other's which ends in a way of total low per capita income of the state. This scenario gradually leads and perpetuates regional disparities that are what happened in the many northern state now. High level of education reinforces a high level of development as in the case of southern districts of the country. Recently concluded global investment meet has assured Corers of rupees of new foreign investment to be made in the country. In this regard inclusive growth and development has become the high priority of the policy-makers today. I am thankful to the Asian Journal of Development Matters, International journal of Social Economic Research publishing under ROAD TRUST® Mysore for permitting me to reproduce these selected articles. I am also thankful the God and other my friends for good support.

Jyothi Lakshmi. S

Content

List of Contributors

Sony Pellissery, Associate Professor, Institute of Rural Management, Anand. Gujarat - India.

M.V. Srinivasa Gowda, Adjunct Professor, National Institute of Advanced Studies, Bangalore.

Sathyanarayana, Junior Research Fellow, State Bank of Mysore Chair, DoS in Economics and Co-operation, Manasagangothri, University of Mysore, Mysore - 570006.

Nader Khedri, Department of Accounting, Aabadan Branch, Islamic Azad University, Abadan, Iran.

B. Venkatraja, Research Scholar DOS in Economics and Co-operation .University of Mysore, Mysore - 6.

M. Indira, Professor, DOS in Economics and Co-operation University of Mysore, Mysore.

Alison C., Palacios Institute of Rural Research and Development (IRRAD), Gurgaon, Haryana, India.

Pradeep K. Mehta, Institute of Rural Research and Development (IRRAD), Gurgaon, Haryana, India.

Skylab Sahu, Independent Researcher, New Delhi.

Dr. Motaleb Azari, and Assistant Professor, Payame Noor University, Iran.

Dr. Nanjunda, Dr. Dinesha, Dr. Sidda Raju and Prof. Ramesh, UGC-CSSEIP, Mysore University - India.

Roohollah Arab, Department of Studies in Commerce, University of Kerala, India.

D. Rangaswamy, Assistant Professor of Law Government Law College, Ramanagara - 571 511, Karanataka, India.

Ramesh, Associate Professor of Law, University of Mysore, Mysore, Karnataka.

Dariyoush Jamshidi, International Business School (IBS), Universiti Teknologi, Malaysia

Neda Pouradeli, Commerce Department, University of Mysore - India.

Dr. M. James Antony, Associate Professor, Department of Economics, Arul Anandar College, Karumathur - 625 514 Tamil Nadu.

S. Saravanan, Research Associate, Department of Economics, Arul Anandar College, Karumathur - 625 514 Tamil Nadu.

Gayathri, Assistant Professor, Economics Wing, Directorate of Distance Education, Annamalai University, Tamil Nadu.

P. Veerachamy, Assistant Professor, Department of Economics, Annamalai University, Tamil Nadu, 608 002.

T. R. Gurumoorthy, Department of International Business and Commerce, Alagappa University, Karaikudi, Tamil Nadu.

AR. Annadurai, Department of International Business and Commerce, Alagappa University, Karaikudi, Tamil Nadu.

Saikumar C. Bharamappanavara, Department of Agricultural Economics, Humboldt University of Berlin, Germany.

Madhulika Sahoo, Senior Research Fellow in Anthropological Survey of India, Central Regional Centre, Ministry of Culture, Government of India

Dr. Anamika Kaushiva, Economics Department, Sahu Ram Swaroop Mahila Mahavidyalay, Bareilly, Uttar Pradesh.

Hema Tripathi, Indian Veterinary Research Institute, Izatnagar (U.P.)

Jyoti Yadav, Indian Veterinary Research Institute, Izatnagar (U.P.)

C. S. Chandrika and Prof. Midatala Rani Department of Studies in Political Science, University of Mysore. Mysore.

Khalid Md. Bahauddin, Bangladesh Society of Environmental Scientists, Bangladesh.

Nayma Iftakhar, International University of Business Agriculture and Technology, Bangladesh.

1

A Critical Governance Issue for Inclusive Growth
Is 'Citizen Centric' Participation Possible?

— SONY PELLISSERY

ABSTRACT

A good number of institutions have been created at macro and meso level to promote and elicit participation since 1970s. Many of these institutions gave representation to the local elites. Thus, in the process of eliciting participation, these elites became alternative power centres to bureaucracy. However, presently these institutions are undergoing tremendous transformation due to the shifts in development aims and processes. One of the most important changes is that of 'dismantling of State' in the arena of welfare provisioning and changes which followed it. Growth of welfare provisioning by agencies other than State redefined the role of local elites in a significant way. This paper is looking-at how the role of local elites is determining the levels of participation in the new context of emergence of multiple agencies of welfare provisioning. We argue that welfare provisioning by multiple agencies will not substantially improve unless mechanisms to contain the power of elites are seriously designed and implemented by these agencies.

While governance is State's ability to bring together the institutions of civil society and market, and thus to benefit the citizens with the 'co-production' of multiple agencies, how would such a 'co-production' be beneficial to the poor people who may be in conflict with local elites, who are stake holders in multiple agencies? How could 'citizen centric participation' be possible at all when the institutions of elites perpetuated by the 'participation model of development' still remains as opposed to 'governance model of development?' Major part of this paper is devoted to sharpen these questions theoretically by examining various concepts of governance and its relation to development and welfare state. Then the analysis is carried forward to a critique of the local elites.

The literature on governance cannot bypass two important questions:

1. Why has this new term of 'governance' become important in recent times?
2. How is governance different from government?

Or does this new term substantially contribute/alter the developmental and re-distributive functions of government? In the process of answering these questions the concept gets sufficient clarification. I will attempt to answer these questions in a rather unsystematic way since the questions are often lapped.

Lexiconical meaning of the term governance has its roots in Latin and ancient Greek which refers to 'steering' – meaning very clearly the manner of governing or guiding rather than government (Jessop, 1998). In a nutshell we can state three core components of governance as:

(i) A well managed state with efficient institutions meeting basic needs of citizens.

(ii) A competitive market economy (promotion of private sector in contrast with public sector).

(iii) A democratic civil society (Archer, 1994).

Theoretically, these are result of the crossbreeding of three 'bringing back', using the buzzword of the day, attempts:

(a) Bring back state: Evans *et al*, 1985.

(b) Bring back market into development intervention: neo-liberal school.

(c) Bring back civil society to make government accountable: Putnam (1993). We will see in detail how these strands have been influential.

Unravelling the history of the concept of governance, Minogue (1999) has shown that there were conscious attempts in institution building during decolonisation period through the transfer of systems such as rule of law, neutral civil service and parliamentary democracy and they were in fact quest for good government. Decentralisation movement with its emphasis on participation in 1960s and 1970s wanted to ensure effective and efficient institutions. The reference of Huntington to the weak political institutions of developing countries as 'governments simply do not govern' (1968: p. 2) or the discourses of governability crisis (Kohli, 1990) also are referring to the concept of governance. If these were quests for improving the mode of governing, why has the term become important now?

The term governance began to be used in a new way since early 1990s. This new use is in the context of development assistance provided through the international agencies and the effective and efficient administration of the funds provided through them. Therefore, the documents of these international agencies have defined the components of good governance to a great extent. UK's Overseas Development Administration (UKODA), United

Nations Development Programme (UNDP) and World Bank (WB) have played crucial role in the development of the concept. A brief survey of the key documents by these organizations (UKODA, 1993; UNDP, 1995; World Bank, 1994) reveals common characteristics of governance: accountability, rule of law, freedom of association, political legitimacy, efficient public sector management, co-operation with institutions of civil society and transparency (see also Kauffman *et al.* 1999; Rhodes, 1997; Leftwich, 2000). However, the documents of bilateral organizations also diverge on their emphasis depending on the objectives of the organizations and their interests in providing development funds rather than defining the concept of governance as a theoretical category. The most crucial distinction is while UNDP defines governance by taking cultural pluralism into account, UKODA ignores the aspect of cultural pluralism and thinks values like democracy are universal. On a different note, WB limits itself to managerial and policy capability of a government, refraining from the question of politics because of the constitution of WB prevents it to enter any political matters of country that WB is transacting with (Minogue, 1998).

Developing on the criteria proposed by these bilateral global institutions, academics have built on theories of governance. Rhodes (1997), distinguishing the terms government and governance notes: "Governance signifies a change in the meaning of government, referring to a new process of governing; or a changed condition of ordered rule; or the new method by which society is governed" (p. 46) (also see Rhodes, 1995). Therefore, understanding what is this new condition is essential to understand the concept. Leftwich (2000) has pointed out that the role of bilateral agencies through structural adjustment lending as only one of the aspects for the rise of the concept of governance. She points out three other major influences or conditions:

1. the dominance of neo-liberalism in the West;
2. collapse of communist regimes; and
3. rise of pro-democracy movements in Eastern Europe and other developing countries.

These influencing factors on governance, and how governance is defined by bilateral agencies as conditions for lending, point out to the vital importance of the concept for any development research in the developing countries.

Though these conditions have given rise to governance, the term is not used in similar sense. Rhodes (1997) pointed out six different uses, of governance:

(i) as the minimal state (with concentration on regulatory function);
(ii) as corporate governance (collaborative effort);
(iii) as the new public management;
(iv) as 'good governance' (principles of management with equity principle as priority);

(*v*) as a socio-cybernetic system (flow of information to decision maker and decision-making system); and

(*vi*) as self-organizing networks (p. 47).

Osborne and Gaebler's (1992) *Reinventing Government* show how these characters act as conditions of a governing structure that can function effectively and efficiently. Further, the structure itself is not the important consideration. "The empirical referents of this process-based, rather than structure-based, definition of governance thus include a range of organizations, public and private, as well as the complex relationship between them" (Jayal and Pai, 2001: 14). However, how does efficiency, effectiveness and capacity of process-based network be measured and assessed?

Various facets of institutional, technical, administrative and political capacity (White, 1984; Mehta, 2000) used to be parameters to understand the goodness of government. The capacity of the State have been examined by political scientists and economists (Almond and Powell, 1996; Myrdal, 1968) using the dependent variables of ability "to *penetrate* society, regulate social relationships, extract resources, and appropriate or use resources in determined ways" (Midgal, 1988: p. 4). If the concept of capability of state was already been investigated, how does its usage improve in defining governance? From the management perspective, the answer would be as follows: World Bank, though emphasises 'sound development management' (1992:1) as the primary objective of governance, it says the function of government is "not as a direct provider of growth but as a partner, catalyst and facilitator" (1997: 1). The new capacity of state latent in the concept of governance is not 'doing' things, but ensuring that things are done (Stoker, 1998; Adironkdack, 2000) in association with market and civil society. Internal working of the public organizations and management skills were the parameter to assess the goodness of 'government'. But, the criterion to assess goodness of governance would be its networking abilities and enablement skills (Salamon, 2002). However, this tendency to de-politicise the re-distributive function of state has its own perils.

Governance and Development Issues

According to us, the newness of the concept of governance has deeper implications. It should be understood in the context of the concept of 'developmental state'. Developmental state can be defined as those states whose "political purposes and institutional structures (especially their bureaucracies) have been developmentally driven, while their developmental objectives have been politically driven" (Leftwich, 2000: 154). Developmental state is a variant of modern state, emerged in the particular socio-economic context of developing countries. In the developmental states, the politico-bureaucratic elites, who enjoyed a relative autonomy or 'embedded autonomy' (Evans, 1995), used their power to achieve a high growth rate and better scale on social indictors, often subordinating the social forces and weakening the civil society.

The literature on developmental state begins with Chalmers Johnson's (1981) works on East Asian economies. He distinguishes two types of states on the basis of their development orientation:

1. The states that plan the economy from an ideological/rational aim with clear targets of socio-economic goals for private sector.
2. The states that merely regulate the other sectors (providing a framework for private sector allowing them to pursue their own goals) (see also Leftwich, 2000: 157).

According to Johnson (1995) this method was successful in the countries like Japan where the elite bureaucracy achieved national objectives.

However, the experiment of the developmental state was not universally successful. In the countries like India, the same practice of developmental state failed (Herring, 1999) due to the size of the country, which was beyond bureaucracy's capability for penetration and subjected to private interests. Factional politics with multi-party system putting pressure from below through various social forces compelled the political-bureaucratic elite to compromise on its developmental vision (Weiner, 1989; Kothari; 1990). The ambivalent results of the experiments of developmental state (strong bureaucracy and weakening of civil society institutions; high growth rate, often through private sector performance, without convincing evidence of 'trickle down') necessitated a revision of the developmental state by keeping the factors producing good results intact and by correcting the deficiencies. Looking from this perspective, the characteristics of governance, which we discussed above, can be seen as extension of developmental state:

(i) Accountability and transparency are the means to improve the bureaucracy (which was very powerful and 'oversize' in the developmental state).

(ii) The emphasis on the networking of the state with private sector is a strategy of involving private sector (which was restricted to pursue profit goals or narrowly defined social goals in the developmental state), for attaining the development goals especially within the fiscal constraints of developing countries to meet the re-distributive objectives.

(iii) Importance for civil society (which was stifled in some of the developmental states) as a mechanism of checking 'agenda setting' by elite bureaucracy of the state.

Recognition of the multiple agencies in the responsibility of development and welfare has given rise to what is known as welfare pluralism (Cook and White, 2001: 25). This has important implications for governance in the welfare states.

Governance in the Welfare State

The existence of multiple agencies, in addition to the state's major welfare services, has been pointed out in the welfare literature (Titmus, 1955;

Mackintosh, 1995). These non-state institutions have generally been pointed out as 'market and civil society institutions'. At the same time concern has been expressed that the net benefit of these multiple agencies are in favour of dominant class in the society (Papadakis and Taylor-Gooby, 1987) as they are likely to have membership or linkages with various organizations and poor would largely depend on the state provisions (Harris-White, 1995; 1999).

It is in this context of unequal availability of various welfare institutions to the citizens, the new role of the state in the context of governance emerges. "The state plays a leading role in integrating economic and welfare institutions and in utilising the market, community and public sector" (Midgley, 1995: 10). This *managed pluralism* implied shift for research focus. The unit of analysis, which used to be public agency in the traditional welfare research, now need to be the "tool through which public purposes are pursued" (Salamon, 2002: 2).

Nation-state functioned on the basis of a 'political contract', which was created through a constitution or conventional practice of a government to which citizens expressed their consent or dissent through their votes. In the traditional welfare state, this 'political contract' gave the responsibility of development to the state. In such a context, other important organs of nation-state – civil society, private sector and local authority – did not have (or was not required) space to engage in the activities of development when government took the responsibility of the welfare of its citizens. In the paradigm of governance, a "formal outcome of a new configuration of institutions resulting in a new social contract and redefining the pluralistic state in the constitution" is ushered (Hye, 2000: p. 7 emphasise is not in original). This clarifies important confusion that has been created by governance discourse in terms of the state's role. As Hirst (2000) puts, though the state's role, as direct provider is redundant, its role as 'orchestrator of social consensus' has been enhanced.

For example, in pluralistic societies like India, where backwardness is linked with socio-ethnic backgrounds of scheduled castes (15.75% of population) and scheduled tribes (7.75%) the state designs policies of positive discrimination for welfare functions. These policies have been source of conflict and disruption of social cohesion (Srinivas, 1966; Beteille, 1998) since they come on the way of larger population. The state's ability to reduce these cleavages in co-ordinating with other welfare institutions would be parameters for judging the goodness of governance in the context of welfare pluralism.

In this 'self-organization of inter-organizational relations' (Jessop, 1998: 33), negotiations and pursuing rather than command and control (Salamon, 2002) becomes methods. But, the power dependence involved in the relationships of involved institutions (Stoker, 1998) cannot be ignored by the state. An independent identity for the bodies of media, trade unions, professional people, NGOs, cultural bodies and social welfare organizations was existent even without the framework of governance. In the framework of governance, an autonomy for these institutions as well as the mutual relationship as a collectivity is stressed.

Theoretically, the importance attached to civic organizations as welfare provider is because civic organizations are presumed to be emanating from the collective action of individuals and groups in a society (Robinson and White, 1997). Ideologically, this alternative political space, created by civil society, outside usual arenas of party and government, though not outside state (Kothari, 1984) is supposed to be efficient and effective than the state machinery itself.

The studies into welfare pluralism involving the sectors of state, market and NGOs are emerging in the industrialized countries and they are negligibly low in developing countries (Wuyts *et al.* 1992; Harriss-White, 1999; Mwabu *et al.* 2001). Even the existing studies have country focus and local governance in the context of welfare pluralism is not at all researched. It is at local level the dynamic interactions of various institutions and organizations become more visible leading to important welfare policy reconsiderations.

Governance, Decentralisation and Participation

The concept of local governance is closely associated with the theory and practice of decentralisation. Therefore, it is essential to review these concepts first. I will first review the origin and application of the concept of decentralisation. Then, I will narrate the experience of decentralised governance in India.

Huntington (1968) suggests that the modernization paradigm with centralised planning considered authoritarian regimes and large bureaucracies as essential components of fast paced development. Efficient and economic allocation of scarce resources was the rationale for this. The dominant paradigm prevalent at this time in the public sector was the Keynesian model of planned growth. Simultaneously, in the private sector, mass production following Fordism was successful. However, both these models underwent radical changes in the late 1970, giving way to planning from below in public sector and organizational restructuring through managerial delegation in private sector. Hambleton and Hoggett (1990) have argued that as the state is becoming more managerial by its nature, changes in the private sector are adopted to deliver public services. However, this argument does not satisfactorily answer the issues of democratisation process, which is a corollary of local government empowerment.

It is increasingly being realised that decentralisation is not a politically neutral concept (Rondinelli, 1981; Conyers, 1986; Ckagnazaroff, 1993) as seen in the managerial state. Origin of the concept, along with its counterpart participation, is clearly political. The concept of participation emerges in the post World War II scenario in the industrialised countries as a demand for political space and representation by the public. The concept of participation received more popularity due to its association with poor people's movements (Piven and Cloward, 1977) and decentralisation was a demand for organizational space for participation. This became 'bottom-up' development strategy in 1970s. However, earlier studies showed that though there were signals of 'participation', genuine participation did not take place from most desired arenas due to low levels of education, mass poverty, cultural barriers, poor communication and lack of technical capacity (Lipset, 1959; Huntington, 1965; Huntington and Nelson, 1976).

Participation is catergorised in to two types according to the approach:

1. The functional approach (emphasising instrumental benefits of participation) was easy to be promoted. Often, central authority may use participation in individual projects and decentralisation of power as a tool to legitimise its own control over power blocs in a state by giving token 'ad hoc' functions to them (Ckagnazaroff, 1993; Robinson, 1998).
2. Political approach (considering empowerment of poor as starting point (Oakley *et al.* 1991)) was considered to be more radical and difficult to be elicited. However, both these approached became piecemeal in reality, and is well evidenced is the comment of Smith *et al.* (1977): "Participation can easily be a trap, by diverting protest and energies into empty consultative structures while the real decisions are taken elsewhere" (p. 237).

These real world experiences of co-option disillusioned the enthusiasm of development interventions using participation as strategy. Besides, in early 1980s, when it became a widely accepted view that a strong and technocratic government was essential for economic reforms, the participation agenda and decentralisation project got subsumed (Robertson, 1984; Robinson, 1999).

Later, in late 1980s when participation made a coming back, it merged functional approach and political approach into the 'stakeholder' concept, *i.e.*, those intended and unintended persons to be affected by proposed intervention. This gave rise to what came to be known as participatory development. OECD definition of participatory development comes very close to the concept of governance we discussed above: "Participatory development stands for a partnership which is built upon the basis of a dialogue among the various actors (stakeholders), during which the 'agenda' is set jointly, and local views and indigenous knowledge are deliberately sought and respected. This implies negotiation rather than the dominance of an externally set project agenda. Thus, people became actors instead of being simply beneficiaries" (Schneider and Libercier, 1994: 3; also see Fortin and Stiefel, 1985). With this renewed approach, as Huntington suggests (1991) participation found a revival within development agenda.

The history of 'decentralisation' had the same trajectory as participation as decentralisation was an attempt for organizational structure for participation. Etymology of the term decentralisation – 'away from centre' (Meenakshisundaram, 1999) – refers to various possible meanings and contexts in which it can be used. Rondenelli (1984) suggests four different applications of deconcentration, delegation, devolution and privatization. The two terms of deconcentration and devolution have been much treated as two sides of the same coin of decentralisation (Mawhood, 1993) in the sense that while deconcentration refers to administrative decentralisation, devolution refers to political decentralisation. But, Crook and Manor (1998) suggests that they have opposite effects. While deconcentration purely strengthens the central authority through relocating the officers at different levels, devolution installs a local authority with legal and financial legitimacy, where a great amount of power is exercised outside the control of central government. Delegation and privatization are treated as specific activities within the process of decentralisation.

Recent studies on the relationship between decentralisation and development have confirmed this when they do not show a convincing correlation (Crook and Manor, 1998; Minogue, 1998; Crook and Sverrison, 2001). These studies have reinforced the hypothesis that the explanatory variable of the success of decentralisation are deeply rooted in the local phenomenon.

A Synthesis: Critique of Local Elites

In a local area various institutions exist. Various institutions follow various rules for welfare provisioning. Etzioni (1961) identified three types of mechanisms or organizational behaviours that are used to gain compliance or cooperation: 'coercive' (control through forces of sanction), 'remunerative' (control over material resources and rewards) and 'normative' (control of symbolic rewards such as prestige, esteem). Uphoff (1993) suggests, in the context of rural development, how the state, the market and NGOs might adopt these mechanisms. Markets operate with profit making motive and individuals interact with markets as clients or customers. In such a framework, markets use remunerative mechanisms through price signals and incentives. Dealing with a NGO, an individual may be member and the NGO functions with the objective of self-help or service towards a common interest. In such a context, the chief mechanism is the normative principle. For example, the consideration for giving a loan to a poor family by a rich landlord may be the ability of the poor family to repay the loan (remunerative). But a NGO may primarily apply the normative principle of the need and secondarily give importance to the repayment of loan. In the state's services through the bureaucracy of local administration and local government, an individual is primarily citizen or voter. And the primary mechanism that the state uses is coercive, *i.e.*, the state has a certain quota of rationed resources; normative and remunerative principles can be applied only to facilitate the coercive mechanisms though there may be welfare rights for citizens.

Though the above agency-wise description is useful for analytical purposes, in close-knit communities, the resources, roles, power, norms and legitimacy all overlap in multiplex relations between individuals and organizations (*e.g.*, a poor household may relate to the same elite in his roles as political leader, landlord and volunteer in some group or religious activity at the same time) of individuals and organizations (Kabeer, 1994). Therefore, how the network between individuals in these agencies function and how the decision-makers involved in the agencies, in different roles, act differently in different relationships becomes very important. It is in this triangular tension of state forces, market forces and societal forces (see the 'shadow state' and informal economy concepts of Harriss-White, 2003; and Meier, 1992) that policy formulation and implementation takes place. Therefore, the impact of redistributive policy and provision should be investigated in a framework of institutions and public authorities responsible for its implementation. Where the agents of triangular tension intersect, *i.e.*, elites, the public authority has the potential to prevent or facilitate the policy process. As Figure 1.1 shows, the elites through the web of their network may be able to link state, market and NGO and to influence the supply of welfare provisions. On the other hand, the non-elite's linkages may be limited to individuals contacting organizations on their own (dealing with the state individually, the market individually or an NGO individually).

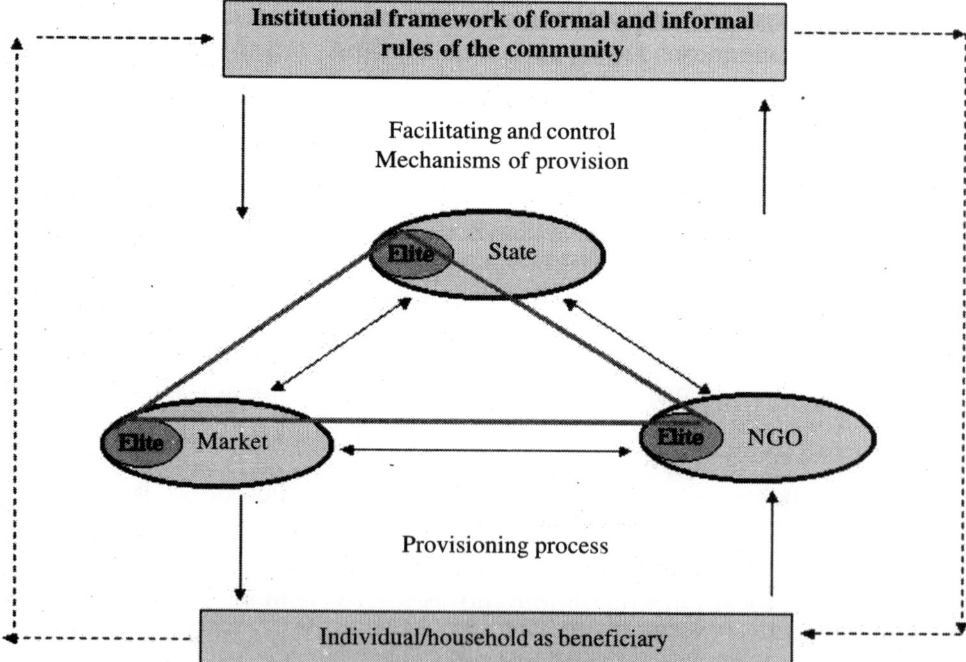

Fig. 1.1: Theoretical Mapping of Elite Influence on Welfare Provision in the Context of Welfare Pluralism

Thus, the above synthesis gives rise to the chief argument of this paper that the elite through their network and control of the organizations may be able to be the decisive force determining welfare provisioning in rural communities despite of the existence of multiple agencies and a governance structure. Therefore, the mechanisms used by the elite to facilitate or prevent provisioning in various agencies need to be researched.

The Elite and Welfare Provisioning

A good number of analytical studies (Pareto, 1935; Mosca, 1939; Mills, 1956; Miesel, 1958; Bottomore, 1966; Parry, 1969; Eldersveld, 1989) and empirical studies (Lasswell *et al.* 1952; Hunter, 1953; Dahl, 1961; Polsby, 1974; Domhoff, 1978; see Singh, 1988 for a range of Indian and international studies) on the elite have clarified the concept. Our attempt here is to reach a definition drawing on this literature (rather than to settle the controversies raised) and to briefly describe how elites could affect welfare provision.

At the heart of elite theory is the idea that in every society a few people with social status and power make decisions that affect the majority of population. This intersection of status and power in the same individuals makes them the reference points of state-society relations in a given community. It also implies that the power of the elite may not necessarily be derived from overt leadership or formal positions they hold. Therefore, elites can be seen not only in elected political positions; they will be visible in the market and NGO operation as well. In fact, the potential power because of the strategic role, control and influence through these organizations is the distinctive feature of an elite. However, the elite in modern India (or for that matter in most societies) are not merely people 'born to power and privilege' (Mitra, 1992: xiv). Various factors such as state-sponsored education, reservations policies for the backward classes, political parties recruiting lower caste cadres (Corbridge and Harriss, 2000) have helped the emergence of a substantial number of elite members from the lower strata of society.

In the context of this research the role of the elite is of crucial concern for three reasons:

(i) The elite may be strategically placed at the critical state-society intersection point and become important actors in the implementation of any provision by the state programmes to rural communities.

(ii) The nexus of wealth and power makes the elite crucial actors in the market provision of social security.

(iii) The elite as formal or informal leaders are likely to take the initiative and control of any collective action.

In a given community the elite may have multiplex relation and may have access to and control over more than one agency. This may allow them to use social security provision as a mechanism to expand their power in the community through the linkages they possess. It also allows the elite to create a network with other elite members of the community to strengthen their own position. For example, a 'market elite' person may, by using his network ability with another elite, prevent public provision or collective action needed for a poor household to serve instead the market 'interest' (*e.g.*, forcing the poor to provide labour at cheaper price at a landlord's farm, which an unemployed person might not have done if had he the opportunity to get public provision). On the other hand, a political elite person may encourage collective effort by a self-help group as long as the group interaction of the members is in his favour, and what may potentially reduce the power of the market elite on the community members.

At this juncture it is useful to identify some of the institutional mechanisms that may be used by the elite in the provisioning process.

The early studies of Lasswell (1950), Hunter (1953) and Dahl (1961) examined the power relations within the community and how they affected decision-making. Then, Smith (1974) argued that both social space and physical space have to be considered as important variables in planning for human welfare. Later, based on examples from industrialised countries Lipsky's (1980) study of 'street-level bureaucrats' made a significant contribution in terms of analysing how local institutional structures could affect access to resources. He pointed out that 'street-level bureaucrats', when they function with limited resources and stringent performance requirements, may use the discretionary power available to them to reduce the cost of decision-making, rather than to serve the stated objective of the programme. Clients experience the effects of policies through interaction with street-level bureaucrats and this in turn contributes to policy changes. Blalock (1991) has taken this discussion further and modelled the allocation process. He argues, from a behaviour-interaction perspective, that unequal resource allocation is a deliberate method to increase social inequality. The strength of the Blalock model is in integrating self-selection behaviour by the applicant, *i.e.*, applicant choosing to make claim for a particular benefit, with the administrative selection behaviour by the allocator, *i.e.*, administrator choosing from many claimants. These developments by Smith (1974), Lipsky (1980) and Blalock (1991) have probably paid too much attention to the detailed technical aspects of resource allocation, and insufficient attention to the wider power relations in society. Recent attempts to view policy through anthropological theories have shown how technical and seemingly evidence-based allocations are entrenched in power relations (Marglin and Marglin, 1990; Shore and Wright, 1997).

Based on the above literature I identify five organizational factors that may be used by the elite and other decision makers to influence differential access to resources:

1. *The Provision or the Nature of Benefit Itself can Determine the Nature of Provisioning Process:* Whether the provision is divisible between

beneficiary and decision maker, how the provision is valued by the stakeholders, whether the provision once made is revocable, whether it is a 'once-and-for-all' provision, depletion or devaluation aspects of provision are some of the variables that would determine the decision-making. A good example is when the benefit is in the form of a cash transfer, how it is directly misappropriated (probably through bribery) while food aid, because it depletes, has to be transferred to cash by selling it (needing an intermediary of shop keeper) before mis-appropriating it.

2. *Another Major Determinant is the Relationship Factor:* Whether the beneficiary is likely to share power with the decision maker in future, the nature of the mediating agency between decision-maker and beneficiary, the relationship of decision-maker with other decision makers, if any, and the need to satisfy them, are some of these factors. Often, at local level, resource allocation is used as a tool to create loyalty.

3. *The Foreseen Cost of Decision is another Important Aspect in Provisioning*: If those who are denied benefits are likely to become organized, the decision-maker might be more cautious in avoiding unequal resource allocation. For example, the apparently better state social allocation in Kerala is often attributed to people's ability to come together/organize to demand accountability from their employers (Sen, 1992). In a similar manner, if there is close surveillance over the provisioning agency there may be substantial difference in the decisions. An example would be the way donor agencies exert pressure on local NGOs (Bratton, 1980) for particular patterns of provisioning.

4. *The Structural Features of the Programme are another Important Aspect:* They include the degree of secrecy in decision-making, monopoly in supply, time and knowledge available to the decision-maker, ideological orientation, such as equity, of the decision-maker and wider society. Examining the case of the Employment Guarantee Scheme, Acharya (1990) had recommended that NGOs and trade unions should be involved in designing programmes for better service provision and to check corruption in the EGS scheme.

5. *Multiple Agency Availability*: And the size and composition of the applicant pool may also be important in differential allocation. When there are many eligible people and few resources, the decision-maker has more discretion (Lipsky, 1980). On the other hand, when there are multiple agencies providing the same or similar services, beneficiaries can exercise their choices to increase their welfare. For example, a study in Maharashtra (Herring and Edwards, 1983) revealed differential behaviour of market elite and political elite when it was reported that women preferred EGS to agricultural labour in the private sector to avoid the sexual tyrannies

of some rural elites. Women also felt a sense of dignity when receiving equal wages with men in the EGS scheme, since there was substantial gender differentiation in the private sector wages.

This brief review suggests that organizational and institutional arrangements, often created by the elite at local level leads to unequal allocation and implementation deficit even in well-intentioned and well-designed programmes. It is these organizational and institutional factors, which have not been sufficiently researched.

Conclusion

The inability of the Indian state to contain poverty despite of *(i)* centrally planned economic development (since independence) and *(ii)* redistributive policies (since 1970s) through state-led development is attributed to "the lack of autonomy of state from organized interests in society which distorted decision-making and prevented the implementation of redistributive policies" (Joseph, 2001: 1011). Development and welfare interventions have been pointed out as benefiting the local elites, rather than the intended beneficiaries, by various researchers. While, agreeing with these researches, this paper has tried to identify some of the mechanisms and pointed out the need to sharpen empirical researches in this area. Further, the paper is pointing out how the institutions of participation can be greater advantage for the elites in the era of governance.

FOOTNOTES

1. The term'embedded autonomy' is defined as "the autonomy of the well developed bureaucracies that has been embedded in a dense web of ties with both non-state and other state actors (internal and external) who collectively help to define, re-define and implement developmental objectives" (Leftwich, 2000: 162).
2. Leftwich (2000) makes a historical survey of the genesis of the thought of 'developmental state' and traces its root to Marx.
3. However, case of China is a success within the framework of'developmental state' despite its larger size than India.
4. Some scholars also consider household as separate institution.
5. At this juncture it is good to bear in mind the argument of Ckagnazaroff (1993) who points out that privatisation strategy, motif. Besides, power transferred to NGOs or local the benefits only among them), excluding certain other groups focusing.

REFERENCES

Achayra, S. (1990), *Maharashtra Employment Guarantee Scheme: A Study of Labour Market Intervention*. Delhi: ILO-ARTEP.

Adirondack, S. (2000), *The Good Governance Action Plan for Medium and Large Voluntary Organizations*. London: NCVO Publications.

Agere, S. (2000), *Promoting Good Governance: Principles, Practices and Perspectives.* London: Commonwealth Secretariat.

Almond, G.A. Powell, G.B. (eds.) (1996), *Comparative Politics Today.* New York: Harper Collins.

Archer, R. (1994), *Markets and Good Government.* In Clayton, A.(Ed.)

Beteille, A. (ed.) (1969), *Social Inequality: Selected Readings.* Middlesex: Penguin Education.

Beteille, A. (1996), *Caste, Class and Power: Changing Patterns of Stratification in a Tanjore Village.* Delhi: Oxford University Press.

Blalock, H. M. (1991), *Understanding Social Inequality: Modeling Allocation Process.* London: Sage Publications.

Boulding, K. (1989), *Three Faces of Power.* Beverly Hills: Sage Publications.

Bottomore, T.B. (1964), *Elites and Society.* Middlesex: Penguin Books.

Bratton, M. (1980), *The Local Politics of Rural Development: Peasant and Party – State in Zambia.* London: University Press of New England.

Bratton, M. (1989), "The Politics of Government – NGO Relations in Africa?" *World Development* 17 (4): 569-87.

Clayton, A. (Ed.) (1994), Governance, Democracy and Conditionality: What Role for NGOs. Oxford: Intrac Publication.

Ckagnazaroff, I. (1993), Decentralisation and Democratisation of Local Government. *Doctoral Working Paper.* No. 11. Birmingham: Aston University.

Conyers, D. (1986), Decentralisation and Development: A Framework for Analysis. *Community Development Journal,* April, 21, No. 2. pp. 88-100.

Cook, S. and White, G. (2001), Alternative Approaches to Welfare Policy Analysis: New Institutional Economics, *Politics and Political Economy.* In Mwabu, G. *et al* (eds.) pp. 26-52.

Crook, R.C. and Sverrison, A.S. (2001), Decentralisation and Poverty-Alleviation in Developing Countries: A Comparative Analysis or is West Bengal Unique? *IDS Working Paper* No. 130.

Crouch, C. (ed.) (1977, *Participation in Politics. British Political Sociology Yearbook. Vol.* 3. London: Croom Helm.

Dahl, R.A. (1961), *Who Governs: Democracy and Power in an American City.* New Haven: Yale University Press.

Domhoff, G.W. (1978), *Who Really Rules? New Haven and Community Power Reexamined.* Santa Monica: Goodyear Publishing Inc.

Eldersveld, S.J. (1989), *Political Elites in Modern Societies: Empirical Research and Democratic Theory.* Ann Arbor: The University of Michigan Press.

Etzioni, A. (1961), *A Comparative Analysis of Complex Organizations: On Power, Involvement and their Correlates.* New York: The Free Press.

Evans, P. Rueschemeyer, D. Skocpol, T. (1985), *Bringing the State back in.* Cambridge: Cambridge University Press.

Evans, P.B. (1995), *Embedded Autonomy: States and Industrial Transformation.* Princeton, N J.: Princeton University Press.

French, J. and Raven, B. (1959), The Bases of Social Power. In Cartwright, D. (ed.) pp. 150-65.

Galbraith, J.K. (1983), *The Anatomy of Power*. Boston: Houghton Mifflin.

George, V. and Wilding, P. (1984), *The Impact of Welfare*. London: Routledge and Kegan Paul.

Harriss-White, B. (1995), Economic Restructuring: State, Market and Collective and Household Action in India's Social Sector. *The European Journal of Development Research*. Vol. 7 (1) pp. 124-147.

Harriss-White, B. (1999), State, Market, Collective and Household Action in India's Social Sector. In Harriss-White, B and Subramanian, S. (eds). pp. 303-328.

Harriss-White, B. (2003), *India Working: Essays on Society and Economy*. Cambridge: Cambridge University Press.

Herring, R.J. and Edwards, R.M (1983), Guaranteeing Employment for the Rural Poor: Social Functions and Class Interests in the Employment Guarantee Scheme. *World Development* 11 (7) pp. 575-92.

Hirst, P. (2000), Democracy and Governance. In Jon Pierre (ed.).

Herring, R.J. (1999), Embedded Particularism: India's Failed Development State. In M. Woo-Cumings (ed.) pp. 306-34.

Herring, R.J. and Edwards, R.M (1983), Guaranteeing Employment for the Rural Poor: Social Functions and Class Interests in the Employment Guarantee Scheme. *World Development* 11 (7) pp. 575-92.

Hirschman, A. (1970), *Exit, Voice and Loyalty: Responses to Decline in Firms, Organizations, and States*. Cambridge: Harvard University Press.

Hirschman, A.O. (1982), *Shifting Involvements: Private Interest and Public Action*. Oxford: Martin Robertson.

Hambleton, R. and Hoggett, P. (1990), The Democratisation of Public Services. In Hambleton, R. and Hoggett, P. (Eds.) *Decentralisation and Democracy: Localising Public Services*. Bristol: School for Advanced Urban Studies. pp. 53-83.

Hunter, F. (1953), *Community Power Structure: A Study of Decision Makers*. Chapel Hill: The University of North Carolina Press.

Huntington, S.P. (1968), *Political Order in Changing Societies*. New Haven: Yale University Press.

Huntington, S.P. and Nelson, J.M. (1976), *No Easy Choice: Political Participation in Developing Countries*. Cambridge: Harvard University Press.

Hye, H.A. (ed.) (2000), *Governance: South Asian Perspectives*. Karachi; Oxford: Oxford University Press.

Jayal, N.G. and Pai, S. (Eds.) (2001), *Democratic Governance in India: Challenges of Poverty, Development and Identity*. New Delhi: Sage Publications.

Jessop, B. (1998), The Rise of Governance and the Risks of Failure: The Case of Economic Development. *International Social Science Journal*. 50 (155) pp. 29-45.

Johnson, C. (1981), Introduction: The Taiwan Model. In J.S. Hsiung (ed.) pp. 9-18.

Johnson, C. (1995), *Japan: who governs?* New York: W.W.Norton and Co.

Joseph, S. (2001), Democratic Good Governance: New Agenda for Change. *Economic and Political Weekly* 36 (12) pp. 1011-14.

Kabeer, N. (1994), Gender-aware Policy and Planning: A Social-relations Perspective. In Macdonald, M. (ed.) pp. 80-97.

Kauffman, D., Kraay, A., Zoido-Lobaton, P. (1999), *Governance Matters.* Policy Research Working paper No. 2196. Washington D.C: World Bank.

Kohli, Atul. (1990), *Democracy and Discontent: India's Growing Crisis of Governability.* Cambridge: Cambridge University Press.

Kothari, R. (1984), The Non-party Political Process. In *Economic and Political Weekly* 19 (5). pp. 45-49.

Kothari, R. (1990), *Politics and the People: In Search of a Humane India.* London: Aspect Publications Ltd. Vol. I and II.

Lasswell, H.D. (1950), *Politics: Who gets What, When, How.* New York: Peter Smith.

Leftwich, A. (2000), *States of Development: On the Primacy of Politics in Development.* Cambridge: Polity Press.

Lele, J. (1981), *Elite Pluralism and Class Rule: Political Development in Maharashtra, India.* Toronto: University of Toronto Press.

Lipsky, M. (1980), *Street-level Bureaucracy: Dilemmas of the Individual in Public Services.* New York: Russell Sage Foundation.

Mackintosh, M. (1995), Competition and Contracting in Selective Social Provisioning. *The European Journal of Development Research.* Vol. 7 (1) pp. 26-52.

Marglin, F.A. and Marglin, S.A. (1990), *Dominating Knowledge: Development, Culture, and Resistance.* Oxford: Clarendon Press.

Mawhood, P. (1993), Decentralisation: The Concept and the Practice. In Mawhood, P. (Ed.) *Local Government in the third World.* Chichester: Africa Institute of South Africa.

Meenakshisundaram, S.S. (1999), Decentralisation in Developing Countries. In Jha, S.N. and Mathur, P.C. (Eds.) *Decentralisation and Local Politics.* New Delhi: Sage Publications.

Mehta, D. (2000), Urban Governance: Lessons from Asia. In Hye, H.A. (ed.) pp. 317-340.

Meier, G.M. (1992), Do Economists Influence the Developing World? In Sharma, S. (ed.) pp. 20-34.

Midgley, J. (1995), *Social Development: The Developmental Perspective in Social Welfare.* London: Sage Publications.

Miesel, J. (1958), *The Myth of the Ruling Class.* Ann Arbour: University of Michigan Press.

Migdal, J.S. (1988), *Strong Societies and Weak States: State-society Relations and State Capabilities in the third World.* Princeton: Princeton University Press.

Mills, C.W. (1956), *The Power Elite.* London: Oxford University Press.

Minogue, M. (1998), *Is good Governance a Universal Value?* Public Policy and Management Working paper series: Paper No. 6. The University of Manchester.

Minogue, M. (1999), *Power to the People? Good Governance and the Reshaping of the State.* Public Policy and Management Working paper Series: Paper No. 14. The University of Manchester.

Mitra, S. K. (1992), *Power, Protest and Participation: Local Elites and the Politics of Development in India.* London: Routledge.

Mitra, S.K. and Singh, V.B. (1999), *Democracy and Social Change in India: A Cross-sectional Analysis of the National Electorate.* London: Sage Publications.

Mitra, S.K. (2001), *Making Local Government Work: Local Elites, Panchayati Raj and Governance in India.* In Kohli, A. (Ed.) pp. 103-26.

Mosca, G. (1939), *The Ruling Class.* New York: McGraw Hill.

Mwabu, G., Ugaz, C. and White, G. (eds.) (2001), *Social Provision in Low-income Countries: New Patterns and Emerging Trends.* Helsinki: WIDER.

Myrdal, G. (1968), *Asian Drama: An Inquiry into the Poverty of Nations.* London: The Penguin Press.

Oakley, P. *et al.* (1991), *Projects with People: The Practice of Participation in Rural Development.* Geneva: International Labour Office.

Osborne and Gaebler's (1992), *Reinventing Government: How the Entrepreneurial Spirit is Transforming the Public Sector.* New York: Plume.

Papadakis, W. and Taylor-Gooby, P. (1987), *The Private Provision of Public Welfare: State, Market and Community.* Sussex: Wheatsheaf Books.

Pareto, V. (1935), *The Mind and Society.* London: J. Cape.

Parry, G. (1969), *Political Elites.* London: George Allen and Unwin Ltd.

Pierre, J. (ed.) (2000), *Debating Governance: Authority, Steering and Democracy.* Oxford: Oxford University Press.

Piven, F.F. and Cloward, R.A. (1977), *Poor People's Movemnts: Why they Succeed, How they fail.* New York: Pantheon Books.

Polsby, N.W. (1974), *Community Power and Political Theory.* New Haven: Yale University Press.

Putnam, R. (1993), *Making Democracy Work: Civic Traditions in Modern Italy.* Princeton: Princeton University Press.

Rappoport, A. (1969), *Two-person Game Theory: The Essential Ideas.* Ann Arbor MI: University of Michigan Press.

Rhodes, R.A.W. (1995), *The New Governance: Governing without Government.* Swindson: Economic and Social Research Council.

Rhodes, R.A.W. (1997), *Understanding Governance: Policy Networks, Governance, Reflexivity and Accountability.* Buckingham: Open University Press.

Robertson, A.F. (1984), *People and the State: An Anthropology of Planned Development.* Cambridge: Cambridge University Press.

Robinson, M. (1998), Democracy, Participation, and Public Policy: The Politics of Institutional Design. In Robinson, M and White, G. (eds.)

Robinson, M. and White, G. (1997), *The Role of Civic Organizations in the Provision of Social Services: Towards Synergy.* Helsinki: UNU/WIDER.

Robinson, M. and White, G. (eds.) (1998), *The Democratic Developmental State: Political and Institutional Design.* Oxford: Oxford University Press.

Rondinelli, D.A. (1981), Government Decentralisation in Comparative Perspective: Theory and Practice in Developing Countries. In *International Review of Administrative Science,* Vol. 47 pp. 136-145.

Salamon, L.M. and Anheier, H.K. (1997), *Defining Non-profit Sector: A Cross-national Analysis.* Manchester: Manchester University Press.

Salamon, L.M. (2002), *The New Governance and the Tools of Public Action: An Introduction.* In Salamon, L.M. (ed.). pp. 1-47.

Salamon, L.M. (ed.) (2002), *The Tools of Government: A Guide to the New Governance.* Oxford : Oxford University Press.

Schneider, H. and Libercier, M-H (1994), Concepts, Issues and Experiences for Building up Participation. in *Participation: Development from Advocacy to Action.* Paris: OECD Development Centre.

Sen, G. (1992), Social Needs and Public Accountability: The Case of Kerala. In Wuyts, M., *et al.*, (eds.) pp. 253-278.

Sharma, S. (ed.) (1992), *Development Policy.* New York: St.Martin's Press.

Singh, R. (1988), *Land, Power and People: Rural Elite in Transition, 1801-1970.* New Delhi: Sage Publications.

Shore, C. and Wright, S. (Eds.) (1997), *Anthropology of Policy: Critical Perspectives on Governance and Power.* London: Routledge.

Smith, D.M. (1974), Who gets What, Where, and How: A Welfare Focus for Human Geography. *Geography* 56 (4) pp. 227-57.

Smith, G., Lees, R., and Topping, P. (1977), Participation and the Home Office Community Development Project. In Crouch, C. (ed.) pp. 237-272.

Srinivas, M.N. (1969), The Caste System in India. In Beteille, A. (ed.) pp. 265-72.

Stoker, G. (1998), Governance as Theory: Five Propositions. *International Social Science Journal* Vol. 50 (155) pp. 17-28.

Titmuss, R. (1955), Essays on 'The Welfare State'. London: Allen and Unwin.

Uphoff, N. (1993), Grassroots Organizations and NGOs in Rural Development: Opportunities with Diminishing States and Expanding Markets. In *World Development* 21 (4) pp. 607-22.

Weiner, M. (1989), *The Indian Paradox: Essays in Indian Politics.* New Delhi: Sage Publications.

White, G. (1984), Developmental States and Socialist Industrialisation in the Third World. *Journal of Development Studies* 21 (1) pp. 97-120.

World Bank (1992), *Governance and Development.* Washington D.C.: The World Bank. *Policy and Public Action.* Oxford: Oxford University Press and Open University Press.

2

Impediments to Inclusive Financing in India
Evidence from A Study of 'No-Frills' Accounts of Banks

— M.V. Srinivasa Gowda
— Sathyanarayana

This paper attempts to examine the impediments to inclusive financing drive initiated recently by the Reserve Bank of India to bring the hither-to unbanked, weaker sections of the society into the modern banking ambit. It is based on the primary-data collected from a sample of 100 'no-frills' accounts of two public sector bank branches. The main findings of the study are:

(i) Majority of the 'No-frills' accounts are inoperative.

(ii) Only 17 per cent of households surveyed have placed a portion of their savings in these accounts' the rest of them prefer other types of investments such as purchasing gold, financing in family business, house construction, investing with private chit funds etc.

(iii) Hardly 6 per cent of the households had availed direct finance from banks, while 82 per cent availed loans from SHGs.

(iv) As high as 35 per cent of the households continued to borrow from private financiers albeit at high rates of interest.

(v) Use of intermediaries like business correspondents and business facilitators assisted by technology products like bio-metric smart cards and hand-held devices, permitting small overdrafts on 'No frills' accounts and tagging health insurance products to these accounts would greatly improve the number and frequency of operation of these accounts.

The main reasons for the inactiveness of 'no-frills' accounts are: low and irregular incomes of poor households; lack of physical access to the bank; unsuitability of bank timings to the informal sector working class; tendency of low-income people to place their savings with local chit funds and also borrowing from chit funds or local money lenders regardless of the usurious interest rates; uneasiness of poor with the rigid banking procedures; lack of awareness about the innovative banking products and their benefits; non-availability of easy bank loans for needs like housing, education and genuine consumption. The 'No-frills' accounts drive can be made more effective if banks extend direct loans and overdrafts to these account holders to part-finance their micro enterprises; meet their children's higher education and other genuine consumption needs; make small loans more customer-friendly and impart financial literacy and credit counseling to the account holders.

Introduction

Inclusive financing or financial inclusion means provision of basic financial/banking services such as savings, credit and insurance at an affordable cost to vast sections of disadvantaged and low-income groups. This enlarges the livelihood opportunities for low income groups which form a large part of the Indian economy. In its relentless attempts to extend modern banking facilities to the weaker sections of the society and to the unorganized sectors of the economy the Reserve Bank of India has initiated a series of steps for the last over four decades.

The latest in this series is the 'No-frills' accounts drive launched since 2006. In pursuance of this drive, all banks, especially the public sector ones, have been urged to open 'no-frills' accounts. Many public sector banks have claimed that they have achieved 100 per cent financial inclusion (hereinafter abbreviated as FI) in some districts by way of opening no-frills accounts. However, close on the heels of its launching, an evaluation of the scheme by some independent external agencies in 26 districts of AP, Gujarat, HP, Karnataka, Orissa, Punjab, Rajasthan and West Bengal, revealed that the actual inclusion was not 100 per cent. Most of the accounts that have been opened as part of the FI drive have remained inoperative due to various reasons such as distance from the Branch, illiteracy, lack of interest, lack of savings and non-availability of Pass books, the study revealed. Based on these findings, RBI directed the State Level Bankers Committees (SLBCs) to take the following steps: actively stepping up the awareness with regard to 'No Frills' accounts; providing banking services to account holders closer to their homes by using a variety of channels such as Business correspondents, mobile offices etc., and providing General Purpose Credit Cards (GCC) and small overdrafts in 'No Frills' accounts to encourage them to actively operate the accounts.

Objectives

The present study attempts to evaluate the implementation of this step by two branches of a public sector bank. Following are the specific objectives of the study.

1. To examine the progress/performance of 'No Frill' accounts scheme and implementation of FI measures at two branches of a public sector bank since the launch of FI Scheme.

2. To identify the factors leading to the success or failure of the FI measures.
3. To suggest improvements in the scheme based on the perspectives given by the 'No frills' account holders themselves and also the concerned bank branches.

Methodology and Data

Two branches of the Union Bank of India were chosen for this study and they are located at Kalkere village, Anekal Taluka, Bangalore Rural District (a rural branch) and Mysore (an urban branch). Primary data were collected through personal interviews of a total of 100 'No Frills' account holders (50 from each of the two branches) by way of responses to a structured schedule. The data collected for the study was for the period from the inception of the scheme in January 2006 upto December, 2009. Primary data were also obtained from the two bank branches by interacting with the branch officials and from the relevant bank records. Secondary data were gathered from the publications/reports of principle bank, namely the Union Bank of India, pertaining to the overall implementation of FI scheme by the Bank. The data collected from the sample respondents covered a wide range of information including their socio-economic traits, institutional credit extended to 'No frills' account holders to meet their livelihood and/or consumption needs either directly or through SHG-Bank linkage, particulars of other services of FI extended such as General Purpose Credit Cards issued, small overdrafts given in 'No Frills' accounts, providing one-time settlement of NPAs, use of IT devises such as smart cards and providing financial counseling.

All the respondents covered by the study belonged to the low income category. Efforts were made to cover people with diverse sources of livelihood such as retail trade, small business, skilled workers, weavers, drivers, self employed, factory workers, construction and farm labourers, etc., so that they represented a cross section of the poor. The schedule used for data collection had two parts: Part A covered the socio-economic traits of the respondents and their households, their assets and liabilities, and their membership in self help groups. Part B covered respondents' perspectives on the success or failure of FI measures/'No frills' accounts scheme, covering mainly: the operation/non-operation of 'No frills' accounts, credit requirements of respondents, their preferred lenders, reasons for continuing to avail finance from private money lenders instead of seeking bank finance and, respondents' awareness and utilisation of other services of FI scheme such as GCC, health insurance, biometric smart cards, etc.

Major Findings

Socio-economic Traits of Respondents

An analysis of the socio-economic traits of respondents would help evaluate the perceptions of the respondents about the 'No frills' account of banks and other matters related to banking/financial transactions. The survey covered households engaged in a fairly wide variety of occupations as shown in Table 2.1. As the Table indicates, majority of households are engaged in labour (construction, domestic) followed by retail trade and small business, skilled workers and weavers.

Table 2.1: Occupation Structure

Sl. No.	Occupation	Number of Households		
		Kalkere Branch	Mysore Branch	Total
1.	Agriculture/Diary	1	–	1
2.	Driver	3	7	10
3.	Retail Trade and Small Business	2	14	16
4.	Self-employed	1	5	6
5.	Weaver	13	–	13
6.	Other Skilled Worker	3	10	13
7.	Construction Labour	11	7	18
8.	Domestic Labour	12	3	15
9.	Salaried employee	4	3	7
10.	Pensioner	–	1	1
	Total	**50**	**50**	**100**

Education Level

As Table 2.2 shows, 81 per cent of the respondents were either illiterate or school dropouts. It was revealed during the survey that most of the latter had dropped out of school before reaching the 5th standard. They could hardly read and write. Only 19 per cent of the respondents had completed matriculation.

Table 2.2: Education Level of Respondents

Education Level	Number of Respondents		
	Kalkere	Mysore	Total
Illiterate	13	21	34
Less than 10th std.	26	21	47
10th std. and above	11	8	19

Household and Monthly and per capita Income

Monthly income of Households was classified into 6 broad categories. Table 2.3 represents the distribution of households under each category.

Table 2.3: Monthly Income of Households – Both Kalkere and Mysore Branches

Category (Income Range in Rupees)	Number of Households	
	Kalkere	Mysore
< or = 1000	7	3
1001 to 2000	23	16
2001 t0 3000	18	15
3000 to 4000	1	6
4001 to 5000	1	5
>5001	0	5

Monthly income per capita has also been classified into 6 broad categories. Maximum percentage of households (39%) fall under category 2, followed by category 3 (33%) and category 1 (10%). A large number of households (42%) lie in category 2, followed by category 3 (26%). Together they account for 68 per cent of the households where the average monthly income per person is less than Rs. 2000. This indicates that the respondents indeed belong to the lower income category.

Household Consumption Expenditure

Branch averages for monthly expenses of respondent households on items such as food, clothing, transport, loan repayments etc., are shown in Table 2.4. Monthly expenses (average total) were Rs. 9082/- for Mysore branch respondents as against Rs. 7263/- for Kalkere branch respondents. Of the total monthly expenses, two heads account for 60 per cent of the total expenses; food accounts for 31 per cent while loan repayments (including interest) for 30 per cent. All other expenses together account for less than 40 per cent, with each head at around 10 per cent. This reflects high cost of living which leaves meager income for savings by poor.

Table 2.4: Break-up of Average Monthly Household Expenses (Absolute and %)

Expenses Items	Kalkere	Mysore	Average
Miscellaneous	545 (8%)	670 (7%)	608 (7%)
Loan Repayment	2294 (32%)	2573 (28%)	2434 (30%)
Medical	369 (5%)	300 (3%)	335 (4%)
Education	453 (6%)	798 (9%)	626 (8%)
Transportation	557 (8%)	896 (10%)	727 (9%)
Clothes	524 (7%)	676 (7%)	600 (7%)
House Rent	267 (4%)	299 (3%)	283 (4%)
Food	2254 (31%)	2870 (32%)	2562 (31%)

Household Savings

Monthly net savings per household are shown under 6 broad categories in Table 2.5. Most of the households of both the branches fall under Rs. 1/- to Rs. 1000/- net savings category. Gold was reported to be the most popular form of savings.

Table 2.5: Net Household Savings per Month

Category (Range of Net Savings per month in Rs.)	Number of Households	
	Kalkere	Mysore
< or = -2000	6	2
-1999 to -1000	8	6
-999 to 0	9	9
1 to 1000	13	7
1001 to 2000	6	8
>2001	8	18

Household Assets

The market value of the assets as stated by the respondents are not quite accurate, especially the immovable assets such as land and housing. The sites/houses could be unauthorized or free (inalienable) and hence do not have much market value. Hence for the purpose of analysis of data, only the number of households owning such assets is shown in Table 2.6.

Table 2.6: Break up of Household Assets – Both Kalkere and Mysore Branches

Type of Assets	Number of Households	
	Kalkere	Mysore
Own House	27	35
Rented out units	6	6
Agriculture land	9	0
Sites	3	3
Vehicles	8	25
Bank Deposit	3	14
LIC	6	10
SHG Savings	39	50
Other Deposits/bonds	2	0
Chit funds	9	5
Gold	40	38
Business assets	6	16
Lease Deposits	8	7

That the maximum percentage of households (89%) have SHG savings, it may be noted that, as SHG members they would have to save compulsorily in SHG savings accounts. The quantum of such savings is rather low, in the range of Rs. 100/- to Rs. 200/- p.m. Jewellery ranks second in terms of the percentage of households (78%) that have invested in it, the quantum of investment in jewellery is very much higher. Next in line comes investment in dwelling house (62% of households) followed by vehicles (33% of households). This clearly implies that bank deposits are not the preferred form of assets/investments for 'No-frills' account holders, as only 17 per cent of them have saved in bank deposits.

Household Liabilities

Table 2.7, depicts the sources of loans availed by the respondents. Majority of them (82%) have availed loans from SHGs, while about 35 per cent had borrowed from private financiers and hardly 6 per cent had borrowed from banks and other institutional sources. (No loans from Micro Finance Institutions were reported). This indicates that although SHG loans have helped poor amortize loans borrowed from private financiers to a significant extent, they were still not able to fully come out of the clutches of private financiers.

Table 2.7: Sources of Household Liabilities

Sources	Number of Households	
	Kalkere	Mysore
SHG Loan	39	43
Bank and other Financial Institutions	4	2
Private Financiers	22	14

Purpose-wise Break up of Loans

Loans availed by the sample respondents were classified into 9 purpose-wise categories. Table 2.8 shows the classification of loans availed from different sources by respondents at both branches. (It may be noted that 'Amount of Loan' shown here pertains to Loan amount availed initially and not the 'Outstanding Loan'.

Of the above four purposes, bank/institutional finance was reported to be relatively easy to get for 'Business Development' for which the banks and other financial institutions have well structured schemes. For the other three purposes, which are essentially non-productive in nature, the poor do not find it easy to get bank/institutional finance. Hence the needy persons in low income categories rely more on private financiers for their non-production needs. About 70 per cent of loans from private financiers are obtained for *(i)* house construction/house repairs and lease deposits (39%) and *(ii)* marriage celebrations (31%).

Table 2.8: Purpose-wise Break-up of Loans availed (in Rs. Lakhs)

Sl. No.	Loan Purpose	SHG Loans		Loans from Banks and Fin. Institutions		Loans from Private Financiers/ Money Lenders		Total Loans			
		No. of Acnts.	Loan Amt.	No. of Acnts.	Loan Amt.	No. of Acnts.	Loan Amt.	No. of Acnts.	% to Total (No. of Loan Acnts.)	Total Loan Amt.	% to Total (Loan Amt)
1.	Business development	27	10.17	4	5.00	5	1.87	36	29.3%	17.04	35.8%
2.	House construction and/ or repairs	9	3.40	2	3.00	8	4.50	19	15.4%	10.90	23%
3.	Lease Deposits	9	2.47	–	–	4	2.30	13	10.6%	4.77	10%
4.	Marriage	9	1.63	–	–	6	5.40	15	12.2%	7.03	14.8%
5.	School/ College fees	16	2.68	–	–	5	0.79	21	17.1%	3.47	7.3%
6.	Consumption	5	0.70	–	–	4	0.40	9	7.3%	1.10	2.3%
7.	Medical expenses	3	0.52	–	–	1	0.30	4	3.3%	0.82	1.7%
8.	Agriculture and allied activities	2	0.33	–	–	1	1.75	3	2.4%	2.08	4.4%
9.	Others	2	0.25	–	–	1	0.10	3	2.4%	0.35	0.7%
	Total	**82**	**22.15**	**6**	**8.00**	**35**	**17.41**	**123**	**–**	**47.56**	**–**

Four important purposes for which loans were availed by the respondents are as follows.

Purpose of Loan	% to Total	
	No. of Loan Accounts	Loan Amount
Business Development	29.3%	35.8%
House construction/Repairs + Lease Deposits	26%	33%
School/College fees	17.1%	7.3%
Marriage	12.2%	14.8%

Interest Rates on Loans

Interest rate on loans from banks/financial Institutions to small borrowers is around 12 per cent p.a. Interest rate on SHG loans ranges between 12 per cent and 24 per cent p.a. Interest rates on private loans are much higher. The number of private loan accounts of respondents and rates of interest charged by private financiers are as follows:

Interest Rate per Annum	No. of Accounts
12%	1
24%	6
36%	10
60%	12
100%	1
120%	1
Variable interest rates (This pertains to chit fund loans which do not have a fixed rate of interest, but they are much higher than Bank rates)	4 Total 35

Respondents' Perspectives on 'No Frills' Accounts Scheme and other FI Drives

The opinions of respondents of regarding the FI drive are presented here under. Most of the 'No Frills' accounts have been opened to fulfill SHG membership requirements. Over 90 per cent of the respondents were members of SHGs which are linked to either of the two UBI branches under study. The SHGs as well as Bank branches have made it compulsory for the SHG members to open 'No Frills' SB account with the Bank branch. It must be mentioned here that the responses analysed below only indicate the respondents' intentions/perceptions, rather than their actual acts, in using the 'No Frills'. In reality most of these accounts are not being operated at all.

(i) Source of Advice/Information to open 'No Frills' Account

Response Options	Number of Responses		
	Kalkere	Mysore	Total
(a) Bank officials/Manager	34	46	70
(b) Village Panchayat Members	7	–	7
(c) Friends/Relatives	–	–	–
(d) SHG Members	33	48	81
(e) NGOs	–	–	–
(f) Others	–	–	–

(ii) Purpose of Opening 'No Frills' Account

Response Options	Number of Responses		
	Kalkere	Mysore	Total
(a) To follow SHG rules	33	48	81
(b) To save money	31	9	40
(c) To apply for Bank loan	22	2	24
(d) To keep money safely	7	8	15
(e) To get identify proof	–	–	–
(f) To receive cheque payments	2	–	2
(g) To receive subsidy, grant, wages etc.	17	–	17
(h) To transfer money to others	2	–	2
(i) No clear purpose	–	–	–

(iii) Current Operating Status of 'No Frills' Accounts

About 86 per cent of the 'No Frills' accounts were inoperative. Only 14 per cent of the sample 'No frills' account holders were found to operate their accounts. This was confirmed by cross-verification at the branch level.

Response Options	Number of Responses		
	Kalkere Branch	Mysore Branch	Total Sample
Yes	6	8	14
No	44	42	86

(iv) Benefits Obtained by 'No Frills' Account Holders who Operate the Account

Response Options	Number of Responses		
	Kalkere Branch	Mysore Branch	Total
(a) Saving money in Banks in the form of RD/FD	3	6	9
(b) Safe custody of money	5	7	12
(c) Encashing crossed cheques received from third parties	5	–	5
(d) Remitting money to family members through the account	1	–	1
(e) Making cheque payments	–	–	–
(f) Helps getting loans from Bank	–	–	–
(g) Helps getting Identity	–	–	–

(h)	Helps getting health Insurance	–	–	–
(i)	Helps avoiding borrowers from money lenders	–	1	1
(j)	Facilitates learning about Banking transactions products and their benefits.	–	1	1
(k)	Not response	44	42	86

The maximum number of responses regarding the benefits obtained through these accounts pertained to: safe custody of money, saving money in Bank RD/FD and encashing cheques received from third parties. All other benefits as shown against 'Response options' were perceived to be negligible. The intentions of the RBI/Government that 'No Frills' account would serve as a gateway to enable the account holders to get the various financial services such as credit, insurance, remittance facility etc., at an affordable cost do not seem to have materialized as yet.

(v) Reasons for not Operating 'No Frills' Accounts

Response Options		Number of Responses		
		Kalkere Branch	**Mysore Branch**	**Total**
(a)	No income/No savings/very little savings	36	22	58
(b)	• High loan repayments towards SHG loans • High loan repayments towards private financiers **Sub Total** *2 accounts reduced from subtotal as they figure under both SHG loans and loans from private financiers.	15 16	11 6	26 **36**
(c)	Bank branch far-away/timings not convenient/Transportation not available	10	21	31
(d)	Investing money in family business and hence not able to operate 'No frills' account.	7	12	19
(e)	Investing with local chit funds because • Interest offered by banks on savings deposits is not attractive and/or • Not confident of getting bank loan when urgently needed/getting loan from chit funds is easy.	12	3	15
(f)	Not comfortable with Bank operations/not aware of Banking products and their benefits.	4	6	10

Regarding the reasons for not operating the accounts, 'Lack of savings' (58%) was reported to be the most prevalent reason.

(vi) Requirements Specified by Respondents to Enable Operation of 'No Frills' Accounts

Based on the responses of No-frills account holders to an open ended question, following requirements were identified. Since the respondents were finding it difficult to go to the Bank branch during its working hours, they expressed the need for these facilities.

Sl. No.	Type of Requirement Specified	No. of Respondents Specifying
1.	ATM card needed	10
2.	Cash depositing facility at ATMs needed	7
3.	Services of pigmy collector needed (This could be interpreted as the need for BC/BF)	7
4.	Branch to work on Sundays	2

(vii) Preferred form of Savings by 'No Frills' Account Holders

Response Options	Number of Responses		
	Kalkere	Mysore	Total
(a) Gold	21	21	42
(b) Bank FD/RD	14	19	33
(c) Investment in Family business	9	20	29
(d) Keeping cash at Home	6	19	25
(e) Chit funds	15	6	21
(f) Bank SB	7	9	16
(g) LIC/Other deposits	6	10	16
(h) Real estate/House construction for renting out	5	4	9

* More than one option chosen by many respondents.

(viii) Interest Rate Expected on Savings

Majority of the respondents desired higher interest on their savings than what is offered by Banks, understandably because, having become used to borrowing/lending in the unorganized money market, most no-frills account holders think in line with the high interest rates charged/offered by private financiers.

Response Options	Number of Responses
(a) 5 to 10 per cent per annum	18
(b) More than 10 per cent per annum	82

(ix) Major/critical Expenses for which the Respondents Prefer to Borrow Loans in Future

Majority of respondents (66%) reported that they would need loans for business and house construction in the near future. Similarly, the outstanding loans were also raised mostly for these two purposes.

Response Options	Number of Responses		
	Kalkere	Mysore	Total
(a) Business development/setting up of business	17	16	33
(b) House construction/purchase/repair/for lease deposits	14	18	33
(c) School/College fees	11	5	16
(d) Marriage expenses	8	6	14
(e) To repay private loans	10	4	14
(f) Vehicle purchase	5	3	8
(g) Others	6	2	8
(h) No requirements for loan at present	3	2	5

Purpose of Loan (Outstanding)	As % to Total	
	Accounts	Amount
Business development	29.3%	35.8%
House construction/purchase/Repairs+ Lease Deposits	26%	33%
School/College fees	17.1%	7.3%
Marriage expenses	12.2%	14.8%

(x) Extent of Loan Respondents Desire to take in the Near Future

Responses regarding the quantum of loan required by the respondents revealed that their future credit requirements were not high, with 71 per cent of the respondents needing between Rs. 10,000 and Rs. 1,00,000 and hardly 20 per cent expressing need credit of more than Rs. 1,00,000. Majority of the respondents (68%) needed loans for less than 3 years duration.

Response Options	Number of Responses		
	Kalkere	Mysore	Total
(a) Less than Rs. 10,000/-	3	1	4
(b) Rs. 10,000 to Rs. 50,000/-	21	13	34
(c) Rs. 50,000 to Rs. 1,00,000/-	14	23	37
(d) Rs. 1,00,000/- and above	9	11	20
(e) No requirement of loan at present	3	2	5

(xi) Repayment Period Preferred by Respondents

Response Options		Number of Responses		
		Kalkere	Mysore	Total
(a)	Less than a year	3	1	4
(b)	1 to 3 years	27	37	64
(c)	Over 3 years	17	10	27
(d)	No requirement of loan at present	3	2	5

(xii) Critical Factors Expected by Respondents from Lenders

Almost all the respondents (99%) had indicated 'lower rate of Interest on loans' as the critical factor they expect from lenders. However respondents had indicated other reasons too, these included: immediate loan disbursement, security not be made mandatory, minimum conditions, sympathetic attitude while recovering loans.

Response Options		Number of Responses		
		Kalkere	Mysore	Total
(a)	Immediate loan disbursal	11	8	19
(b)	Security should not be mandatory	11	10	21
(c)	Specific purpose of loan should not be a criterion for sanction	3	1	4
(d)	Lower rate of interest	50	49	99
(e)	Minimum restrictions	14	1	15
(f)	Sympathetic attitude while recovering loans	11	7	18
(g)	Others	3	–	3

(xiii) Comparative Advantages of Loans from Banks and Private Money Lenders

Banks score over money lenders in two of the critical aspects, *viz.*, 'Lower interest on Loans' and 'Sympathetic attitude while recovering loans'. But private money lenders were considered better in three other critical aspects *viz.*, 'Security not mandatory', 'Speedy loan disbursement' and 'Minimum restrictions'. But 'Lower Interest rate on loans' being the overriding factor, 96 per cent of the respondents have overall preference to borrow from banks as against only 4 per cent preferring private financiers/money lenders.

(xiv) Usefulness of Bank/SHG Loan for Earning Livelihood

SHG loans were considered together with bank loans as the former were simply bank loans through the backdoor. About 27 per cent of respondents have indicated that bank loans/SHG loans had helped them earn better livelihood. However, 55 per cent have replied in the negative because bank/SHG loans have been utilised for meeting consumption needs, purchase of household articles etc., and not for livelihood generation. Remaining 18 per cent had replied 'Not applicable' because they had not availed any bank loan/SHG loan. So banks need to go a long way to devise suitable schemes to suit all borrowers and also to market them because majority (73%) of the respondents perceived they were helped by Banks to earn their livelihood.

Response Options		Number of Responses		
		Kalkere	Mysore	Total
(a)	Yes	11	16	27
(b)	No	27	28	55
(c)	NA (Not applicable)	12	6	18

(xv) Whether Bank/SHG Loans can Prevent Respondents from Borrowing from Money Lenders

Fifty-two per cent of the respondents had stated that Bank/SHG loans had helped them stop seeking loans from money lenders. This is a very encouraging revelation. This means that with easier access to bank loans, loans from private financiers would definitely be reduced.

Response Options		Number of Responses		
		Kalkere	Mysore	Total
(a)	Yes	21	31	52
(b)	No	17	13	30
(c)	NA (Not applicable)	12	6	18

(xvi) Reasons for not Availing Bank Loan in Spite of Expressing Preference

Response Options		Number of Responses		
		Kalkere	Mysore	Total
(a)	Not aware of Banks' loan products/ not comfortable to deal with Banks	29	12	41
(b)	Difficult to fulfill Banks' requirements	9	28	37
(c)	Unable to provide security for Bank loans	10	26	36
(d)	Not having any bankable activity	17	13	30
(e)	Already availed loan from money lenders and others but not cleared yet	11	5	16
(f)	Loan asked but not sanctioned	3	5	8
(g)	Others	11	2	13

(xvii) Willingness of Respondents to Avail Certain Financial Services

Responses	GCC	Health Insurance
Yes	8	92
No	92	8

(xviii) Type of Assistance Specified by Respondents for Availing Loans from Banks

Most of the respondents wanted guidance for getting bank loans for various purposes, the break-up for which is as follows: business development (30%), housing (27%), marriage expenses (9%), clearing private finance (7%), paying school/college fees (4%), meeting consumption (3%), and general guidance about Banks' loan products (17%). This pattern is more or less in line with the purpose-wise break-up of existing loans.

Conclusion

The present study revealed that only about 10 per cent of the 'No frills' accounts opened by banks were operated regularly and only 6 per cent of the households under study had availed direct loans from banks and other financial institutions. About 5 per cent of the respondent households continued to borrow from private financiers. The all-India situation in this regard seems to be no different. It is estimated that out of the 250 million 'No frills' accounts opened during 2009 and 2010 by the Indian banks, only 11 per cent were operational. (Source: UBI's Financial Inclusion Plan 2010-13). Apparently, the FI drive and 'No frills' accounts mission had shown only a limited success so far. However, FI is a long-term plan. Decades of financial exclusion cannot be eliminated in a few years. After all, the journey in the right direction has begun. Many significant steps are being taken by the Reserve Bank, public sector banks and other government agencies for bringing thousands of hitherto financially excluded individuals under the umbrella of financial inclusion.

But within the broad framework of these major institution level measures, suitable modifications must be made to these measures to suit the different parts of the country, different areas (rural, urban etc.) and the micro-environment of different branches. More detailed studies are needed to identify these specific measures. The present study is an effort in this direction, where the focus has been on the Financial Inclusion of the poor living in towns/cities and their outskirts. The study revealed that the problems faced by the urban poor were somewhat different from those faced by rural poor. Based on the findings of the study, certain key suggestions are as under. Some of these are already being implemented, and others need to be implemented. These measures can be broadly grouped as follows:

(a) *Measures to Improve Access to Financial Services:* These include increasing the village outreach, establishing branchless banking units with the help

of BCs/BFs, introduction of new technology products like smart cards, hand-held electronic devices etc. For initiating these measures, greater focus is on rural/unbanked areas at present, where the need for these measures is higher. But these measures have to be extended to urban branches as well.

(b) *Capacity Building Measures:* These would enable the urban poor to use the financial services better. They include:

- Increasing the savings potential of the poor by providing low-cost credit to improve their livelihood and/or meet their necessary expenses and giving better returns on their savings.
- Provision of affordable low-cost housing.
- Providing micro insurance (life as well as health).
- Providing financial literacy including counseling for credit management, investments, professional knowledge, social reforms etc.

These measures would help improve not only the frequency of operation of 'No Frills' accounts but also the savings potential of the account holders which would be beneficial to them as well as the banks. The poor have so many essential but unfulfilled needs to run their daily lives that their savings are not enough to meet them. They need credit to purchase the required productive assets and also to meet the necessary household expenses. It is only after these essential needs are met that there would remain a saving to be put in their 'No Frills' Bank accounts. This state may not occur in the initial stages of inclusive growth but may materialize down the road. We are still in the initial stages of implementing financial inclusion. Thus, it is for the Banks and the Government to continue their efforts without getting disheartened by the present status of 'No Frills' accounts and wait for the positive results.

REFERENCES

Agarwal, Prakash, 2009, Financial Inclusion/Financial Literacy in Select Districts of Jharkhand – A Project Report under RBI Young Scholar Scheme, Ranchi.

Ananthaswamy B. N, Moses, J. S, Vidyasagar P. S. S, Kumar N.A.V. and Suraj S, 2009, Financial Inclusion in India: Recent Initiatives and Assessment, RBI Staff Studies, December.

Gangopadhyay, Shubhashis, How can Technology Facilitate Financial Inclusion in India? A Discussion Paper, http://rmi.sagepub.com/cgi/content/abstract/1/2/223.

Government of India, 2010, Report of the Expert Committee on Harnessing the India Post Network for Financial Inclusion.

Kochhar, Sameer, 2010, Speeding Financial Inclusion, Skoch Development Foundation, New Delhi.

Mehrotra N, Puhazhendhi V, Gopakumaran Nair G and Sahoo, B B, 2009, Financial Inclusion – An Overview, National Bank for Agriculture and Rural Development Occasional Paper 48.

Prasad, Chowdari, 2009, Financial Inclusion in India – Yet another Ritual or an Integrated Tool for Poverty Alleviation? Alliance Business School, Bangalore; http://www.authorstream.com/presentation/chowdarip-179120-financial-inclusion-micro-finance-rural-banking-millineum-development-goals-chowdari-prasad-fi-nitte-2008-final-business-ppt-powerpoint/

Ramanathan, Smita and Kamath, Rajalaxmi, Financial Inclusion – A View from Below; http://www.iimb.ernet.in/microfinance/ramnagar/index_files/fin_inlcusion.pdf

Reserve Bank of India, 2008, Financial Inclusion, Report on Currency and Finance, Ch. VII, http://rbi.org.in/scripts/publicationsview.aspx?id=10494

Reserve Bank of India, 2009, Report of the Working Group to Review the Business Correspondent Model.

Reserve Bank of India, 2010, Report on Trend and Progress of Banking in India 2009-10.

Subbarao, Duvvuri, 2010, Financial Inclusion: Challenges and Opportunities, Reserve Bank of India Bulletin, January.

Thyagarajan S. and Venkatesan, J, 2008, Cost-Benefit and Usage Behaviour Analysis of No-Frills Accounts: A Study Report on Cuddalore District, IFMR, Chennai.

3

Growth and Outreach of Self-Help Groups Micro-credit Models in India
A Literature Insight

— Saikumar C. Bharamappanavara

The SHGs micro-credit concept in India started on a pilot basis in the year 1991 and presently has become the biggest micro-finance programme in the world. This glints for the research review paper to looking to Indian micro-credit industry from its emergence to present status. It begins with curtaining the terms poverty, origin of Self-Help Groups (SHGs) and micro-credit concept. The literature goes through the different dimensions of SHGs concept and infers that SHGs forms the essence of co-operation with an ambience of dynamism, cohesion and collective action in group members. After looking into the past studies on micro-credit coverage, it is apparent that still larger section of poor are not yet covered under the micro-credit umbrella; entails still a bigger population is waiting to harness the SHGs micro-credit to escape poverty. Further, the paper deeply elucidates the Indian widespread and diversified micro-credit delivery system existing, namely Model-I: Bank promoted, Model-II: Government Agency and Model-III: NGOs promoted. The commonalities and differences in existing in these models are unveiled. This marks the existing scope and arenas for micro-credit expansion and reveals the role of Banks, Non-Governmental Organization (NGO) and other related institutions in filling the gap to reach the poor in the widespread micro-credit models. The paper ends with recommending the research in vital direction which helps to achieve success in explaining SHGs' micro-credit as a tool for rural development.

Introduction

The prosperity of India lies in the prosperity of its villages. In spite of being an agrarian economy, India's rural sector reveals a despondent picture

(Bardhan and Dabas, 2007). Hence, in India – right from its independence, in fact even in the pre-independence era – rural development *vis-a-vis* poverty alleviation had been considered as a major challenge to the country (Athena, 2009). In fact, one in five of the world's people live in absolute poverty – two-third of them are women (State for International development report, 2000). There are estimated to be about 1.2 billion people in the world who are blighted by poverty and are unable to meet their basic needs of food, clothing, shelter, and acquire minimum healthcare. Today, India retains the dubious distinction of having the largest number of poor people on the planet, where almost three out of four Indians and close to 80 per cent of the poor live in rural areas (Hanstad *et al*, 2002), in which 77 per cent (836 million) live on less than half a dollar a day (2009).[1] Though the Indian economy is witnessing GDP growth rates of 6.5 to 7.0 per cent, and despite the significant growth in agricultural production and employment over the past five decades, one out of every three persons in India is poor and two out of every three are undernourished or malnourished. If we include those who are deprived of safe drinking water, adequate clothing, or shelter, the number is considerably higher. Though the percentage of poverty has been reduced in India since 1947, the absolute numbers of poor who are still below the poverty line has doubled to about 300 millions. Based on poverty estimates of 2009-10, about 33.8 per cent of the population in rural areas and 20.90 per cent in urban areas live below the poverty line (Planning Commission, 2012).

There are about 0.638 million villages in India and 75 per cent of the total population lives in rural areas,[2] of which 70 per cent of the population depends on agriculture for their livelihood (Bendapudi, 2007). The rural sector is typically characterised by subdivisions and fragmentation of landholding, which encourages under employment, malnutrition, poverty, and results in lack of financial resources, leading to increased poverty. Thus, poverty in India is associated with an imbalance between the population and land resources. Landless and near-landless sections of the population live close to the margins of existence, experiencing seasonal unemployment and nutritional stress under severe poverty. Seeing the burden of poverty that falls heavily upon women, *Pandit Jawaharalal Nehru* (The first prime minister of India) envisioned that women can be the driving force to eradicate poverty. This sentimentis reflected very well in one of his statements, "When women move forward, the family moves, the village moves and the nation moves." Witnessing this, presently more than 90 per cent of SHGs are women groups showing tremendous progress in extending micro-credit to the vulnerable (Government of India, 2007; Nabard Report, 2009).

Poverty

At the world level, though 'globalisation' and 'global village' are discussed, poverty is still a major curse faced by many countries. The word 'poverty' has a number of definitions – it is not easy to give an absolute definition and has relative definitions that depend on the situation. If we see some of the important definitions used globally, poverty, according to the CGAP report (CGAP, 2005), can be defined as "The proportion of population living below $1 a day (PPP)[3] or is the percentage of the population living on less than $1.08 a day at 1993 international prices." Whereas poverty is defined by the World Bank (World Bank, 2000) as the condition of poor households or persons – interpreted conventionally as those lacking access to the assets necessary for a higher standard of income or welfare – assets are thought of as human (access to education), natural (access to land), physical (access to infrastructure), social (access to networks of obligations), or financial (access to credit). Thus, poverty has a relative definition confined to the particular environment and situation. In order to eradicate poverty, a number of programmes for free education, free health, and food-for-work programmes, etc., have been implemented globally. The Lessons from these experiences is that these programmes did not fix the predicament, and when the quandary was analysed by experts, it led to the evolution of micro-credit as an alternative means for poverty eradication. Later in the beginning of this decade, micro-credit revolution has made to achieve progress in this facet. The next question is how micro-credit has helped poverty alleviation. A study by Ellerman (2008) answers the question, wherein micro-credit is described as being mainly sustaining those at the brink of survival who have low savings and no investments. Hence, the credit rarely re-enters the production capital, which can contribute meaningfully to farm growth. He further argues that targeting vulnerable, asset-less, non-entrepreneurial farmers who lack clear business ideas may help them to escape the vicious cycle of poverty. Thus, from the last decade onward, it is being realised that instead of targeting individuals, it is more advantageous from many perspectives to target the group. Currently, 'micro-credit' is recognised as an effective tool to fight poverty from the bottom-up approach in society (Neils and Robert, 2007). Hence in recent years, SHGs have become the significant means of reaching the micro-credit target groups at the world level.

Origin of Self-Help Groups

SHGs in their basic form existed in rural society long prior to the period when rural planners formulated this concept. The groups have also been termed 'affinity groups' due to the existing natural bonds of neighbourhood, blood, caste, community, or activity, as well as being termed 'solidarity groups', as they provide monetary and moral support to each other in difficult times. SHG is not a new concept in Indian society. Traditional Indian society functioned mainly on the basis of self-help and mutual aid. However, in recent years, SHGs have been emerging as a major strategy for the promotion of informal credit to the poor. The concept of SHG in India can be traced back to the Gandhian Grama Swaraj movement. It is mainly concerned with the poor and helping each other through the motto, "of the people and for the people". Unlike many other countries that implemented SHGs after the mid-1970s as a part of the formal credit delivery system, India has been experimenting with the concept for decades (Karmakar, 1998).

However, the origins of SHGs in their present form can be traced back as the brainchild of Grameen Bank of Bangladesh, founded by Prof. Mohammed Yunus of Chittagong University, Bangladesh, in the year 1975 (Jayaraman, 2001). This innovation has proved that credit is not only for the privilege of a few fortunate people, but that the poor and vulnerable can also afford it to assist in their development. This argument of Prof. Mohammed Yunus, which acknowledges people's human rights and offers a unique vision, merited him a Nobel Prize. In fact, the dependence of the rural poor on non-institutional sources of credit like moneylenders is one of the major causes perpetuating poverty. SHGs are identified as substitutes and an antidote for that poverty. In Bangladesh, it has developed into a national programme and has shown remarkable results regarding poverty mitigation. These SHGs have emerged as alternative credit sources for the poor with the recovery performance of 99 per cent, with mutual trust, solidarity, group accountability, and collective action as inherent operational mechanisms (Rajagopalan, 1998). Indeed, the impetus of the present-day SHG movement can be attributed to the success of the Grameen Bank. Presently, it functions in over 52 countries and has been operational for a long time in Bangladesh, Malaysia, Korea, Philippines, and Indonesia.

In Indian rural villages, neighbourhood groups are informally named with different local names but widely known as Self-Help Groups. These are informal groups of 10 to 20 members who have a common vision of the need and importance of collective action (Khun, 1985). These groups promote savings among members and use the pooled resources to meet the emergency needs of their members, including consumption needs. It is obvious that collective work, leadership with fixed tenure, mutual trust, and co-operative philosophy would be the underlying driving forces for these SHGs. The basic tenet of SHGs is to develop savings capabilities among the poorest sections of the society, which in turn reduces dependence on financial institutions and thereby develops self-reliance. However, unlike savings activities found in SHGs of several other countries, these SHG's in India also obtain loans from micro-finance banking institutions and then re-lend them to the members of the group. Thus micro-credit through SHGs has become a fulcrum for developmental initiatives for the poor, particularly in India and in developing countries. It has been practiced in varying forms in different countries and it has been regarded as an important tool for poverty alleviation.

Definition and Concept of Self-Help Groups

Self-Help Groups, in essence are a form of co operation with a definite ambience of dynamism and cohesion, collective action surfaced in the group members by their association within and outside the groups, which are formed in their neighbourhood. There are different definitions given by different experts for the SHG concept and a few are presented below.

SHG is not a new concept in development. SHGs are the grassroot-level organizations that are based on the principles of need and collective action. While explaining about SHGs and its members, Harper said that an SHG is not a static institution (Harper, 1996). It grows on resources and management skills of its members and their increasing confidence to get involved in issues and programmes that require their involvement in the public and private sectors. Through an SHG, the members are automatically empowered economically, politically, and socially in a holistic way for developing their own institution for common benefit. Many studies have shown that creating savings through thrift and credit has been one of the important activities of SHGs, and it became very popular among the poor, particularly among women in the rural areas (Kumaran, 1997). However, SHGs cannot be considered as credit or savings groups alone; they also conduct the mobilisation and organization of women into groups, because these groups form the basis for solidarity, strength, and collective action (Khun, 1985). Organizing such groups has a way to go yet in addressing not only economic problems but also social and political issues.

Author	Definition
Hagenbuch (1958)	SHGs are mutual help organizations formed by a group of people to help each other and are essentially democratic in nature.
Chawla and Patel (1987)	Self-Help organizations are entities that are set up and run by local people who are also the beneficiaries of the programme; it has a loose organizational structure but strong commitment and sense of purpose.
Royal Tropical Institute (1987)	SHG is a membership organization or group wherein risks, costs, and benefits are shared among its members on an equitable basis; its leadership and managers are liable to be called to account by the membership for their needs.
Singh (1995)	SHG is an informal association of individuals who come together voluntarily for promotion of economic and social objectives.
Roul (1996a)	SHG is an institutional framework for individuals or households who have agreed to co-operate on a continuing basis to pursue one or more objectives.
Indian Bank (1996)	SHG is a homogenous group of not more than 25 individuals who have come together to undertake thrift and credit for economic and social strength on the basis of equality, nurturing trust, and mutual help.

These groups were first organized as savings groups for women to overcome the lack of credit access for their needs. Once the group is able to accumulate the sufficient amount of money, it will be encouraged to take up various income-generating activities, either as a form of group initiative or as an activity of the individual member. The money saved by women is used not only for meeting their emergent consumption needs but also for income-generating activities (Rao, 1994).

Emergence of Micro-credit Concept

The micro-credit concept was first introduced in Bangladesh for experiment in the 1950s and 60s; on the other hand, all government efforts to empower peasants' households were not showing the targeted impact until late 1970s and 80s. This has led to the emergence of a new micro-credit-lending programme by the Bangladesh Grameen Bank and Bangladesh Rural Advancement Committee[4] in the 1980s to reach poor landless households. Beneficiaries of the micro-credit loans were poor women who did not have assets to present as collateral in banks and hence never had access to formal banking institutions before (Jayaraman, 2001). One important feature of micro-credit is that it gives credit 'based on trust' without any collateral security. Even then it has achieved on an average more than 90 per cent credit recovery. Literature confirms that this success is mainly because of group-lending, where each group member experiences pressure from the neighbourhood regarding loan repayment (Sa-Dhan, 2008). In Bangladesh most of the micro-credit funds were put towards paddy husking, livestock rearing, aquaculture, vegetable production, poultry farming, and petty business. In another study, the researcher Ledgerwood (1999) enunciated that micro-credit is not just a credit, but it is also a development tool that involves activities such as small loans (micro-credit) for working capital, informal assessment of borrowers and investments, collateral substitutes (group guarantees or compulsory savings), and access to subsequent loans based on repayment performance. In fact, micro-credit groups are used for a range of activities at the world level. In India Self-Employed Women's Association – which has given micro-credit for strong social components like labour advocacy, healthcare, and education – proves that micro-credit groups can be expanded to any extent based on successful participation of rural households.

The concept of micro-credit has emerged and expanded, going beyond Asia, America, and Africa and even reaching Eastern Europe in the name of micro-finance at Mercy Corps[5] at the world level. Professor Muhammad Yunus launched a €150 million global micro-finance outfit styled by Grameen-Credit Agricole Foundation in Paris on 18 February 2008. Credit Agricole SA and Grameen Trust have teamed up to create a dedicated foundation (Star, 2008). It is intended to provide micro-finance institutions with a complete range of financing facilities in the form of credits, guarantees, and equity capital along with advisory services. Grameen Trust is a sister organization of Grameen

Bank, which stepped in to support micro-finance initiatives in 38 countries. In China, the Chinese Foundation for Poverty Alleviation[6] in Beijing – a government NGO under the State Poverty Alleviation Office – developed successfully its own micro-credit model based on the Grameen Bank model. Mercy Corps is another important organization supporting micro-credit in dozens of countries ravaged by wars, conflict, and civil unrest. By and large the micro-credit experiment has been tried all over the world due to the problem of rising poverty. The Association of Social Advancement is an international NGO providing assistance to 30 organizations in 17 countries. One assisted organization was also an NGO from India called Bandhan located in West Bengal, which had women as the primary borrowers. At the global level, the study conducted on the micro-credit summit campaign reported that 1.6 million were served micro-credit in the year 1997, and in last decade there are about 3,100 micro-finance institutions providing micro-credit to the 92.9 million poor people at the world level, indicating micro-credit is no longer micro in its global approach (Kabir, 2002). Out of the 92.9 million people in the world, Asia's share is 59.6 million.

Micro-credit – Spring Board in Rural India

The need for rural credit in India had been recognised even before independence by the erstwhile British government as early as 1793, when it issued regulations for *Taccavi* loans to farmers and subordinate tenants for various purposes (Government of Jharkhand, 2007). Measures were initiated to reduce indebtedness and regulate money-lending activities for agricultural purposes, but it failed to provide a long-term solution. The Co-operative Societies Act, which was passed in 1904 to provide necessary legislative support for financing agriculture and for regulating credit in the interest of cultivators, signalled the entry of credit for agriculture from the institutional sector. These co-operatives are formal organizations that were started long before the concept of SHGs in India, but were based on similar principles as neighbourhood groups or thrift-oriented, member-led, autonomous organizations, etc. Since then and till the late 1950s, co-operatives have been the major institutional source for all agricultural loans in rural areas. At that time, it focussed only on ensuring production credit loans for farmers through primary credit societies. But for non-farm credit needs, farmers paid very high interest rates to private moneylenders. As a result it became difficult for the poor to access funds for starting even small income-generation activities like tailoring, buying buffalo, goat-and sheep-rearing, and petty shop business for self-consumption needs, etc.

Later, for the first time, the Syndicate Bank, which started functioning in 1921, concentrated on raising micro-deposits as daily or weekly savings and providing micro-loans for its constituents. After the nationalisation of banks in 1969, the micro-finance concept in the banking institutions was discussed once again. Despite having a broad network of bank branches in the rural parts of the country, a large number of the poor remained outside the fold of the formal banking system. On average, there is at least one retail credit for about every 5,000 people in the rural population – or for every 1,000 households. The rural credit share from non-institutional sources (informal credit) is more than 36 per cent (Government of Jharkhand, 2007), indicating the role of moneylenders in the rural credit system. This emphasises that India is home to a growing and innovative micro-credit sector.

The structure of rural financial markets in India is dualistic, with formal, semi-formal, and informal intermediaries such as:

- *Formal Sector Institutions:* These include private and public institutions that are funded by government or foreign capital. The transactions involve some bureaucratic procedures with a bias for larger loans, for example, the commercial and co-operative banks, state-owned rural banks.
- *Semi-Formal Institutions:* These are not regulated by banks, but usually licensed and supervised by donor or government agencies that fund such institutions. These include some NGOs, credit unions.
- *Informal Sector Institutions:* These operate outside the structure of government regulation or supervision, including many Self-Help Groups and NGOs supporting micro enterprises.

The study by Adolph (2003) emphasised that the formal financial market failed in effectively serving the rural population in fulfilling their basic functions such as:

- Production credit to finance income-generating activities.
- Consumption credit to maintain and expand human productive capacity.
- Micro-saving schemes for increasing risk-bearing capacity of the rural households.

In fact, the cooperative credit was introduced in India as a defence mechanism against the exploitation of the rural poor. However, with the growth of co-operatives as formal organizations, they have ceased to be thrift-oriented, member-led, and autonomous organizations. Though conceptually the rich and the poor members can participate equally in the cooperative effort, the needs of the poor often get marginalised (Panda and Mishra, 1996). As a result, the performance of formal co-operative credit institutions – particularly with respect to rural India – has been unsatisfactory.

On the other hand at the world level, the micro-credit system gained momentum in the mid-1990s after the World Summit for Social Development,[7] held in Copenhagen in 1995. The summit – which emphasised the easy access to credit for small producers, landless farmers, and other low-income individuals, particularly women – urged governments of various nations to take appropriate actions in order to provide easy accessibility to credit by the poor. Subsequently, in 1997, the Micro-credit Summit in Washington, DC, announced a global target of ensuring delivery of credit to 100 million of the world's poorest families, especially to the women of those families, by 2005. In the past, despite the vast institutional credit network, the attempt to serve the weaker section of society, particularly women and the deprived, had yielded only limited success (Gabaand Abha, 2003; Justus and Mohiba, 2000). Micro-credit Summit 2006 set goals to be reached by 2015 that were aimed at:

1. Reaching 175 million of the poorest families with micro-credit.
2. Ensuring that 100 million families rise above the US$1-a-day threshold, which would lift 500 million people out of extreme poverty (UNFPA, 2006).

To reach the summit goal of 100 million families, each country must reach 50 per cent of the poor families in their country. As a solution to overcome the previous limitations and to achieve the target, SHGs are used as a springboard to reach the rural poor to help them meet their financial demands in the present world (Roy, 1994; Ojha, 2001).

Progress of SHGs Micro-credit Models in India

Self-Help Groups are voluntary groups that come together to obtain loans from financial institutions in order to meet their financial needs to improve standards of living. It is seen as a good means both from the perspective of group members, who do not have direct access to bank loans, and also from the view point of financial institutions regarding recovery success, since members with loans will experience neighbourhood (group) pressure to repay loans. In many of the cases, micro-credit has also helped Self-Help Groups to start self-employment projects in groups as well. Thus since last decade, SHG banking is the primary mode of micro-finance in India. Today, financing through SHGs is becoming the best medium to include the rural poor in the formal financial sector. Reaching over six million families presently in India, the following three models have primarily evolved for the purpose of linking SHGs with banks (Adolph, 2003; Robert, 2005).

Model-I: SHGs formed and financed directly by banks (Bank-promoted):

In this model, the SHGs are organized and promoted directly by banks. Banks provide credit in bulk directly to the SHG, which might be an informal or registered body. Then, SHGs would lend to its members with terms and conditions. NABARD[8] provided refinance assistance to the lending banks. In this model there was no involvement of NGOs.

Model-II: SHGs formed by other agencies but directly financed by banks (Government department):

In this model, government agencies organize and promote the SHGs and then refer those SHGs to the bank for lending either to the SHGs or directly to individual members of the SHGs. The government agency stands only as a support to both the bank and the SHGs for monitoring and evaluating the projects, the proper functioning of the SHGs, the repayment of the loans, the training of members of SHGs, etc.

Model-III: SHGs, financed by banks but NGOs, act as financial intermediaries (NGO-promoted):

Here, the SHGs are organized and promoted by NGOs and referred to the bank for linkage and the bank provides finance directly to the NGO for lending to the SHGs or to individual members of the SHGs. NGO will be fully responsible for making repayment to the bank and it also performs the functions that are in Model-II.

In India the first effort was taken up by the National Bank for Agriculture and Rural Development (NABARD) in 1986-87 on a pilot basis, and then the Reserve Bank of India (RBI) from 1991 prepared the concept of SHGs for banking, finance, and development onwards. Later NABARD launched a project to provide micro-credit by linking SHGs with the bank after 1991-92 (Nabard, 1995). In a research study (Nabard, 2007) it is stated that from a modest beginning in 1992-93 with 255 SHGs in 10 states, the number of SHGs increased substantially by a hundredfold, to 0.717 million in 2002/03, covering all states and union territories. Cumulatively, 0.717 million SHGs were provided micro-finance loan aggregating Indian Rupees (INR)[9] 20,487.00 million, benefiting 7.8 million poor households in India. Total micro-finance loans disbursed to SHGs during 2003 are aggregated to INR 10,223.00 million involving a refinance of INR 6,223.00 million by the national banks. Recent statistics based on NABARD report on SHGs and micro-finance in 2010 is presented in Table 3.1. In Table 3.1 we can see that more than 75 per cent of the financed groups are women-run SHGs, which amount to about 6.953 million. This covers about 97 million poor household families (Nabard Report, 2010. This will be more than 18 per cent growth in outreach to rural areas (Srinivasan, 2008).

Table 3.1: SHGs' Progress Highlights in India

Sl. No.	Particulars	Data
1.	No. of SHGs micro-financed (million)	6.953
2.	% ofwomen groups	76.37%
3.	No. of participating banks	498
	1 Commercial banks	27
	2. RRBs	81
	3. Cooperative banks	318
	4. Foreign Banks + Private banks	19
4.	Total Savings of Women SHGs (in INR billion)	44.99
5.	Bank loan discoursed to women SHGs (in INR billion)	124.29
7.	Refinance INR in billion	128.61
8.	No. of poor households assisted (in millions)	97
9.	Average loan (INR)/SHG	57795
10.	Average loan (INR)/Group member	4128

Source: NABARD, 2010. *(Note: All the above data are as on 2010).*

Outreach of Micro-credit Models

According to a study by Sa-Dhan (2007), India is performing well regarding micro-credit, with a Compound Annual Growth Rate of 76 per cent. NABARD conducted research on the impact assessment of micro-credit in 2005. It inferred that micro-credit clients have diversified their risks and thus reduced the vulnerability to external factors and that they also were able to provide regular and more years of schooling to their children. Women were empowered in decision-making.

Following successes with micro-credit, micro-credit operations in India became the centre of discussion globally in 2002. Consequently, SHGs and micro-credit are considered very essential for the complete eradication of poverty. On the other hand, researchers emphasise that, in context of the magnitude of poverty and flow of funds for poverty alleviation through micro-credit, there has been very little intervention in India (Thankha, 2002). Figure 3.1 explains the present outreach and scope for micro-credit expansion in context of the depth and intensity of outreach in India.

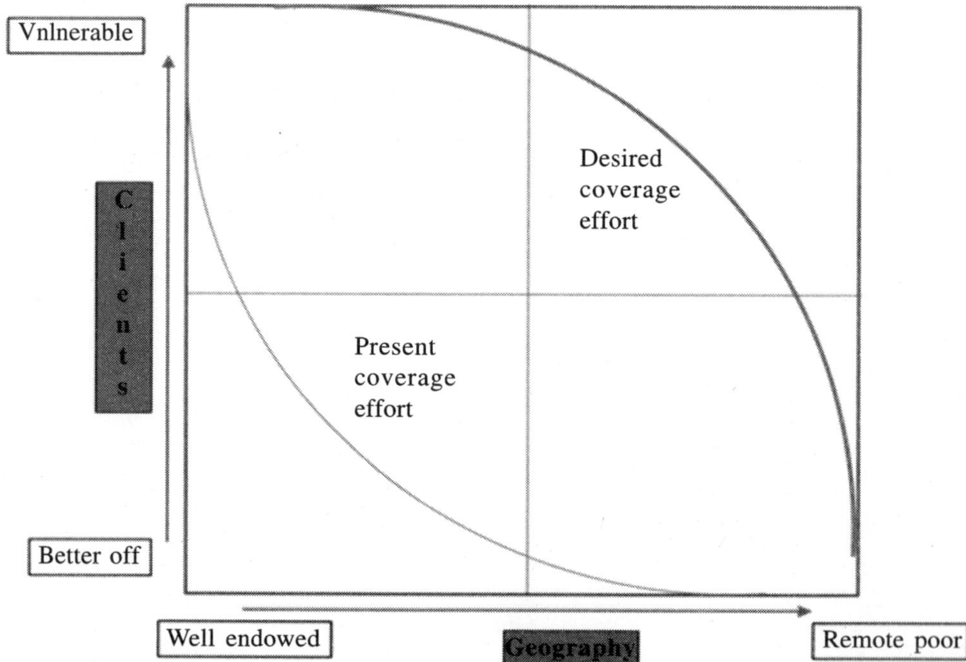

Fig. 3.1: Micro-finance Coverage in India

Source: Srinivasan, 2008.

Figure 3.1 explains the distribution of the micro-finance services across the country and also the coverage of the most vulnerable sections of population through SHGs. In terms of its coverage of the poor clients, the four southern states in India, namely Tamil Nadu, Karnataka, Andhra Pradesh, and Kerala, which have made outstanding progress in SHG credit linkage, have reached both targeted groups: the upper strata of poor and the ultra-poor. In the other six major north Indian states, there are very few clients, constituting less than one per cent of the total clients. In terms of geographical coverage, well-endowed and high-growth areas have been prioritised. Another study finding mentions that in terms of outreach Andhra Pradesh, Karnataka and Tamil nadu has 52 per cent share in number of clients and 59 per cent in loan volumes, clearly indicating the outreach disparities (Reddy and Malik, 2011). The expansion within such areas has also not been consciously targeted towards the poor. The most vulnerable are not clients of choice for most organizations engaged in SHG promotion or micro-finance institution lending (MFI) in such areas. In poorly endowed, backward, and remote areas, even the better-off among the poor do not get covered, as these areas are not yet on the microûnance map. The critically poor remain excluded, indicating that a vast sample of the population is still waiting to harness micro-financing benefits through SHGs to escape poverty.

Many research studies have proved that micro-credit through SHGs seems impressive and found it to be one of the potential weapons for eradicating poverty in India. This necessitates in expounding on the institutional structure of the three micro-credit delivery models of SHGs in reaching the poor in India – explained in figures 3.2, 3.3, and 3. 4 (Adopted and Modified from Rakesh Malhotra, 2005).

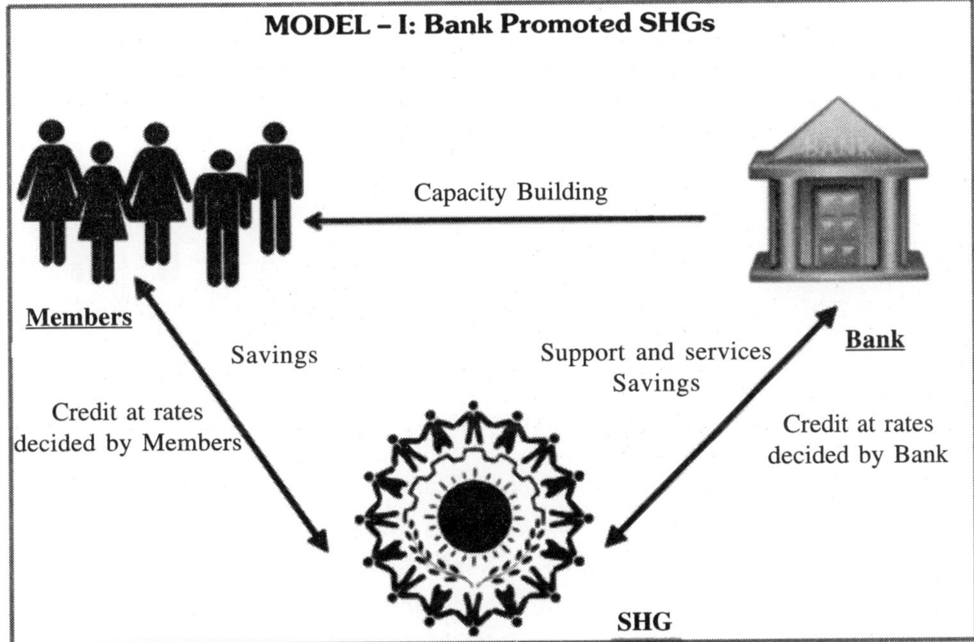

Fig. 3.2: Model-I Showing Bank-Promoted SHGs Working Structure

Source: Adopted and Modified from Rakesh Malhotra, 2005.

Bank-promoted (Model-I) SHGs are one of the three micro-credit delivery models of SHGs operating explicitly in India. In this model, banks play a key role in all SHG activities. This model has succeeded in meeting the main objectives of micro-credit and SHG programmes, both from an institutional perspective and from the member's side. The Consultative Group to Assist the Poor (CGAP) in its study (Cgap, 2007) recognises that the model has met the target of reaching the poor, and it might be due to directed lending and priority-sector quotas imposed on public sector commercial banks. Indian commercial banks, most of which are government-owned, began lending to SHGs because of government-imposed, priority-sector lending quotas (Rbi, 2007). The fact is that lending via micro-credit accounted for less than 1 per cent of the priority-sector lending done by banks and less than 0.40 per cent of total credit of commercial banks as of 31 March 2007, leaving a lot of scope for further expansion of the programme.

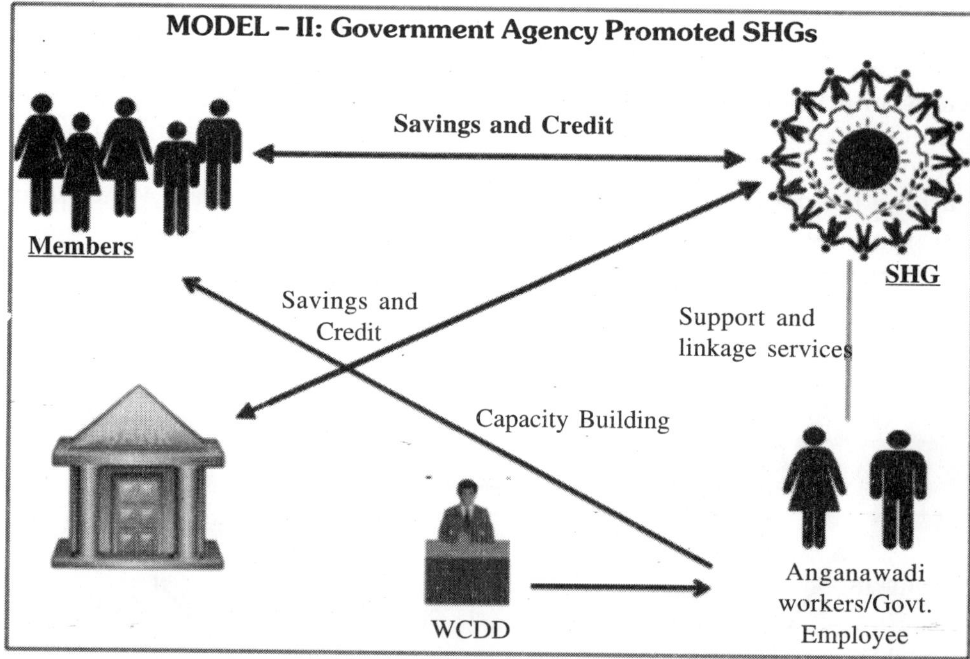

Fig. 3.3: Model-II Showing Government Agency-Promoted SHGs Working Structure

Source: Adopted and Modified from Rakesh Malhotra, 2005.

The second model of micro-credit delivery by SHGs is through a government agency. It forms the group and facilitates linkages to the bank, gives training, capacity-building, and regular monitoring. The Government of India had come up with the *Sthree Shakti* (government agency)[10] scheme in 2000/01. It mainly supported the SHG movement in rural areas to empower women to fight against poverty and to assist rural women in understand their rights as well asgaining economic independence, freedom of participation, and access to credit. At the village level, school teachers (*Anganwadi* workers) are the grassroot workers from the government side; they work with SHGs with an objective to make members self-reliant and to achieve financial stability through neighbourhood Self-Help Groups.

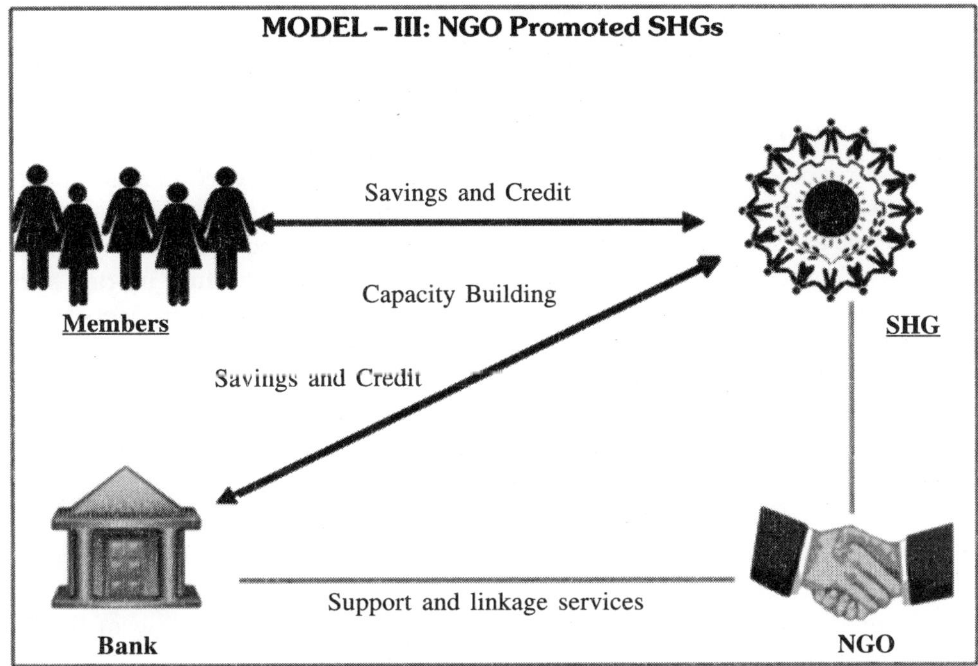

Fig 3.4: Model-III Showing NGO-Promoted SHGs Working Structure

Source: Adopted and Modified from Rakesh Malhotra, 2005.

The third model includes micro-credit delivery for the SHGs, which are formed by NGOs and linked to banks. In fact, the concept of NGOs (voluntary organizations) was already there in India from the early 19th century, when the country was still under the clutches of the British (SMITH and FREEDMAN, 1972). In the beginning, micro-credit started only under the flagship Grameen Bank in Bangladesh; later NGOs emerged to fill the void left by the failure of banks to serve the poor effectively and have become the true pioneers at the world level (BRIGHT, 2006). As time advanced micro-credit began being championed and monitored by thousands of NGOs around the globe, often combining small business training, consulting, and marketing support and then adopting different national governments as part of a development programme at the international level (SNOW and BUSS, 2001). In the same way in India, NGOs are playing a crucial role by providing their own ways for SHGs formation, bank linkage, support, and services through active and meaningful participation and thereby making an impact on rural members that is different from the other two models. Supporting this statement is the example of the Dhan Foundation working in India, which, along with giving credit to the poor, also provides training on income-generating activities like tailoring, hand looming, food processing, etc., so that the SHG members can develop their own livelihood strategy (Sa-Dhan, 2007).

The literature indicates that there is wide variation in the shares of the implemented models in India, wherein Model-II covers about 75 per cent of SHGs, Model-I about 17 per cent, and the remaining eight per cent of SHG micro financing is done through Model-III (Nabard, 2007; Government of Kerala, 2004). The above models operate under different frameworks of rules and regulations; they also differ in the amount of government support, purpose of loan, amount of loan disbursement, interest rate, mode of repayment, etc. Numerous studies have been conducted on the impact of micro-credit and SHGs and the performance of each individual model, and each of these models has been found to have varying positive impacts from an objective point of view in an Indian context. But there has been no attempt to compare the performances between these three models. In nutshell can be inferred that in spite of its considerable outreach, successful savings mobilisation and high repayment rates, as with most other micro-credit models the comparative financial viability of SHG banking has not been clear due to dualistic participation of both formal and informal institutions. However, all the three models have basic commonalities that are pictured here below.

In all the three models, commonality in inflow and outflow of SHGs are...

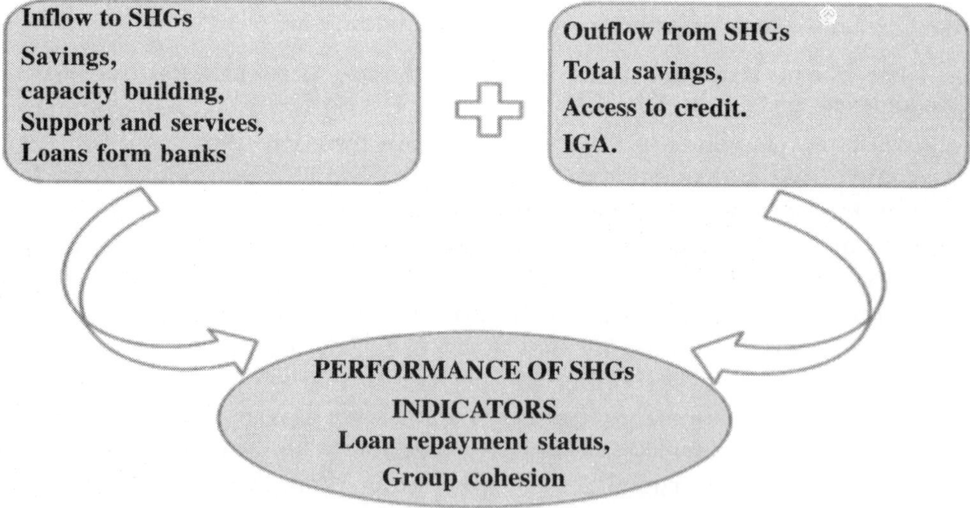

Fig 3.5: Commonality in Inflow and Outflow of SHGs

Conclusion

The SHGs micro-credit concept in India started on a pilot basis in the year 1991 and presently has become the biggest micro-finance programme in the world. The Indian micro-credit sector is known for its diversity of micro-credit delivery models of SHGs. In India, SHGs of all three micro-credit delivery models are working simultaneously with the same objectives and target group. But they diverge in their framework, approach, and execution and outreach also as well in performance. In the above flow chart, we can see that all three models have few important common features in their functioning such as savings, capacity-building, support, and services, loan from bank linkages on inflow side to SHGs and on the outflow side they have total savings of the members and access to credit by the group, purpose of credit like income-generating activities (IGA) or other purposes. In all the models the group performance at the outset depends on its loan repayment status and group cohesion as economic and social indicators respectively. Further, it is suggested that the three models can be compared to analyse and to find the better one, so that the results can assist for further improvement of the programme in a vital direction. In turn, emerging research in this direction helps to achieve success in explaining SHGs' micro-credit for rural development.

FOOTNOTES

1. http://www.expressindia.com/news/print.php?newsid=90717, accessed on 20 June 2009.
2. http://www.nationmaster.com/graph/peo_per_liv_in_rur_are-people-percentage-living-rural-areas.
3. Purchasing Power Parities (PPPs) are Currency Conversion Rates that both Convert to a Common Currency and Equalise the Purchasing Power of Different Currencies. In Other Words, they Eliminate the Differences in Price Levels between Countries in the Process of Conversion. (Source: http://www.oecd.org/department/0,3355,en_2649_34357_1_1_1_1_1,00.html.)
4. Bangladesh Rural Advancement Committee (BRAC) was Established in the Year 1970 on Pilot Basis and Became an NGO and was Implemented in Many Developing Countries.
5. Mercy Corps is an International Humanitarian Aid and Development Charitable Organization that Focuses on Emergency Relief Services, Economic Development, and Civil Society.
6. http://www.cfpa.com.
7. http://www.un.org/documents/ga/conf166/aconf166-9.htm.
8. The National Bank for Agricultural and Rural Development (NABARD) is An Apex Bank for Rural Development in India. It is Accredited with all Matters Concerning Policy, Planning, and Operations Related to Credit for Agriculture and Economic Activities in Rural areas.
9. The Currency Exchange Rate of Euro to INR is 1 Euro = 70 Indian Rupees.
10. http://wcd.nic.in/ and http://www.kar.nic.in/dwcd/.

REFERENCES

Adolph B., 2003, The Role of Self-Help Groups in Rural Non-farm Employment, Rural Non-farm Economy: Access Factors. Discussion Paper, Department of International Development, Natural Resource Institute.

Athena, C., 2009, A Study on the Levels of Living of Self-Help Groups in Coimbatore District, Tamil Nadu. Language in India, Strength for today and Bright Hope for Tomorrow. Vol. 9:1, Feb. ISSN 1930-2940.

Bardhan, D. and Dabas Y.P.S., 2007, Micro-finance Initiatives through Self-Help Groups: Some Issues, *Agricultural Extension Review*. January-June.

Bendapudi, Ramkumar., Shiferaw, Bekele, Wani, S.P., Nageswara Rao, G.D., and Sreedevi, T.K., 2007, Socio-economic Proûles, Production and Resource Use Patterns in Selected Semi-arid Indian Watershed Villages. *ICRISAT Report: Global Theme on Agroeco Systems*, Report No. 34.

Cgap, 2005, CGAP Report – Consultative Group to Assist the Poorest.

Chawla, O.P. and Patel, K.V., 1987, Change and Development in the Village-Role of Self-Help Organizations. *Prajnan*, 16(3):283-298.

Ellerman D., 2008, "Social Funds and Micro-finance Programmes, Paper Presented by David Ellerman. The World Bank at Fundamental Conundrum of Overseas Development the Institute of Development Policy and Movement, University of Antwerp, Belgium, March 4, 2008.

Gaba G. and Abha A., 2003, Perception of Women about their Status as Members of Selected Self-Help Groups of Udhamsinghnagar District. Pantnagar, *Journal of Research*. Vol. I, June.

Government of India, 2007, Government of India Report.

Government of Jharkhand, 2007, Study on Self-Help Groups-Micro-credit: An Innovative way to Help Poor People Improve their Lives.

Government of Kerala, 2004, A Comparative Study of Self-Help Groups Organized and Promoted by NGOs and *Kudumbasree* (A Government Organized NGO) in Kerala. Government of Kerala.

Hagenbuch , W., 1958, Social-economics. Nishet and Company, Cambridge, Britain.

Hanstad T., Brown J. and Prosterman R., 2002, Larger Homestead Plots as Land Reform, International Experiences and Analysis from Karnataka. *Economic and Political Weekly*.

Harper, M., 1996, Self-Help Groups, Some Issues from India. Small Enterprise Development, 7:(2).

Indian Bank, 1996, Financing Self-Help Groups 'Swayam Seva', Indian Bank Central Office, Madras.

Jayaraman, B., 2001, Micro-finance Retrospect and Prospects. Occasional Paper Micro-finance Programmes Other Country Experiences, NABARD.

Justus, E., Raja and Mohiba, M., 2000, Participatory Micro-enterprises: A Case Study of PASA. *Kurukshetra: Journal of Rural Development*. 49 (3):40-4.

Kabir H., 2002, The Experience Revolution and the Grameen Bank Experience in Bangladesh. *Financial Markets Institutions and Instruments*, 11. No. 3.

Karmakar K.G., 1998, SHGs in Orissa – Some Conceptual Issues. *Prajnan*, 26 (2): 123-131.

Khun, J., 1985, The Role of Non-governmental Organizations is Promoting Self-Help Organization. Seminar Papers, Druchari Tranz, Paffernholz Bomheins, pp. 265.

Kumaran, K.P., 1997, Self-Help Groups: An Alternative to Institutional Credit to the Poor: A Case Study of Andhra Pradesh. *Journal of Rural Development*, 16(3):515-530.

Ledgerwood, J., 1999, "Sustainable Banking with the Poor; An Institutional and Financial Perspective" Micro-finance Handbook, *The World Bank*, Washington DC.

Nabard, 1995, Linking SHGs with Banks – An Indian Experience. NABARD Bombay, pp. 1-25.

Nabard, 2007, Annual Report for 2006-07. District NABARD Branches, Dharwad, Karnataka.

Nabard, 2010, Status of Micro-finance in India 2009-10, NABARD Head Office, Mumbai.

Nabard, 2009, Potential Linked Credit Plan 2009-10, National Bank for Agriculture and Rural Development, Davanagere District, Karnataka Regional Office, Bangalore.

Neils Hermes and Robert Lensink, 2007, The Empirics of Micro-finance: What do We know?. The *Economic Journal*, 117 (Feb): F1-F10.

Ojha, R.K., 2001, Self-Help Groups and Rural Employment. *Yojana: A Development Monthly*. 45(2):20-3.

Panda, A.K. and Mishra, A.K., 1996, SHG-Informal Co-operatives in Orissa. Rediscovering Co-operation, IRMA, Anand, Gujarat, 2:216-235.

Planning Commission, 2012, Planning Commission, Poverty Estimates, Government of India.

Rajagopalan, B.K., 1998, SHGs and Social Defence. *Social Welfare*. pp. 30-34.

Rakesh Malhotra, 2005, NABARD-District Development Manager, NABARD, Bareilly, India.

Rao, K., 1994, Self-Help Group and Credit. *Arthavijnana*, 36(3):194-208.

RBI, 2007, Revisiting Bank Linked Self-Help Groups – A Study of Rajasthan State, *RBI Occasional* Paper, Monsoon 2007, by Navin Bhatia, DGM, RBI, Mumbai.

Reddy, Amarender., and Malik, Dharm Pal, 2011, A Review of SHG-Bank Linkage Programme in India. *Indian Journal of Industrial Economics and Development*. Vol. 7 (2): 1-10.

Robert, Christen., 2005, "Micro-finance and Sustainability: International Experiences and Lessons for India." Conference paper for NABARD Workshop, "Micro-finance: Challenges for the Future," New Delhi, 3-6 May.

Roul, S., 1996a, Co-operative in the Emerging Contest. *National Seminar on Rediscovering Co-operation*, IRMA, Anand.

Roy, D.K., 1994, Peasant Movements Grass root Mobilization and Empowerment of Rural Women: Some Sociological Observation. *Women's Link*. 4(4):17-8.

Royal Tropical Institute, 1987, Royal Tropical Institute – Rural Economic Development and Food Security, Amsterdam, Netherlands.

Sa-Dhan, 2007, Maturing Micro-finance-Emerging Challenges. Sa-Dhan. The Association of Community Development Finance Institutions.

Sa-Dhan, 2008, The Bharat Micro-finance Report, Quick Data 2008. Sa-Dhan-The Association of Community Development Finance Institutions.

Singh, S., 1995, Self-Help Groups in Indian Agribusiness-Replications from Case Studies. Arthavijnana, 37(4):380-388.

Smith, C. and Freedman, A., 1972, Voluntary Associations: Perspective on the Literature, Cambridge (mass), Harvard University Press.

Snow Douglas R., and Buss, Terry F., 2001, Development and the Role of Micro-credit. *Policy Studies Journal*, Vol. 29(2), (296-307).

Srinivasan N., 2008, Micro-finance India, State of the Sector Report 2008, SAGE Publications.

Star, 2008, Star Report. The Daily, Dhaka: Transcraft Limited.

State for International Development Report, 2000, Eliminating World Poverty: Making Globalisation Work for the Poor. White Paper on International Development. Presented to Parliament by the Secretary of State for International Development by Command of her Majesty, December.

Tankha, Ajay, 2002, Self-Help Group as Financial Intermediaries in India: Cost of Promotion, Sustainability and Impact. Sa-Dhan, New Delhi. A Study Report Prepared for ICCO and Cordaid, The Netherlands, August.

Unfpa, 2006, From Micro-finance to Macro Change. Integrating Health, Education and Micro-finance to Empower Women and Reduce Poverty. Micro-credit Summit Campaign, New York.

World Bank, 2000, World Development Report 2000-01: Attacking Poverty, Washington DC: World Bank.

4

The Effects of Economic Value Added and Intellectual Capital on the Firms Market Value
Evidence from Iran

— NADER KHEDRI

ABSTRACT

The purpose of this research is to study and compare the explanatory power of economic value added and intellectual capital in determining the firm's value. This research uses the Ohlson valuation method. Statistical universe containing accepted companies in Tehran Stock Exchange (TSE) in period from 2005-07. In order to test the hypotheses and comparing the explanatory power of model we used R^2 co-efficient and adjusted R^2 co-efficient to test hypotheses and comparing explanatory power of models.

The results show that residual income calculated in accounting method, explain the value of the firms better than economic value added. Also, results show that the determinant models of the firm's value that intellectual capital variables have been added to theme, have a higher explanatory power.

Keywords: Firm's value, Economic value added, Accounting earning, Intellectual capital.

Introduction

Now-a-days, by introducing value based management concept, the direction and purpose of many firms have switched to create value and shareholders expect from managers to maximize shareholder wealth as the firm goal. Shareholders wealth is reflected in the firm's stock price. Studying the factors and systems that affect the firm's stock price are important in understanding the assessment of capital market and the change in stock price. In current knowledge-based societies, capital market assessment is not limited to tangible factors. Analysts, in addition to the financial statements of firm, consider other factors too. Intangible assets have become important factors in creation of firm's value. Today's business world is the age of the knowledge-based organizations. In this economy, factors such as income, profitability and assets indicate only a small part of the organizations success and real wealth of organizations is utilisation of expertise and superior human resource, knowledge and skills of them, internal processes and procedures, fame and reputation from customers and stakeholders viewpoint and in other words, intangible assets and intellectual capital (Ashton, 2005).

The role and importance of intellectual capital efficiency in stable and continuous potential profitability is not less than the financial capital (Mouritsen, 1998). In another view, the firm's market value is equal to total of financial capital and intellectual capital. In many cases, developed model by Ohlson (1995) is used in the capital market as a basis for firm's valuation. Ohlson (1995) proposed a residual income valuation model, in which the market value of a firm can be determined by its book value, by the discounted value of its expected future abnormal earnings, and other information. The Stern Stewart Company has argued that the aim or goal of Economic Value Added (EVA®) is to evaluate a firm's market value directly in a way similar to residual income; that it is a financial performance measure integrating accounting and economic concepts. According to this concept, some accounting items in the financial statements are adjusted to present the firm's whole economic value, and shareholder's value is increased only after its earnings exceed its cost of capital (Huang and Wang, 2008).

In this research we use the Olson model and developed it by using EVA and adding the aspects of intellectual capital provided by Edvinsson and Malone (1997). The questions of this research are: Does the Economic value added provide better information than accounting profit in determining the market value of the firms? Does firm's value increase by adding the aspects of intellectual capital?

Literature Review

In the financial literature, there are various theories for valuation of securities. Stewart (1997) believes that measures such as earning per share and profit growth are misleading measures for measurement of firm's performance and EVA is noteworthy as the only measure of wealth or value created by firms.

Lev and Zarowin (1999) found that the usefulness of financial information has been decreasing in the past twenty years, the main reason they argue being that financial information cannot fully reflect major changes in a firm's operating activities. This study will consider the roles of EVA® and intellectual capital in valuation of firms.

Stewart (1997) show that the EVA is the best tool for creating value in firms. The result of this study provides the important evidence that show the advantage of Economic value added compared to traditional criteria such as accounting earning.

Lehn and Makhija (1996) and Mouritsen (1998) state that EVA explicitly considers the necessary cost of capital, where capital is derived from adjusting certain items on the balance sheet to more closely reflect the real cash flows invested; and that therefore EVA can better reflect a firm's risk, and is more representative of the value creation ability of the firm than are the accounting earnings

Chen and Dodd (1997) found that EVA does not provide incremental information content beyond operating income, suggesting that accounting measures are still important in the valuation of firms.

Stewart (1997) argues that intellectual capital is the knowledge and ability that employees bring to their firms and that it is something which will increase firms' competition advantage. He believes that intellectual capital is a set of Knowledge, information, intellectual property, experience, competition and organizational learning that can be used to create wealth. In fact, Intellectual capital include all of the staff, organizational knowledge and its abilities for create value added and causes the continuous competitive advantage.

Edvinsson and Malone (1997) state that intellectual capital is information and knowledge used in order to create value. They decompose firm value into financial capital and intellectual capital, and the latter into complementary human capital and structure capital. Capital structure is divided by them into customer capital (or relation capital) and organizational capital (or structure capital) (Bontis, Keow and Richardson, 2000). The development of the knowledge economy has brought these issues to public attention. Organizational capital can itself be further divided into innovative capital and procedure capital (Bukh, Larsen and Mouritsen, 2001).

Chauvin and Mark (1993) examined the relation between advertisement, R and D expenditure and a firm's market value, and showed that firms which report greater expenditures on advertisement and R and D are more highly valued in security markets.

O' Donnell *et al.* (2003) adopted a case study approach to measure how much value firms place on intellectual capital. Their study showed that chief executive officers and chief financial officers believes that 60 per cent of a firm's value is constituted by intellectual capital, up to 50 per cent is human capital, while external and internal structure capital are 30 per cent and 20 per cent respectively.

Mahdavi and Rastegari (2007) study the information contents of EVA to predict the profit. The results of this study imply that EVA has no increasing information contents as compared with the current operating profit.

Palliam (2006) investigate the relationship between EVA and firm's value. The results show that use of EVA is somewhat invalid, unreliable and controversial.

Maditinos *et al.* (2009) study the explanatory power of two value-based performance criteria that includes EVA and shareholding value added and traditional accounting performance criteria such as earnings per share and return of assets in determining the efficiency of Greek stock exchange. The results show that the earnings per share is related with stock market efficiency more than EVA and other performance criteria.

Wang (2008) study the relationship between intellectual capital and firm's market value in electronic firms that their stock is traded in the US exchange. He used the Ohlson model to determine the value of firm. Results show that there is a positive relationship between the intellectual capital and market value.

Hypotheses Development

For studying the explanatory power of economic value added and intellectual capital in determining the firm's value, we test the following hypotheses:

Hypothesis 1: There is no difference between the residual income that is calculated by the EVA and accounting earnings, in determining changes in the firm's market value.

Hypothesis 2: The affects of residual income that is calculated by the method of accounting principles on the firm's market value is significantly greater in presence of intellectual capital's proxies.

Hypothesis 3: The affects of residual income that is calculated by the method of EVA on the firm's market value is significantly greater in presence of intellectual capital's proxies.

Research Variables

Dependent Variable

In this research, dependent variable is market value of firms stock and this is equal to amount that investor is willing to pay for each share in official stock exchange.

Independent Variable

In addition to book value per share at the end of period and shareholder's expected rate of returns, residual income per share, EVA, return of investment and intellectual capital are other independent variables that described below.

Residual income per share

Based on Wang (2008), in order to calculate this variable, we use following equation:

$$EPS_r = EPS_t - (BV_{t-1} * R)$$

Where:

EPS_r = Residual income per share.

EPS_t = Earnings per share at the end of t term.

BV_{t-1} = Book value per share in the previous period.

R = Shareholder's expected rate of returns.

Return of investment

For calculating this variable, we use following equation:

$$ROI = NOPAT/Capital$$

Where:

ROT = Return of investment.

NOPAT = Net operating income after tax..

Economic value added

Based on Stewart (1991), EVA is calculated by following equation:

$$EVA = (ROI - R) * Cuplial$$

Intellectual capital

In this research we use intellectual capital aspects provided by Edvinsson and Malone (1997) as follow:

- Customer capital. It is the strength and loyalty of customer relations. Its proxies are advertising expense per share and operating revenue growth.
- Process capital. Process capital includes the techniques, procedures, and programmes that implement and enhance the delivery of goods and services. Its proxy is administrative expense per staff.
- Innovation capital. Innovation capital includes intellectual properties and intangible assets. Intellectual properties are protected commercial rights such as copyrights and trademarks. Intangible assets are all of the other talents and theory by which an organization is run. Its proxy is ratio of research and development expense by net operating revenue.
- Human capital. Human capital includes knowledge, skills, and abilities of employees. Human capital is an organization's combined human capability for solving business problems. Its proxy is operating revenue per staff.

Sample Selection

The statistical universe for this study comprises firms listed on the Tehran Stock Exchange (TSE). All financial firms (including banks) and firms with insufficient data about variables used in this research (such as R and D) are excluded. Based on these limitations, the final sample includes 37 firms. The sample period is from 2005-07. Financial and accounting data needed to estimate models are obtained from TSE reports on CDs and web.

Research Model

In this research, we use the following model (first model) for firm's valuation:

$$Pt = \alpha_0 + \alpha_1 BV_t + \alpha_2 X + \varepsilon_t$$

Where:

Pt = Market value of the equity per share.

BV_t = Book value per share.

X = Accounting residual income per share or economic value added per share.

Because Ohlson (1995) is not clearly defined the other information in his model so, researchers have tried to determine such information as much as possible and enter the factors that affect firm's value in this model. In this research, we use aspects of intellectual capital as the other information. So, by adding these aspects, the final model that used in this research is as follow (second model):

$$P_t = \alpha_0 + \alpha_1 BV_t + \alpha_2 X + \alpha_3 RPE_t + \alpha_4 SP_t + \alpha_5 RG_t + \alpha_6 RD_t + \alpha_7 AEPE_t + \varepsilon_t$$

Where:

RPE_t = Operating revenue per share.

SP_t = Advertising expense per share.

RG_t = Growth of operating revenue.

RD_t = Ratio of research and development expense by net operating revenue.

$AEPE_t$ = Administrative expense per staff.

Based on Edvinsson and Malone (1997), We expect that all independent variables have a positive relationship with firm's market value.

Results

The purpose of this research is to compare the effects of EVA, earning per share and aspects of intellectual capital in firms value. For compare the explanatory power of research models and hypotheses testing, we use R^2.

The R^2, adjusted R^2 and F-statistic of estimating the first model and second model are shown in Table 4.1, 4.2, 4.3 and 4.4.

Table 4.1: First Model with Earnings per Share

Model: $Pt = \alpha_0 + \alpha_1 BV_t + \alpha_2 EPS + \varepsilon_t$			
R^2	Adjusted R^2	F-statistic	Sig.
0.552	0.526	20.978	0.000

As shown in Table 4.1, F-statistic of this model is 20.978 and is statistically significant at the 1 per cent level. This issue indicates that the model is significant in general. R^2 in this mode is 0.552 and this issue shows that the independent variables (book value and earnings per share) could determine the 55 per cent of firms value.

Table 4.2: First Model with Economic Value Added

Model: $Pt = \alpha_0 + \alpha_1 BV_t + \alpha_2 EVA + \varepsilon_t$			
R^2	Adjusted R^2	F-statistic	Sig.
0.188	0.140	3.931	0.000

As shown in Table 4.2, *F*-statistic of this model is 3.931 and is statistically significant at the 1 per cent level. This issue indicates that the model is significant in general. R^2 in this mode is 0.188 and this issue shows that the independent variables (book value and economic value added) could determine the 18 per cent of firms value.

Table 4.3: Second Model with Earnings per Share

Model: $P_t = \alpha_0 + \alpha_1 BV_t + \alpha_2 EPS + \alpha_3 RPE_t + \alpha_4 SP_t + \alpha_5 RG_t + \alpha_6 RD_t + \alpha_7 AEPE_t + \varepsilon_t$			
R^2	Adjusted R^2	F-statistic	Sig.
0.622	0.531	6.825	0.000

As shown in Table 4.3, *F*-statistic of this model is 6.825 and is statistically significant at the 1 per cent level. This issue indicates that the model is significant in general. R^2 in this mode is 0.622 and this issue shows that the independent variables (book value, earnings per share and intellectual capital proxies) could determine the 62 per cent of firms value.

Table 4.4: Second Model with Economic Value Added

Model: $P_t = \alpha_0 + \alpha_1 BV_t + \alpha_2 EVA + \alpha_3 RPE_t + \alpha_4 SP_t + \alpha_5 RG_t + \alpha_6 RD_t + \alpha_7 AEPE_t + \varepsilon_t$			
R^2	Adjusted R^2	F-statistic	Sig.
0.305	0.138	1.822	0.021

As shown in Table 4.4, *F*-statistic of this model is 1.822 and is statistically significant at the 5 per cent level. This issue indicates that the model is significant in general. R^2 in this mode is 0.305 and this issue shows that the independent variables (book value, economic value added and intellectual capital proxies) could determine the 30 per cent of firms value.

Results of Testing the First Hypothesis

In first hypothesis we compare the residual income based on EVA and accounting earnings. Based on results of estimating the first and second hypotheses that are shown in Table 4.5 and 4.6, we can test this hypothesis.

Table 4.5: Results of Estimating the First Model

Model: $Pt = \alpha_0 + \alpha_1 BV_t + \alpha_2 X + \varepsilon_t$				
Variables	α_0	BV_t	EPS_t	Adjusted R^2
co-efficients	1840.25	0,378	4.833	0.526
Variables	α_0	BV_t	EVA_t	Adjusted R^2
co-efficients	2279.13	1.250	0.06	0.140

Table 4.6: Results of Estimating the Second Model

Model: $P_t = \alpha_0 + \alpha_1 BV_t + \alpha_2 X + \alpha_3 RPE_t + \alpha_4 SP_t + \alpha_5 RG_t + \alpha_6 RD_t + \alpha_7 AEPE_t + \varepsilon_t$									
Variables	α_0	BV_t	EPS_t	RPE_t	SP_t	RG_t	RD_t	$AEPE_t$	Adj. R^2
co-efficients	1709.4	0.486	4.613	-3.76	0.159	-43.15	60.48	-2.01	0.531
Variables	α_0	BV_t	EVA_t	RPE_t	SP_t	RG_t	RD_t	$AEPE_t$	Adj. R^2
co-efficients	2145.3	1.348	8.69	-2.72	0.266	-66.53	66.954	-4.32	0.138

As shown in Table 4.5 and 4.6, adjusted R^2 in first and second model in a situation that we use accounting method for calculating the residual income is more than situation that we use EVA method. This result indicates that earnings per share can better determine changes in firm's market value than economic value added. So, the first hypothesis is not supported and this means that there is difference between the residual income that is calculated by the EVA and accounting earnings, in determining changes in the firm's market value.

Results of Testing the Second and Third Hypotheses

In order to testing hypotheses 2 and 3, we compare R^2 related to first and second model. This comparison is shown in Table 4.7.

Table 4.7: Comparison between first and Second Model's

Residual income	First Model's R^2	Second Model's R^2
Accounting method (EPS)	0.552	0.622
Economic value added per share	0.188	0.305

Results in Table 4.7 show that the second model's R^2 is more than first model's R^2 in both situations. This issue indicates that by adding intellectual capital proxies to models, the determination power of models increased. So, hypotheses 2 and 3 are supported and this means that the affects of residual income calculated by both accounting method and EVA, on the firm's market value is significantly greater in presence of intellectual capital's proxies.

Conclusion and Limitations

Analysis of results show that both economic value added and earnings per share have a positive relation with firm's market value. But, based on comparison between determination co-efficients of models, market value determination by residual income calculated by EVA is less than earnings per share. The weaker relationship between EVA and firms market value could be derived by several reasons.

First, there were special conditions in Tehran Security Exchange in period 2005-07. The most important feature in this period is depression in market and significant reduction in bourse index (Table 4.8). Due to changes in viewpoints of economic managers in Iran government, most of investors exited from TSE, stock price decreased, fear and despair atmosphere increased and investors had no hope to earn revenues from stock price increases and therefore, they more consider and attend to the firm's dividend payment. So, it seems that stock price had more correlation with accounting income.

Table 4.8: Changes in Bourse Index

Year	2004	2005	2006	2007
Index	13608	10532	9501	9999

Second, economic value added is a new concept in Iran and due to complexity of computing, it is not familiar and understandable as much as prevalent ratios such as price to earnings ratio.

Finally, considering the equity cost in economic value added is necessary and because of high inflation rate in Iran and its affect on equity cost calculation, less attention paid to economic value added.

The study is subject to a number of potential limitations. *First,* the model may be subject to omitted variable bias. *Second,* most of Iranian's firm have not research and development expense or do not report it separately and this issue makes our research sample too small. High inflation rate in Iran and historical data in financial statements are other limitations of this study.

REFERENCES

Ashton, R. H., (2005), Intellectual Capital and Value Creation: A Review, *Journal of Accounting Literature,* Vol. 24, pp. 230-242.

Bontis, N. (2001), Assessing Knowledge Assets: A Review of the Models used to Measure Intellectual Capital., *International Journal of Management Review,* Vol. 3 No. 1, pp. 41-60.

Chauvin, K.W. and Hirschey, M. (1993), Advertising, R and D Expenditures and the Market Value of the firm, *Financial Management,* Vol. 22 No. 4, pp. 128-40.

Chen, S. and J. L. Dodd (1998), Usefulness of Operating Income, Residual Income and Eva: A Value Relevance Prespective, *Working Paper, Clarion University and Drake University.*

Edvinsson, L. and Malone, M. (1997), Intellectual Capital: Realizing your Company's True Value by Finding Its Hidden Roots, *Harper Collins,* New York, NY.

Huang, G. and Wang, M. C., (2008), The Effects of Economic Value Added and Intellectual Capital on the Market Value of Firms: An Empirical Study, *International Journal of Management,* Vol. 25, No. 4, pp. 722-731.

Maditinos, D. I., Sevic, Z. and Theriou, N. G. Modelling Traditional Accounting and Modern Value-based Performance Measures to Explain Stock Market Returns in the Athens Stock Exchange (ASE), *Journal of Modelling in Management,* Vol. 4 No. 3, pp. 182-201.

Mahdavi and Rastegari (2007), Information Content of EVA for Income Prediction, *Accounting Advances Journal,* Shiraz, Vol. 50, pp, 137-156.

Mouritsen, J. (1998), Driving Growth: Economic Value Added *vs.* Intellectual Capital. *Management Accounting Research,* Vol. 9, pp. 461-482.

Mouritsen, J., Nikolaj, P. N. and Marr, B. (2004), Reporting on Intellectual Capital: Why, What and How?, *Journal of Measuring Business Excellence*, Vol. 8, No. 1, pp. 46-54.

O'Donnel, D., O'Regan, P., Coates, B., Kennedy, T., Keary, B. and Berkery, G. (2003), Human Interaction: The Critical Source of Intangible Value, *Journal of Intellectual Capital*, Vol. 4, No. 1, pp. 82-99.

Ohlson, J.A. (1995), Earning, Book Values, and Dividends in Equity Valuation, *Contemporary Accounting Research*, Vol. 11 No. 2, pp. 661-87.

Palliam, Ralph. (2006), Further Evidence on the Information Content of Economic Value Added, *Review of Accounting and Finance*, Vol. 5 No. 3, pp. 204-215.

Stewart, G. B., (1990), The Quest for Value: the EVATM Management Guide, *New York: Harpner Business.*

Stewart, G. B., (1994), EVATM – Fact or Fantasy, *Journal of Applied Corporate Finance*, Vol. 7, No. 2, pp. 71-84.

Stewart, G. B., III, (1996), The Quest for Value, *New York: Harpper Collions Publisher Inc.*

Stewart, T.A. (1997), Intellectual Capital: The New Wealth of Organizations, New York: Doubleday.

Wang, J. C. (2008), Investing Market Value and Intellectual Capital for S and P 500, *Journal of Intellectual Capital*, Vol. 9 No. 4, pp. 546-563.

5

From 'Wealth of Nations' to 'Happiness of Nations'

Tracing the Path to the Concept of 'Gross National Happiness'

— Dr. Anamika Kaushiva

IT is increasingly being acknowledged that for true well-being and for a fulfilling life, social and economic development should be accompanied with happiness or subjective well-being. Development theories encompass growth, rise in GDP, human development but often ignore deeper issues of happiness. Economists have confined themselves to a narrower concept of wealth basically because it can be measured and accounted. Well-being including subjective well-being is a broader concept. Both Aristotle in the western tradition ages ago and Dalai Lama today in the East, agree that happiness is an end in itself and man pursues all other goals because they lead to happiness. The concept of happiness in economics was confined for many years to issues of growth and development. However realising that social well-being and happiness cannot be reduced to a simple quantitative index like GNP/GDP, thinkers have developed a comprehensive model to define and measure quality of life in holistic and psychological terms – Gross National Happiness (GNH). The paper attempts to explore and understand the concept of Gross National Happiness as developed in Bhutan. It is an attempt to trace chronologically the various theoretical approaches in the sphere of social well-being and happiness. The paper discusses in detail the ideas of defining the criterion of a happy society, identifying the metrics of GNH measuring Gross National Happiness and the possibilities of actually using the concept in assessing economic and social welfare.

Background

IT is increasingly being acknowledged that for true well-being and for a fulfilling life, social and economic development should lead to or should be accompanied with happiness or subjective well-being. Development theories encompass growth, rise in GDP, socio-economic equity, human development but often ignore deeper issues of subjective fulfilment and happiness. Economists, no doubt, know that wealth alone does not bring happiness yet they have confined themselves to a narrower concept of wealth basically because it can be measured and accounted. Well-being including subjective well-being is a broader concept. Both Aristotle in the western tradition ages ago and Dalai Lama today in the East, agree that happiness is an end in itself and man pursues all other goals because they lead to happiness.

The concept of happiness in economics has been confined for many years to issues of growth and development. Promotion of economic growth has been stressed since long as a means of achieving the goal of socio-economic well-being. Income – Happiness relationship within a single country, at a given time period, has been treated as a measure of material happiness. GNP has remained the most dominant guideline in adopting national development plans, rationalising development programmes and evaluating the success of development projects across the world. GNP per capita has been treated as the primary measure of development objectives, economic success, and people's national welfare. It is used to determine a country's economic status and rank in the overall global hierarchy of levels of national development and ranking of nations into categories such as 'least developed', 'developing', 'developed', and so on. However social well-being and happiness is a complex measure comprising of many measurable and non-measurable factors. It cannot be reduced to a simple quantitative index like income, wealth, consumption.... GNP/GDP as has been the case.

The first section of this paper attempts to explore limitations of the measure of GNP as a measure of development and its existing critique. The second section is an attempt to trace chronologically the various theoretical approaches, across the world, that are emerging in the sphere of measuring development, social well-being and happiness. The third section discusses in detail the concept of Gross National Happiness – its definition, origin, four pillars, and its metric measures.

Introduction

Aristotle advocated the concept of happiness 'eudemonia' most fully in 'Nicomachean Ethics' wherein he said "happiness is the meaning and purpose of life, the whole aim and end of human existence". He stated that "It must be most final.... It must be self sufficient.... It must be generally available... And it must be relatively stable."[1] Political Economy too emphasized on happiness in its sociological approach. In the period 1750-1780, when Italian Economic thought *i.e.*, 'Neapolitan School' was dominant, 'Public Happiness' figured in the title of most of the works of Ferdinando Galiani and Antonio Gevonesi. Genovesi, in Lectures on civic Economy 1765, wrote "labour in your own interest; no man can work other than for his own happiness; for he will be less than a man; but.... If you are able and as far as you are able, strive to make others happy. It is the law of nature that we cannot achieve our own happiness without achieving that of others".[2] Their concept of civic humanism contributed two central ideas to economics that technology must be studied as a means of civilizing and improving people's well-being and public faith is the main resource to human development – similar to the present day concept of social capitalism.

With Adam Smith's 'An inquiry into the Nature and Causes of Wealth of Nations' happiness started being pushed into the background and was slowly forgotten in the scope of economics. It became the subject matter of philosophy, psychology and ethics. J.S. Mill's 'Utilitarianism' treated pleasure as identical with happiness. However his idea did not get much attention.

Bentham equated pleasure with happiness defined utility as property of an object whereby it finds to produce benefit, advantage, good or happiness. He thus defined happiness as "greatest good for greatest number of people" and stated that wealth was the means to happiness *i.e.*, the wealthier a person is, the greater the happiness he can attain. The critical question Bentham puzzled over was whether the unhindered pursuit of individual happiness could be reconciled with morality. Despite his attempts, he failed to develop any convincing account of happiness, or of social utility. Happiness came to be reduced to utility.

As economics grew more and more quantitative, utility, preference, choice, income and budgetary constraints came to the forefront. Political Economics inspired thinkers to the hope that satisfaction of basic material needs would lead to happiness. Since 1970's human happiness began creeping back into economic thought. It entered into the arena as a debate on the 'Paradox of Happiness' which began explicitly with the paper published by the Psychologists Brickman and Campbell, 1971, "Hedonic Relativism and Planning the Good Society". According to their view, improvement in material well-being (income/wealth) has no effect on personal well-being. Richard Easterlin was the first modern economist to reintroduce the concept of happiness in economics in the early 1970s. In 1974, in his paper "Does Economic Growth Improve Economic Lot? Some Economic Evidence", he presented the 'Easterlin Paradox' that within a country, people of higher income are more likely to report being happy, however in international comparisons, the average reported level of happiness does not vary much with national income per person, at least with countries with income sufficient to meet the basic needs. Using two types of data – Gallop Poll type of survey and data from research conducted by human psychologist Hadley Cantrell in 1965 in 14 countries, Easterlin arrived at a result that "In every single survey, those in the highest group were happiest on the average than those in the lowest group" In cross sectional differences among countries on the other hand, positive association between wealth and happiness, although present, is neither general, nor robust and poor countries do not appear to be less happy than richer countries. Further between 1946-70 average reported happiness showed no long-term trend and declined in 1960-70 *i.e.,* no link between economic development and average level of happiness was established according to his study.

In 1976, Tibor Scitovsky's, 'Joyless Economy', too focused on happiness and developed an analysis to explain why increase in consumer goods in opulent society is not making people happy and based his answer on the distinction between pleasure and comfort. Today happiness is a fast emerging research focus of economists around the world and many thinkers today support the view that happiness should once more occupy a central place in economics. Recently Richard Layard, Professor at the London School of Economics in his book, *Happiness: Lesson from A New Science,* 1980 argues that public policy should be devoted to increasing happiness rather than wealth or success. Ideas being explored include definition of happiness, indicators of happiness and ultimately accounting of happiness and these are gaining greater and greater attention.

Happiness is also emerging as a major subject of discussion in Philosophy, Sociology and Religion. The Dalai Lama's book, *The Art of Happiness,* 1988, contains conversations with a western psychiatrist Howard Cutler emphasizing the power of compassion and love for all as a happiness therapy.

Gross National Product and Development as a Measure of Happiness

In general, Gross National Product of a country represents the total money value of all goods and services produced by its residents in one year. More specifically, GNP includes the money value of total annual domestic product of a country, plus incomes (*e.g.,* investment earnings and remittances) earned abroad by its residents, minus payments made to non-residents and foreign institutions. GNP measure has come to represent the principal measure of economic progress.

GNP Accounts assess value with units of measurement expressed in common monetary terms. Two types of accounts or systems of economic valuation are used-stock accounts and flow accounts. The conventional stock and flow accounts account for only a fraction of a nation's true wealth and spending, and are therefore narrow and distorted. The accounts count only the value of manufactured and financial capital, and entirely ignore the value of natural, human, social, and cultural capital. These too are subject to depreciation and in need of re-investment as is manufactured capital and therefore cannot be ignored. While the latter are accounted for in GDP and GNP, the former goes unaccounted. Further, the accounting system has a convenient term for everything it excludes *i.e.,* 'externalities', a term which simply helps ignoring the true costs of resource depletion, pollution, health hazards, crime, and declining moral and social values. Simon Kuznets, the primary architect of national income accounting, had himself stated that GDP should never be used as a measure of nation's welfare. "Welfare of a nation can scarcely inferred from a measurement of national income.... goals of 'more' growth must specify of what and for what".

Another limitation of the GNP measure is that it is incapable of measuring non-economic (social) dimension of human welfare, which constitutes an essential part of overall development. In addition, this measure assumes all outputs as beneficial, without making any distinction between "productive and destructive activities".

Thirdly, there is no direct compatibility between GNP growth rate and actual human development.

Fourthly, GNP measure fails to include unpaid labour involved in household activities such as caring for children and elderly parents at home, growing and preparing foods for family consumption, providing volunteer services to the community, and so on. In developing economies, with dominant rural sector and underdeveloped market systems, many household and economic activities are unpaid. These outputs and services outside the market do not appear in the GNP figures. Thus, the measure of GNP is quite misleading to compare the standards of living between the developed and the developing countries.

Thus since GDP measures only quantity of market activity without accounting for social and human costs involved, it is both inadequate and misleading as a measure of prosperity. These issues lead to the realisation that there is need to re-examine and replace GNP as the indicator of human development with a more comprehensive measure of sustainable development and well-being.

Chronologically it is possible to trace various theoretical approaches around the world in the sphere of measuring happiness which attempt to step outside the domains of GDP and introduce indicators of standard of living and welfare.

From 'Wealth of Nations' to 'Happiness of Nations'

The *First* UN decade of Development 1960-70 saw the beginning of a shift from emphasis on growth to development. Secretary-General U Thant said, "Development is not just economic growth, it is growth plus change. Change, in turn, is social and cultural as well as economic, and qualitative as well as quantitative. The key concept must be improved quality of life".[3] However, these various aspects of development were not really yet treated as integrated with economic growth; social development and economic development were still addressed as quite separate components in the proposals for action.

The Cocoyoc-Declaration (23, October 1974) emphasized that human beings have basic needs: food, shelter, clothing, health, education and any process of growth that does not lead to their fulfillment – or, even worse, disrupts them – is a farce. The primary purpose of economic growth should be to ensure the improvement of conditions of the poorest section of society. A growth process that benefits only the wealthiest minority and maintains or even increases the disparities between and within countries is not development. The hope that rapid economic growth benefiting the few will 'trickle down' to the mass of the people has proved to be illusory and economic and social thinkers have begun to reject the idea of 'growth first, justice in the distribution of benefits later' and began to emphasise on 'development'.

Development encompasses much more than growth. Development means "to ensure the quality of life for all with a productive base compatible with the needs of future generations........ Rational use of the available labour force to implement programmes aimed at the conservation of natural resources, enhancement of environment, creation of the necessary infrastructure and services to grow more food as well as the strengthening of domestic industrial capacity to turn out commodities satisfying basic needs." (Cocoyoc-Declaration) With this declaration, development became the goal of all economic policies across the world and various index and indicators to measure the level of development attained began to emerge. Many economists working outside mainstream of pure economic theory began trying to find operational solutions for quantifying the concept of development and to evolve the concept of 'social accountability'.

The Physical Quality of Life Index (PQLI) was developed for the Overseas Development Council in the mid-1970s by Morris David Morris as an attempt to measure the quality of life or well-being of a country. The index is the average of three statistics: *(i)* basic literacy rate, *(ii)* infant mortality, and *(iii)* life expectancy at age one, all equally weighted on a 0 to 100 scale.

The International Index of Social Progress (ISP) and the Weighted Index of Social Progress (WISP) were developed in 1974 by Richard Estes of the University of Pennsylvania's social work faculty. WISP measures economic development, social and political conditions, and the ability of nations to produce welfare services for their citizens using 46 indicators.

The Brundtl and Commission convened by the United Nations in 1983 to address growing concern 'deterioration of economic and social development', gave birth to the concept of 'Sustainable Development'. Sustainable development is development which meets the needs of the present without compromising the ability of future generations to meet their own needs.

The Capability Approach began the 1980s wherein Amartya Sen brought together a new range of ideas and argued for the importance of real freedoms in the assessment of a person's advantage, individual differences in the ability to transform resources into valuable activities, the centrality of the distribution of welfare within society, the multi-variate nature of activities that give rise to happiness, and against excessive materialism in the evaluation of human welfare. The approach emphasizes 'substantive freedoms', such as the ability to live to old age, engage in economic transactions, or participate in political activities; these are construed in terms of the substantive freedoms people have reason to value, rather than in terms of utility or access to resources. The approach was first fully articulated in Sen (1985) and discussed in Sen and Nussbaum (1993). Applications to development are discussed in Sen (1999), Nussbaum (2000). Nussbaum framed ten capabilities, *i.e.*, real opportunities based on personal and social circumstance which should be supported by all democracies. The key dilemma for the capabilities approach was how to measure what people could do, as opposed to what they actually do and to develop new survey instruments to operationalize Nussbaum's list.

The Preamble of the final text of The Earth Charter, (1987, United Nations World Commission on Environment and Development) an international declaration of fundamental values and principles, approved at a meeting of the Earth Charter Commission at the UNESCO headquarters in Paris in March 2000, stated that "We must join together to bring forth a sustainable global society founded on respect for nature, universal human rights, economic justice, and a culture of peace." The four pillars of the Earth Charter – Respect and Care for the Community of Life, Ecological Integrity, Social and Economic Justice, Democracy, Non-violence, and Peace and sixteen principles in the above pillars were outlined to achieve its objectices.

The Genuine Progress Indicator (GPI) was developed by Clifford Cobb and co-authored by Ted Halstead and Jonathan Rowe in 1994 as a concept in green economics and welfare economics that has been suggested to replace gross domestic product (GDP) as a metric of economic growth. GPI is an attempt to measure whether a country's growth, increased production of goods, and expanding services have actually resulted in the improvement of the welfare. It distinguishes between worthwhile growth and growth. Some economists, notably Herman Daly, John B. Cobb and Philip Lawn asserted that a country's growth, increased goods production, and expanding services have both 'costs' and 'benefits' – not just the 'benefits' that are calculated in GDP. According to Lawn's model, the 'costs' of economic activity include the following potential harmful effects like resource depletion, ozone depletion, family breakdown, air, water, and noise pollution, crime, family breakdown. The GPI starts with the same personal consumption data that the GDP is based on, but then makes some crucial distinctions. It adjusts for factors such as income distribution, adds factors such as the value of household and volunteer work, and subtracts factors such as the costs of crime and pollution. Income distribution, house work volunteering, leisure time, higher education, crime, resource depletion, pollution, environmental damage, defence expenditure, dependence on foreign resources are among the 51 socio-economic and environmental indicators included in the index. The index was upgraded in 2005.

In 1990 Mahbub-ul-Haq, (UNDP), launched the concept of Human Development Index – statistical index to rank countries based on statistics for life expectation, education and GDP was introduced using Sen's capabilities approach as the basis of its conceptual framework and used a group of economists – P. Streeten, F. Stewert, G, Ranis etc., to draw up a list of fundamental human needs.

The Canadian Council for Social Development developed 'Life Quality Index' as an index wherein quality of life is assessed. It was first initiated at the Institute for Risk Research, University of Waterloo, Ontario, Canada in the early 1990s. The principal investigators involved in the development of the Life Quality Index were Professors Niels Lind, Jatin Nathwani and Mahesh Pandey. The three components of the Life Quality Index, G, E and K reflect three important human concerns: *(i)* the creation of wealth, *(ii)* the duration of life in good health and *(iii)* the time available to enjoy life are used to measure LQI. The LQI is a summary indicator of net benefit to society for improving the overall public welfare by reducing risks to life in a cost-effective manner.

The Happy Planet Index (HPI) as an index of human well-being and environmental impact was introduced by the New Economics Foundation (NEF) in July 2006. The HPI is based on general utilitarian principles – that most people want to live long and fulfilling lives, and the country which is doing the best is the one that allows its citizens to do so, whilst avoiding infringing on the opportunity of future generation.

The above survey of Economic thought across time and countries on different well-being, socio-economic indicators/accounting measures being developed reveals that they use some common indicators – fulfillment of basic needs, work and leisure, knowledge, relationships, empowerment and participation, and harmony and peace (within and outside) – to assess welfare and happiness.

Gross National Happiness

While countries across the world were coming up with ideas to define and measure well-being and happiness, Bhutan, a very small nation, had already developed a comprehensive model to define and measure quality of life in holistic and psychological terms – Gross National Happiness (GNH). The term GNH was first coined in 1972 by Bhutan's former King Jigme Singye Wangchuck who in speech said "Gross National Happiness is more important than Gross National Product."

The concept of GNH claims to be based on the premise that true development of human society takes place when material and spiritual development occur side by side to complement and reinforce each other. GNH refers to the concept of a quantitative measurement of well-being and happiness. Since the world is increasingly obsessed with numbers, the Centre for Bhutan Studies in Bhutan along with the international academia and development practitioners came up with a formula after several international conferences on GNH. The first conference was held in 2004 in Thimphu, Bhutan.

Dimensions and Indicators of GNH

The efforts towards developing a GNH index was undertaken to provide Bhutan with a valuable set of indicators that can be utilised in making its development efforts more holistic and harmonious in its goals and means.

The single number GNH index and its component indicators provide Bhutan with three different levels and types of indicators: GNH status indicators, GNH demographic indicators and GNH causal and correlation indicators.

The definition of happiness in the kingdom of Bhutan and the Bhutanese, are much broader than those that are referred to as happiness in the Western literature. Happiness according to their perspective covers a range of dimensions of human well-being. Some of these are quite traditional areas of socio-economic concern such as living standard, health, and education while others are new issues such as time use, emotional well-being, culture, community vitality, or environmental diversity.

According to Prime Minister Lyonpo Jigmi Y Thinley "The four pillars of GNH are the promotion of equitable and sustainable socio-economic development, preservation and promotion of cultural values, conservation of the natural environment, and establishment of good governance."

The nine dimensions have been selected on normative grounds, and are equally weighted. Within each dimension, several indicators have been selected. The nine dimensions are:

1. *Psychological Well-being:* Satisfaction with all elements of life, life enjoyment, and subjective well-being. The psychological well-being index covered three areas: general psychological distress indicators, emotional balance indicators, and spirituality indicators.
2. *Time Use:* The nature of time spent within a 24-hour period, as well as activities that occupy longer periods of time. The time available for non-work activities such as sleeping, personal care, social-cultural activities, education and learning, religious activities, sports and leisure and travel contribute to levels of happiness. Measurement of time devoted unpaid work activities like care of children and sick members of household, and maintenance of household, can provide a proxy measure of contribution made by unpaid activities to welfare though

the value of such activities are completely underestimated in national accounts. In the GNH index, time use component was divided into benchmark indicators of sleeping hours and of total working hours.

3. *Community Vitality:* The strengths and weaknesses of relationships and interactions within communities. The community vitality indicators consist of: family vitality indicator, safety indicator, reciprocity indicator, trust indicator, social support indicator, socialisation indicator, and kinship density indicator.
4. *Cultural Diversity and Resilience:* The diversity and strength of cultural traditions. The indicators of cultural diversity consist of: dialect use, traditional support, community festival, local artisan skills, value transmission and basic percept indicator.
5. *Health:* The health status of the population, the determinants of health and the health system. The health index consists of: health status indicator, health knowledge indicator, and barrier to health indicator.
6. *Education:* The knowledge, values, creativity, skills, and civic sensibility of citizens. The education index consists of: education attainment indicator, Dzongkha language indicator, and folk and historical literacy indicator.
7. *Environmental Diversity and Resilience:* The impact of domestic supply and demand on Bhutan s ecosystems. The ecological diversity and resilience indicators consist of: ecological degradation indicator, ecological knowledge indicator, and afforestation indicator.
8. *Living Standard:* The basic economic status of the people. The living standard indicators consist of: income, housing, food security, hardship indicators.
9. *Good Governance:* How people perceive various government functions in terms of their efficacy, honesty, and quality. The indicators of good governance consist of government performance, freedom, institutional trust indicators.

Method for GNH Index Construction

The Gross National Happiness Index (GNH) is constructed in two steps, one of which pertains to identification and one to aggregation. The first step is to define whether each household has attained sufficiency in each of the nine dimensions. This is done by applying a sufficiency cut-off to each dimension using an innovative methodology.

In poverty measurement, it is quite common to apply a poverty line, which distinguishes people who do not have enough money from those who are non-poor. Bhutan holds that it is possible to distinguish, additionally, between those people who have attained sufficient level of achievement and those whose attainments fall short of sufficiency. The sufficiency cut-off is set at a higher level than a poverty line. In some indicators it is set at the top level of achievement for that indicator while in others indicators it is set at a level that is deemed sufficient for most people. A person is identified as having a sufficient quality of life if his or her achievements in that indicator meets or exceeds the cut-off. If the achievements do meet or exceed the cut-off, the person's actual achievements are replaced by the sufficiency level. For example, if actual income were 1,000 and sufficiency cut-off were 150, and then the person would be treated as if they earned 150. Thus achievements above the sufficiency cut-off do not further increase someone's quality of life score. The level at which the sufficiency cut-off is set is a value judgment and it is difficult to set an exact cut-off.

The sufficiency cut-offs are applied as follows: The value of each indicator in which a household attains sufficiency or above sufficiency is given a 0. Subsequently all achievements that are less than sufficient are replaced by the distances from the cut-offs. It is calculated by subtracting the actual achievement from the sufficiency cut-offs, and that difference is divided by the sufficiency cut-off itself. This way, the depth (distances from the cut-offs) will rise if any poor person drops further away from the sufficiency cut-off. This reflects the inequality of achievements among the persons below the cut-offs, thereby placing a greater penalty to low achievements. Any shortfall from sufficiency that any household experiences in any indicator within any dimension is considered to depress Gross National Happiness. A person who has achieved sufficiency in all nine dimensions is considered happy.

The second step is to aggregate the data of the population a decomposable measure that is sensitive to the depth as well as severity of achievements. That is, first we identify the shortfalls from gross national happiness and calculate the squared distances from the cut-offs. The resulting measure is the GNH.

GNH = 1 - Average squared distance from cut-off

Having calculated the Gross National Happiness index, it is very easy to break down the index to identify how achievements in each dimension extend or dampen Gross National Happiness. The number of indicators in each of the nine domains is different and so, in order to avoid biasness the domains are attached with equal weights. Thus when the GNH is calculated it is one number. This GNH is comparable across districts surveyed and across time. Further it is possible to decompose the GNH by dimension (or indicator), by district, by gender, by occupation, by age group etc. The data so derived reveals immediately in what dimensions of life shortfalls from sufficiency are most acute. The decomposition of GNH across time reveals in which dimensions sufficiency is increasing or decreasing. In these ways, the GNH has been developed to be used as an instrument of policy evaluation.

Conclusion

Happiness has usually been looked upon as a utopian issue. The economists have not been very successful in developing suitable tools for its measurement. Thus while the goal of development is happiness, it is regarded as subjective and beyond the realm economic analysis. Most socio-economic indicators are an attempt at measuring means of attaining development; they do not measure ends.

Problems persist about finding cross-cultural and meaningful measures of subjective well-being. The need of the hour is thus changing the system of accounting and economic valuation. Many new indicators and new accounting systems have been proposed by thinkers across the world in the last five decades. All have a common element – stress on the need of valuing natural, social, and human capital properly. While indicators of varying nature have been suggested, work is needed on development of data sources and methodologies. What was once just a concept and an aspiration is now feasible and measurable in Bhutan and Nova Scotia, and all economies across the world should implement the new indicator and accounting tools as guides to policy. The new indicators and accounts must be adopted as core measures of progress and valuation, in order to demonstrate their feasibility, utility, and policy relevance. This is a matter of political will.

New parameters should not be introduced as mere 'add on' to the existing measures, but as an entirely new concept.

Happiness Economics and the GNH index are being applied to a range of issues in many countries today. Some of the issues are relationship between income and happiness, inequality and poverty, the effects of macro-policies on individual welfare. This can deepen understanding of poverty beyond the narrow poverty line concept. It can be used to examine the effects of different macro-policy socio-economic on well-being.

Once the new accounting system are adopted by government, a system of financial incentives and penalties designed to encourage sustainable behaviour that contribute to well-being and happiness and to discourage unsustainable behaviour has to be evolved. This can include measures like taxes, fines, penalties on unsustainable activities like pollution, forest clearing and incentives like tax relief and subsidy on use of renewable energy development, organic farming, social work etc. The GNH approach and practice offers positive solutions to the current global economic crisis. Including GNH principles, practices, and examples in educational curricula, training our youth in the GNH measurement methods, and a wide GNH movement is perhaps the most path for realisation of GNH in practice. GNH should be made the measurement index of an overall strategy to maximize socio-economic well-being. The first step in this direction will be defining the criterion of a happy society and identify the metrics of GNH. Hopefully, the combination of GNH measures and econometric techniques will allow economists in better assessment of macro-economic policies economic welfare and the degree of economic development in the future.

FOOTNOTES

1. As Quoted in Bruni, l
2. As Quoted in Screpenti Ernesto, Stefanzo Zamgani; An outline of the History of Economic Thought, Oxford University Press, 2006.
3. "United Nations Development Decade: Proposals for Action", Report of Secretary General, New York, UN 1962.

REFERENCE

Bruni, L, and Pier Luigi Porta, (2005), Economics and Happiness, Framing the Analysis, Oxford University Press, New York.

Colman, Ronald, *"Measuring Progress towards Gross National Happiness: From GNH Indicators to GNH National Account"*, http://www.bhutanstudies.org.bt/pubFiles/1.GNH4.pdf

Dalai Lama His Holiness, Howard C. Cutler, M.D, (1998), Art of Happiness A Handbook For Living, Riverhead Books.

"The Genuine Progress Indicators", http://www.cyberus.ca\sustain1\gpi.html.

Easterlin, R.E. (1974), "Does Economic Growth Improve the Human Lot? Some Empirical Evidence" in P.A. David and M.W. Reder (eds), *Nations and Households in Economic Growth: Essays in Honour of Moses Abramowitz*, (1995), Academic Press, New York.

Kahneman, D., and Krueger, A.B. (2006), Developments in the Measurement of Subjective well-being, *Journal of Economic Perspectives*, 20(1), 3-24.

Lawn, P.A. (2003), A Theoretical Foundation to Support the Index of Sustainable Economic Welfare (ISEW), Genuine Progress Indicator (GPI), and other Related Indexes. *Ecological Economics*, 44 , 105-118.

Layard, Richard. (March 2003), "Happiness: Has Social Science a Clue?", in *Lionel Robbins Memorial Lectures, 3 - 5,* The London School of Economics, London.

Layard, Richard, (1980), Human Satisfaction and Public Policy, *The Economic Journal*, 90:737-5.

Lyonpo Jigmi Y. Thinley. (1998), Values and Development: Gross National Happiness, *Text of the Keynote Speech Delivered at the Millennium Meeting for Asia and the Pacific*, 30 October ~ 1 November 1998 Seoul, Republic of Korea.

Nassumbaum, Martha C. (2005), "Mill between Aristotle and Bentham", in L. Bruni and Pier Luigi Porta, *Economics and Happiness, Framing the Analysis*, 54 - 90, (Oxford University Press, New York.

Oswald, A.J. (1997), Happiness and Economic Performance, *The Economic Journal*, 107/445, 1815-31.

Prahlad Singh Shekhawat, Prahalad Singh, *"Rethinking Development and Well-Being and a Search for New Indicators"*, Alternative Development Centre, Jaipur. Http://www.gnh-movement.org/papers/shekawat.pdf

Robert, H, Frank. (2005), "Does Absolute Income Matter", in L. Bruni and Pier Luigi Porta *Economics and Happiness, Framing the Analysis*, Oxford University Press, New York.

The Cocoyoc Declaration (1974), *UNEP-UNCTAD Symposium*, October 1974, Cocoyoc, Mexico

"The Genuine Progress Indicators" http://www.cyberus.ca\sustain1\gpi.html.

United Nations, (1962), The United Nations Development Decade: Proposals for Action, Report of the Secretary General, Forwarded by U. Thant, Department of Economic and Social Welfare, United Nations, New York.

UNDP, (2004) Human Development Report 2004, Oxford University Press, New York http://www.grossnationalhappiness.com/

6

Role of NGOs in Human Development
An Empirical Analysis

— Venkatraja. B
— M. Indira

The main objective of the present paper is to analyse the contribution of Non-Government Organizations (NGOs) to human development in Dakshina Kannada (D.K) district of Karnataka state based on micro level data. Inorder to analyse the impact of NGO interventions on human development, Amartya Sen's capability approach has been employed. Human development being multi-dimensional in approach, special care has been taken to ensure that important elements which influence development are not excluded from measurement. That is why, in this study, due consideration has been given to five functionings of development such as economic, social, political, organizational and environmental. Data pertaining to these functionings are collected separately in NGO villages (where NGOs are actively involved in development process) and Non-NGO villages (where NGO activities are absent). Inorder to incorporate all these functionings in the assessment, UNDP's HDI methodology has been applied with modification. Results of the study show that people of NGO villages have higher rate of achievement of functionings but the people of Non-NGO villages have higher rate of deprivation of functionings. Thus, human development is more in NGO villages. This is the clear reflection of the positive impact of the NGO interventions on the overall well-being of the community. Non-Government Organizations (NGOs) are generally regarded as functional agencies and integral part of participatory development of the modern welfare state in India and elsewhere in the world. Of late, there is a gradual withdrawal of the state from providing services to the poor in favour of NGOs. This is because they have better access than government agencies to the project population by virtue of their familiarity with local conditions. With the introduction of neo-liberal policies, state is withdrawing from providing some of the services and they are placed in the market domain. Since market forces are impersonal and do not distinguish between rich and poor, there is a need for agencies to protect the interests of poor. NGOs are filling that gap created by the withdrawal of the state. These are the best suited agencies because of their flexibility in operations, willingness to take risk, ability to act quickly, capacity to involve people in their decision making process, and low administrative and staff costs. They often have a significant cost – benefit advantage over those undertaken by the government. They also act as a watchdog of legitimate interest of women and create confidence among the landless-labourers. This makes a case for increasing role of NGOs in development process.

On these grounds, several scholars have argued in support of NGOs and considered them as catalysts in development of human-beings. Despite having good characteristics, a major question is raised about the impact of NGO interventions on the lives of the people. The important question is – do NGO interventions leave an impact on the lives of the people? This is due to several factors. The major ones to be highlighted are:

(i) There are thousands of registered NGOs operating in India but still poverty, unemployment, illiteracy, exploitation etc., are rampant all over the country.

(ii) Several of the registered NGOs are inactive in the field.

(iii) The methodologies for evaluating the impact of NGO interventions still at evolving stage. These are not standard methodologies.

(iv) The existing literature, evaluative reports are fragmented and are oriented towards the specific objective of either the funding agency or the implementing agency.

It is challenging task to evaluate the impact of NGO interventions on lives of the people. The research problem that the present study addresses is how to measure the impact of NGO interventions on the lives of people who are addressed by the NGOs.

Objectives

The main objective of the paper is to analyse the contribution of NGOs to human development in Dakshina Kannada (D.K) district of Karnataka state based on micro level data. The specific objectives are:

1. To develop a broad based methodology to measure human development.
2. To map the intervention strategies of the NGOs in the study area.
3. To analyse the impact of these interventions on human development.

Methodology

Study Area

The present study is based on the micro level household survey conducted in ten villages of Karnataka state. A sample of 250 households from ten villages of five taluks (such as Mangalore, Belthangady, Puttur, Bantwal and Sullia) in Dakshina Kannada district, Karnataka was selected randomly. In each taluk two villages were selected, of which one village is NGO village and the other village is Non-NGO village. In Mangalore taluk Moodushedde was considered as NGO village and Koikude was the Non-NGO village. Kuvettu and Kukkula villages of Belthangady taluk were selected as NGO village and Non-NGO village respectively. In Puttur taluk Aryapu village was considered as NGO village and Kabaka as Non-NGO village. From Bantwal taluk Alike was selected as NGO village and Kepu as Non-NGO village. The NGO village of Sullia taluk was Jalsoor and Non-NGO village was Aranthod. The villages were selected purposively based on the NGO interventions. Out of the ten villages, five villages represent NGO villages, meaning, villages with NGO interventions and the other five are Non-NGO villages representing the villages without any NGO presence. Data were collected through a pre-tested questionnaire. The reference unit is the individual. This is because of the nature of the functioning selected which mainly pertain to the personal situation. Information about the socio-economic background of the individual and the environment in which he/she lives was collected at the household level.

Functionings of Human Development

Income approach, basic needs approach and other approaches to development measure welfare only on the basis of either income or commodities. In their assessment of well-being several dimensions of life, though they are important are not covered. Therefore, Amartya Sen (1985) has evolved an alternative tool called capability approach to earlier economic frameworks for thinking about poverty, inequality and human development. The major constituent of the capabilities approach is functionings. A functioning is an achievement of a person: what she or he manages to do be. It reflects as it were, a part of the 'state of that person' (Sen, 1985). In other words, functionings are the 'doings of a person' (Robeyns, 2005) and are 'constitute of a person's being' (Alkire, 2005). Therefore, assessment of the achieved functionings provide clear well-being status of individuals.

While measuring human development special care has to be taken to ensure that important elements which influence development are not excluded from measurement. That is why, in this study, due consideration has been given to five functionings of development such as economic, social, political, organizational and environmental. Appropriate indicators were developed to represent each of the five dimensions. The functionings selected and their co-related indicators are the following:

1. *Economic Functioning:* It indicates the economic well-being attained by the people. In the present study economic functioning is measured by six main indicators. They are: *(i)* employment, *(ii)* income, and *(iii)* energy, *(iv)* transport, *(v)* communication and *(vi)* ownership of assets.

2. *Social Functioning:* This functioning throws light on various aspects of social dimension of life. It is measured by twenty one variables divided into the following six groups of indicators such as: *(i)* education, *(ii)* health, *(iii)* empowerment, *(iv)* safety and security, *(v)* ability to go about without shame and individual perceptions about meaning and *(vi)* value in one's own life.
3. *Political Functioning:* Political functioning has been included in the study inorder to understand the level of achievement of political dimension of life. It is indicated by two sets of indicators referring to political awareness and political participation. Political dimension of human development is measured by six variables which describe the awareness and degree of interest in political issues.
4. *Organizational Functioning:* Indicates the dependence of people on organizations, both formal and informal. By measuring five variables relating to the membership, and involvement in associations or other kinds of organizations, this functioning has been calculated.
5. *Environmental Functioning:* This is a very important functioning of human life. This is mainly because environmental factors determine the sustainable development. This functioning is measured by means of five indicators related to: the weather, rainfall, fertility of soil, and steps taken to protect from pollution.

Measurement of the Functionings

Subsequent to the selection of a list of relevant functionings and their indicators, first step in the assessment of human development requires us to assign the rank order score to each variable ranging from one to five, one signifying the least achievement of functionings, whereas five the most. With the aim of realising a more defined picture of the achieved functionings, some elementary indicators have subsequently been merged. In this regard averaging method has been applied. Finally, the individual index for each of the indicators is computed. A general formula, derived from UNDP methodology, has been applied for the computation of the individual index for each of the indicators. The formula is:

$$\text{Concerned Index} = \frac{\text{Actual Value} - \text{Minimum Value}}{\text{Maximum Value} - \text{Minimum Value}}$$

Through this operation, seventeen elementary indices are obtained with reference to the five functionings included in the development assessment. By aggregating the elementary subsets, five composite sets have been derived for each functioning (as shown below) and these five composite sets refer to the five dimensions of human development as discussed earlier.

1. Economic Functioning Index (EFI) = $\frac{EI + YI + EyI + TI + CI + DAI}{6}$

Where, EI=Economic Index, YI= Income Index, EyI = Energy Index, TI= Transport Index, C I= Communication Index, DAI= Durable Assets Index.

2. Social Functioning Index (SFI) = $\frac{EdI + HI + EmpI + SSI + EHI + MVI}{6}$

Here, EdI =Education Index, HI = Health Index, EmpI = Empowerment Index, SSI =Safety and Security Index, EHI = External Humiliation Index, MVI= Meaning and Value Index.

3. Political Functionig Index (PFI) = $\frac{PAI + PPI}{2}$

Where, PAI = Political Awareness Index, PPI= Political Participation Index.

4. Organizational Functioning Index (OFI) = $\frac{BHI + OPI}{2}$

Where, BHI= Banking Habit Index and OPI= Organizational Participation Index.

5. Environmental Functioning Index (EnFI) = $\frac{\text{Actual Value} - \text{Minimum Value}}{\text{Maximum Value} - \text{Minimum Value}}$

Finally, an overall index called Human Functioning Index (HFI) has been computed by calculating the simple average of the five resultant indices, giving equal weightage to each.

Human Functioning Index (HFI) = $\frac{EFI + SFI + PFI + OFI + EnFI}{5}$

Here, EFI = Economic Functioning Index, SFI = Social Functioning Index, PFI= Political Functionig Index, OFI= Organizational Functioning Index and EnFI= Environmental Functioning Index.

- *Range:* Each of the indicators, functionings and finally HFI have been rated on the scale of zero to one, where zero shows the absolutely defined worst achievement and one represents the absolutely defined best achievement of the indicator/functioning/HFI by the individual respondent.
- *Classification of the Respondents:* On the basis of the human functionings achieved, the individual respondents are classified into three groups such as:

(i) *Low Human Functionings Group*: It consists of individuals with index values ranging between 0 and 0.499.

(ii) *Medium Human Functionings Group*: This group includes households with HFI value between 0.5 and 0.799.

(iii) *High Human Functionings Group*: All households achieved HFI above 0.8 are classified under High Human Functionings group.

Research Background

In India, there is a burgeoning size of literature on NGOs and their intervention strategies. They are analytical, theoretical or case studies. Very little efforts have been made by the researchers in the direction of analysing empirically whether such interventions lead to well-being of the people. Further, such studies in Indian context provide us only the partial view of human development. This is because different studies have examined the impact of NGO interventions on a particular area of development like economic development or social development or rural development or women empowerment. Therefore, such studies have failed to ascertain the impact of NGO interventions on all dimensions of life. Most of the empirical studies have considered income as index of positive impact. Indicators like meaning and value in one's own life, ability to go about without shame, safety and security, etc., which are very important for the well-being of people have not been included in these studies. Amartya Sen's (1985) capability approach is a comprehensive theoretical framework of human development giving importance to all dimensions of well-being. This concept has been extensively used in Human Development Reports (UNDP, 1990-99). State level human development reports are prepared in India based on this concept. However, these reports have taken into consideration only three indicators (income, health and education) and they are aggregated at the district level. Therefore, this study fills the gap of developing a comprehensive index incorporating all the dimensions of human development and measures the impact of NGO interventions in human development.

NGO Sector in D.K District

Dakshina Kannada District is perhaps in the forefront in terms of voluntary work. Several social services institutions are working in the district. Some of the existing NGOs in the district have sustainable interventions. The Bassel Mission, Sri Ramakrishna Mission, Fr. Muller's Charitable Institution, Indian Red Cross Society and several other institutions have served the less fortune people in the district.

D. K district also witnessed social reform movements and had a branch of Arya Samaj, Bramho Samaj, Theosophical Society, Narayanaguru movement and so on. These movements were basically against the oppressive caste order existed in the society. However, the nature and method of voluntary action in the district has undergone a lot of changes when compared to its history. Also nature and method of voluntary action differs within the district among different taluks. For *e.g.*, voluntary effort on rural development is much more in Belthangady taluk when compared with other taluks of the district and voluntary social welfare activities are more in Mangalore when compared to other taluks of the district (Kalluraya, 2002). Today, there exists a burgeoning size of NGOs in the district and their activities have stretched to diversified areas.

The NGOs are able to intervene into the issues of different nature. Interventions of NGOs in the community life can be broadly divided in to nine areas. They are: *(i)* Aged and differently abled, *(ii)* alcoholism, *(iii)* agriculture, *(iv)* education, *(v)* environment, *(vi)* health, *(vii)* SC/ST welfare, *(viii)* training, and *(ix)* women and child welfare. The issues addressed by various organizations in D. K shows that majority are development organizations, focusing on either rural or urban development. This includes organizations implementing programmes for women and child welfare, education, health etc. Aged and differently abled, environment and training, also received great attention. SC/ST welfare, agriculture and alcoholism also appear to be areas of growing concern.

Organizations involved in the activities in these areas may be classified as religious based, charities, historical based Christian missionaries, registered voluntary organizations, youth clubs, mahila mandals/clubs, and trusts, branches of international/national associations, corporate philanthropy and individual contributions. Therefore, voluntary interventions are seen both in formal and informal types. Thus, the kinds and sectors involved in intervention and strategies adopted by the NGOs of D. K are wide and diversified.

Mapping of Intervention Strategies

Strategies are the guiding concepts on what to do and what not to do in terms of resources. All organizations have their own characteristic ways of using their resources. The objectives, target groups, areas of intervention, projects undertaken and area covered under programmes vary from NGO to NGO A brief note on the various strategies adopted by different NGOs to intervene in the social life of the community in D. K district is given below.

Anand Ashram Seva Trust came in to existence in Puttur to render services mainly to the elderly people and the children. It has extended its services network nation-wide. The Ashram helps the target group by conducting eye camps, providing old age home, and Anganavadi centre for children. Asha Jyothi, an NGO at Mangalore taluk, works for disabled children of 15 years and above. The strategies devised by it to reach the target group are: conduct meetings regularly for the disabled, provide recreation, special talks to build confidence and improve standard of living and arrange picnics and sight seeing etc. Similarly, Seon Ashram trust at

Belthangady taluk provides home for orphans and destitutes. St. Joseph's Prashanth Nivas is one of the oldest NGOs in Mangalore. It promotes the interests of children, elderly people and the differently abled. It provides old age home and home for the people with different abilities, and also orphanage to orphans and disowned.

Kripa Foundation located in Mangalore, works to create a drug and alcohol free generation. It makes the public aware of the problem and helps the alcoholics and drug addicts to lead a new life. For this the Foundation provides family counseling, brings patients closer to their families. Later it follows up discharged patients for five years. Link Counseling and De-addiction Centre also promotes positive values and work for drug free culture in the district. Its programmes include: de-addiction and rehabilitation of chemical dependents, community based de-addiction camps, preventive educational and awareness programmes on substance abuse and training of personnel in the field.

Cauchin Krishik Seva Kendra (Dayabagh) works with the marginal farmers and landless agricultural labourers in Belthangady taluk. Its programmes are: formation and training of SHGs, integral family development, micro-credit, education, health, awareness, and training programmes for women. These programmes are implemented through SHGs. Harekala Landless Poor and Marginal Farmers Development Society, another NGO, operates for environment protection, creation of job opportunities and conservation of medicinal plants. Its projects include: horticulture, afforestation, training centre, tailoring institute, blacksmith training and agriculture, nurseries, social forestry, Nandanavana Growers Club etc. Syndicate Agricultural Foundation was established to work for rural development. The Foundation has organized Farm Information Exchange Clubs, Future Farmers Clubs and Farm Clinic Project for this purpose.

Prajna Counseling Centre works from Mangalore covering the district. Its focus groups are individuals and families in distress. The projects undertaken by the Centre are therapeutic and family counseling, de-addiction and rehabilitation, entrepreneurship guidance and de-institutionalisation for abandoned children. YMCA, a voluntary agency in Mangalore, provides full fledged adolescent health education programmes in 24 high schools, HIV/AIDS and life skill education in 12 colleges. It also organizes health education programmes to reach dropouts and marginalised rural youth and women through SHGs in and around Mangalore.

Urban Research Centre focuses on urban communities in Mangalore. The important programme are:

(i) Policy research and action research on issues of governance, decentralisation, globalisation, environment, etc. concerning urban areas,

(ii) Coalition with NGO Forum-Mangalore and Nagarika Chinthana Okkoota, Udupi.

UNESCO Co-Action Centre operates in the district by organizing seminars, career guidance course, health and eye camps, and awareness programmees on tribes through street plays, puppet shows, dance and music. It has a hostel for SCs and STs, a nursery classes for children and a garment co-operative society. The Centre extends programmes like literacy, non-formal education, and income generating programmes, village adoption and symposium.

Nagarika Seva Trust was established mainly to work towards protecting environment in D. K. It undertakes following activities: awareness on mega industries and pollution they cause, promotion of human rights, women empowerment, sustainable farming, issues based networking and promotion of environment etc. It has a network of SHGs to implement programmes. Nethravathi Nadi Parisara Jalachara Samrakshana Adhyayana Trust was established at Bantwal with the objective of protecting water and water animals. The main programmes organized by it are: study of water resources, protection and sanitation of water and conduct awareness programmes about the importance of water.

Inorder to organize the backward communities and to improve the quality of life, Jana Shikshana Trust came into existence. The Trust is involved in human resource development, literacy, promotion of SHGs, legal education, health education, community organization and Koraga Tribal education and their organization. The main thrust of the organization is non-formal education and promotion of people's organizations at grass root level. Swayam Seva Yuva Ghataka operates at Sullia taluk. Target groups are SC/ST women, children and old aged people. It promotes local culture by organizing the weaker sections of the society through self-help groups. Dhalitha Sangarsha Samithi and Dr. B. R. Ambedkar Samaja Seva Sangha also work for the upliftment of the backward communities.

Cheshire Home is a NGO set up to provide training and impart skills to target group to enable them to take up either self-employment or wage-employment. The target group is disabled persons. It organizes vocational training programmes and free tailoring school for the poor. RUDSET is another NGO to train rural poor youth to take up self-employment. Its programmes include: entrepreneurship development programme, programmes for established entrepreneurs, rural development and human resource development programmes and technology transfer programmes. Rural Self Employment Programme (RUSEMP) is yet another NGO to provide training. It covers many districts including D. K. Rural unemployed youth are its focus group. Trainings are given to them in many areas and they are helped financially through banks to take up self-employment.

Canara Organization for Development and Peace was established for women, youth and child welfare. It undertakes developmental, educational and welfare projects for focus groups. They are implemented by setting up two federations, SHGs and forming coalition with other NGOs and NGO Forum. In 2000 Disha Trust was established for empowerment of women and the Koraga tribes covering Mangalore taluk. Even Jeevan Dhara Social Service Trust, set up in 1998, desires to empower women in all walks of life. It undertakes activities for women development, community health programme, non-formal education, family programmes through schools.

Thus, NGOs in D.K operates in different areas like aged and differently abled, alcoholism, agriculture, education, environment, health, SC/ST welfare, training and women and child welfare. Though all NGOs have same objective *i.e.*, well-being of the focus group, but adopt different strategies to achieve the goal.

Impact Analysis

These intervention strategies employed by different voluntary organizations and their programmes and activities have profound influence on the lives of the people. In the present study, inorder to examine the impact of NGO interventions on human well-being, Human Functioning Index (HFI) has been developed in line with Human Development Index of UNDP.

(a) *Impact on Human Functionings:* Human development is measured in terms of functionings achieved by the individuals. In this study, due consideration has been given to five functionings of development such as: *(i)* economic, *(ii)* social, *(iii)* political, *(iv)* organizational and *(v)* environmental. Let us analyse the impact of intervention strategies of NGOs on these functionings in the study area.

(i) *Economic functioning:* The first functioning of HFI is economic functioning, which is measured in terms of Economic Functioning Index [EFI]. Economic Functioning Index is the reflection of the economic well-being achieved by the sample population. Higher EFI indicates greater economic well-being of the people, whereas lower EFI means lesser economic well-being. Examination of EFI (Table 6.1) clearly shows that people of NGO villages have EFI more than the people of Non-NGO villages. EFI for NGO villages is 0.584, where as it is only 0.525 for Non-NGO villages. This means that the rate of deprivation of indicators pertaining to economic functioning is less in NGO villages and more in Non-NGO villages. It is clear from Table 6.1, that index values of all indicators of economic functioning such as employment (EI), income (YI), energy (EnI), transport (TI), communications (CI) and durable assets (DAI) are more in NGO villages than Non-NGO villages. Therefore, people of the NGO villages are economically more sound than the residents of Non-NGO villages.

Table 6.1: Index Values of Economic Functioning and its Indicators

Village	EI	YI	EnI	TI	CI	DAI	EFI
NGO	0.463	0.278	0.6	0.754	0.794	0.553	0.584
Non-NGO	0.402	0.184	0.556	0.723	0.76	0.526	0.525
District	0.433	0.231	0.578	0.739	0.777	0.54	0.555

Source: Sample Survey.

Table 6.2 divides respondents of NGO and Non-NGO villages into three groups *i.e.,* Low, Medium and High on the basis of EFI achieved by them. 24.8 per centof the respondents of NGO villages are found to be achieving Low EFI *i.e.,* below 0.499, but their proportion is as high as 49.6 per cent in Non-NGO villages. Therefore, more deprivation of economic functioning is found among a large proportion of respondents of Non-NGO villages. In NGO villages 69.6 per cent of the respondents have attained EFI in the range of 0.5-0.799 and they are placed in the Medium EFI achievement group. However, in Non NGO villages only 45.6 per cent are able to achieve EFI in this range. Further, relatively more number of people in NGO villages (5.6%) have achieved high EFI, *i.e.,* 0.8 and above. But only 4.8 per cent of the respondents in Non-NGO villages could achieve it.

Table 6.2: Different Levels of Achieved Economic Functioning Index [EFI]

Village	Low EFI (0 < 0.499)		Medium EFI (0.5<0.799)		High EFI (0.8< 1)	
	Number of Respondents	%	Number of Respondents	%	Number of Respondents	%
NGO	31	24.8	87	69.6	7	5.6
Non-NGO	62	49.6	57	45.6	6	4.8

Source: Sample Survey.

(ii) *Social functioning:* It is the second functioning of HFI. This functioning is measured by Social Functioning Index [SFI]. Table 6.3 shows that NGO villages have attained higher SFI than Non-NGO villages. In NGO villages SFI is 0.667 and in Non-NGO villages it is only 0.612. Therefore, respondents of NGO villages have greater achievement of social functioning. Table 3.3 also shows that NGO villages have achieved higher index values in case of all indicators of social functioning such as education (EdI), health (HI), empowerment (EmpI), safety and security (SSI), external humiliation (EHI), and meaning and value (MVI). Various social development programmes of Shree Kshetra Darmastala Rural Development Programme such as de-addiction, awareness capms etc., efforts of Loka Seva Trust in providing quality education and health infrastructure to poor might have improved the conditions of social living of people in NGO villages.

Table 6.3: Index Values of Social Functioning and its Indicators

Village	EdI	HI	EmpI	SSI	EHI	MVI	SFI
NGO	0.39	0.808	0.657	0.792	0.663	0.695	0.667
Non-NGO	0.366	0.76	0.586	0.736	0.593	0.633	0.612
District	0.378	0.784	0.622	0.764	0.628	0.664	0.64

Source: Sample Survey.

An examination of achieved SFI at different levels (low, medium and high) shows a wide difference between NGO and Non-NGO villages (refer Table 6.4). A large proportion of people (32%) of Non-NGO villages is deprived off with social functioning, while it is only 9.6 per cent in NGO villages. In NGO villages more number of respondents (80%) have achieved SFI at medium range than in Non-NGO villages (67.2%). Further, 10.4 per cent of the respondents of NGO villages have obtained social functioning at high range (above 0.8). But in Non-NGO villages only 0.8 per cent of the sample population has attained such high range of SFI. These statistical informations detail us that people of NGO villages have greater realization of social well-being.

Table 6.4: Different Levels of Achieved Social Functioning Index [SFI]

Village	Low SFI (0 < 0.499)		Medium SFI (0.5<0.799)		High SFI (0.8< 1)	
	Number of Respondents	%	Number of Respondents	%	Number of Respondents	%
NGO	12	9.6	100	80	13	10.4
Non-NGO	40	32	84	67.2	1	0.8

Source: Sample Survey.

(iii) *Political functioning:* The third functioning/dimension of HFI is political functioning. Achievement of political functioning is measured in terms of Political Functioning Index [PFI]. Higher attainment of PFI indicates that people have greater political awareness and participation. Results of field investigation show that people of NGO villages are taking part in political field more actively than Non-NGO villages. It is also observed that they have higher awareness of political developments. More number of people in NGO villages have developed the habit of reading news paper and listing to news everyday. Thereby their knowledge on current political issues has been enhanced. Due to this people of NGO villages have achieved more political functioning (0.549). However, the respondents of Non-NGO villages are deprived off with political functioning. This is clear from Table 6.5. It indicates that the achieved PFI in Non-NGO village is only 0.469. The presence and wide spread activities of voluntary organizations like Ngarika Seva Trust (NST) in villages (NGO villages) might have partly played role in enhancing the political awareness of the people and their participation in political activities. NST educates people on various political issues and awakes them on recent government programmes by explaining the benefits and effects.

Table 6.5: Index Values of Political Functioning and its Indicators

Village	PAI	PPI	PFI
NGO	0.722	0.38	0.549
Non-NGO	0.573	0.36	0.469
District	0.648	0.37	0.509

Source: Sample Survey.

From Table 6.6 one can observe that in Non-NGO villages people's participation in political activities and their political awareness is very low. But it is high among the people of NGO villages. This is clear from the field data that 34.4 per cent of the respondents of NGO villages have low achievement of PFI but it is more in Non-NGO villages (48.8%). Attainment of Medium PFI is concerned, in NGO villages 53.6 per cent of people are in this group. But only 48 per cent of the respondents of Non-NGO villages are able to enter in to this group. However, 12 per cent of the respondents of NGO villages are able to attain PFI at high range. But a meager proportion (3.2%) of respondents of Non-NGO villages has achieved High PFI. This indicates that deprivation of Political Functioning is more in Non-NGO villages and less in NGO villages.

Table 6.6: Different Levels of Achieved Political Functioning Index [PFI]

Village	Low PFI (0 < 0.499)		Medium PFI (0.5<0.799)		High PFI (0.8< 1)	
	Number of Respondents	%	Number of Respondents	%	Number of Respondents	%
NGO	43	34.4	67	53.6	15	12
Non-NGO	61	48.8	60	48	4	3.2

Source: Sample Survey.

(iv) *Organizational functioning:* This is another functioning of HFI. Attainment of this functioning is measured in terms of Organizational Functioning Index [OFI]. This index examines the banking habits of the people and their participation in organizational activities. Results of the study presented in Table 6.7 indicate a glaring difference in the achievement of organizational functionings between NGO and Non-NGO villages. The achieved index of the organizational functioning of the respondents of NGO villages if 0.617. But in Non-NGO villages it is only 0.511. Therefore, NGO villages are better off with higher attainment of OFI and Non-NGO villages are worse off with higher deprivation of this functioning. Larger achievement of OFI in NGO villages is the manifestation of high banking habit and more participation in the activities of several organizations.

Table 6.7: Index Values of Organizational Functioning and its Related Indicators

Village	BHI	OPI	OFI
NGO	0.788	0.446	0.617
Non-NGO	0.668	0.354	0.511
District	0.728	0.4	0.564

Source: Sample Survey.

Table 6.8 divides respondents into three groups on the basis of OFI achieved. It is noteworthy that a large proportion of respondents (24.8%) of Non-NGO villages has achieved this functioning at a low range of below 0.499. However, the number of people with low achievement of OFI is very less (4.8%). Further, a comparison of the achieved OFI at medium and high range between NGO and Non-Ngo villages shows that more people of NGO villages have achieved OFI at these ranges. This indicates that people of NGO villages have more access to banking services and organizational activities, whereas in Non-NGO villages these indicators of organizational functioning are achieved less.

Table 6.8: Different Levels of Achieved Organizational Functioning Index [OFI]

Village	Low OFI (0 < 0.499)		Medium OFI (0.5<0.799)		High OFI (0.8< 1)	
	Number of Respondents	%	Number of Respondents	%	Number of Respondents	%
NGO	6	4.8	108	86.4	11	8.8
Non-NGO	31	24.8	92	73.6	2	1.6

Source: Sample Survey.

(v) *Environmental functioning:* This is the fifth and the last dimension included in the measurement of human development. While measuring Environmental Functioning Index [EnFI], this dimension considers variables like weather of the area surrounded, rainfall, fertility of the soil, organizational efforts in making area free from pollution, creating environmental awareness etc., the study reveals that in NGO villages these indicators of environmental functioning is much lower than NGO villages. The EnFI for NGO villages is 0.787 and it is only 0.640 for Non-NGO villages (refer Table 6.9). This shows a wide gap in the achievement of this functioning. This difference must have emerged due to the campaigns, awareness programmes and other programmes and services of NGOs rendered in their villages, which are abscent in non-NGO villages.

Table 6.9: Index Value of Environmental Functioning

Village	EnFI
NGO	0.787
Non-NGO	0.64
District	0.714

Source: Sample Survey.

Unlike in other functionings, as shown in Table 6.10, more proportion of people in NGO villages (10.4%) have achieved Low EnFI than Non-NGO villages (9.6%). However, the difference in the achievement of low EnFI between two villages is minimum. It is noted that a huge proportion of respondents in NGO villages (73.6%) have achieved High EnFI. Whereas, in Non-NGO villages only 20.8 per cent of the sample population has derived High EnFI. This shows that the people of NGO villages have achieved environmental functioning in high scale. And the people of Non-NGO villages have high deprivation of this functioning. Higher achievement of OFI in NGO villages might be partly due to the active participation of NGOs in environmental issues in their villages. NGOs like Nagarika Seva Trust, Shree Kshetra Darmastala Rural Development Programme etc., have not only created environmental awareness but also launched several programmes to protect environment. Therefore, NGOs are to be considered as lynchpin in protecting environment and maintaining ecological balance.

Table 6.10: Different Levels of Achieved Environmental Functioning Index [EnFI]

Village	Low EnFI (0 < 0.499)		Medium EnFI (0.5<0.799)		High EnFI (0.8< 1)	
	Number of Respondents	%	Number of Respondents	%	Number of Respondents	%
NGO	13	10.4	20	16	92	73.6
Non-NGO	11	9.6	88	69.6	26	20.8

Source: Sample Survey.

(b) *Aggregate Analysis:* Inorder to understand the attainment of human functionings in both NGO and Non-NGO villages, an aggregate index comprising all the five functionings has been developed and the average

Human Functioning Index (HFI) of these two groups of villages is presented in Table 6.11 and 6.12. From Table 6.11, it can be observed that the HFI in NGO villages is relatively higher compared to the Non-NGO villages. While average HFI in Ngo villages is 0.641, it is 0.538 in the case of Non-NGO villages. HFI in NGO villages is higher than the district average of 0.590.

Table 6.11: HFI and Values of its Related Functionings

Dimensions Village	EFI	SFI	PFI	OFI	EnFI	HFI
NGO	0.584	0.667	0.549	0.617	0.787	0.641
Non-NGO	0.525	0.612	0.469	0.511	0.640	0.538
District	0.555	0.640	0.509	0.564	0.714	0.590

Source: Sample Survey.

At the individual level, it can be observed from Table 6.12 that there are no respondents who attained more than 0.8 HFI in Non-NGO villages. But 3.2 per cent of respondents in the NGO villages have attained more than 0.8 HFI. It is also observed that while only 8.8 per cent of the respondents in NGO villages are in less than 0.499 HFI category, 28.8 per cent of the respondents from Non-NGO villages are in this category. However, more than 70 per cent of the respondents in both the category of villages reported an achievement of HFI between 0.5 and 0.799.

Table 6.12: Different Levels of Achieved HFI

Village	Low HFI (0 < 0.499)		Medium HFI (0.5<0.799)		High HFI (0.8< 1)	
	Number of Respondents	%	Number of Respondents	%	Number of Respondents	%
NGO	11	8.8	110	88	4	3.2
Non-NGO	36	28.8	89	71.2	0	0

Source: Sample Survey.

Conclusion

From the above analysis three major observations are made. They are:

(i) Human development is more in NGO villages. This is depicted by higher HFI in NGO villages (0.641) and poor HFI in Non-NGO villages (0.538).

(ii) Not only the aggregate index *i.e.*, HFI, but also its all five constitutive functionings such as: *(i)* economic, *(ii)* social, *(iii)* political, *(iv)* organizational and *(v)* environmental are better in NGO villages. This indicates that people of Non-NGO villages have higher rate of deprivation of individual functionings.

(iii) In the present study five functionings are measured in terms of sixteen indicators. Surprisingly, people of NGO villages have higher achievement of all sixteen indicators over Non-NGO villages.

The study clearly indicates the positive impact of the NGO interventions in the form of influencing the lives of the people. They are successful in influencing the overall well-being of the community through various activities and programmes. But the absence of voluntary organizations in Non-NGO villages left people with no additional support to government programmes. Therefore, the standard of living of the people in such villages is relatively lower. In order to harness the benefits of the government programmes, people need inputs to claim political rights, improve socio-economic conditions and to preserve their environment. These inputs are supplied by NGO interventions. Though the NGO interventions are helpful in improving the well-being of the people, they are limited and restricted only to some specified areas. There is a need to widen their network and strengthen the effectiveness with appropriate policies.

REFERENCES

Alkire, Sabina (2005), "Human Development and Capability Approach: Basic Ideas" HDCA Pre-conference Training Paper, Paris, 11 Sept.

Anon (2000), "Empower, Directory, Non-Governmental Organizations of Dakshina Kannada, Udupi District" Samanvaya Prakashana, Mangalore.

Anon (2007), "Directory of Non-Governmental Organizations", School of Social Work, Roshani Nilaya, Mangalore.

Kalluraya, Shripathi (2002), "Role of Voluntary Agencies in Rural Development: A Study in Dakshina Kannada and Udupi District", A Project on Non-Profit Organizations submitted to University of Mysore, Mysore.

Robeyns, Ingrid (2005), "The Capability Approach and Welfare Policies" Presented at the Conference on 'Gender Auditing and Gender Budgeting', Bologna, Italy, 28 Jan.

Sen, Amartya (1985), "Commodities and Capabilities", Elsevier Science Publishers, Oxford.

Sen, Amartya (1999), "Development As Freedom" Knopf Publishers, New York.

UNDP (1990-1999), "Human Development Report" Oxford University Press, Oxford.

7

Role of Gender in Food Security of Agricultural Households in Rural Mewat – India

— Alison C. Palacios
— Pradeep K. Mehta

This paper examines the food security situation and its gender dimension in one of the most backward and underdeveloped districts of India, Mewat. The regional level investigation of food security reveals that on the whole, the commercial region, as compared to the subsistence region, have higher incomes, higher crop yields and total production, less yield variability, and have more diversified cropping patterns. Still, the volume of food available to households is approximately the same with negligible difference in the diversity of diets in both the commercial and subsistence regions. Therefore, it cannot be concluded that either of the regions is food secure since widespread micronutrient deficiencies are suspected based on reported food intake. Overall, size of landholding is found to be the most important determinant of household level food security. Regarding the individual food security of women, male education and the presence of an income-earning woman is correlated with women's food security. Most importantly, this study finds that women's status or women's food security does not improve as household income or household level food security improves.

Introduction

Food security is the basis for social, political, and economic development. Food is a basic human entitlement and no effort to educate, employ, empower or govern can be sustained in the absence of sufficient availability of food. A recent report by the United Nations' Food and Agriculture Organization (FAO) estimates that approximately 925 million people in the world are undernourished (FAO, 2010). Women around the world are extensively involved in all aspects related to food security. However, due to socially-constructed gender inequalities ingrained in the society, they are usually the first ones to sacrifice and the last to benefit. Work done by women is often statistically invisible and therefore unseen by policy-makers. It is therefore, extremely important to make the gendered aspects of food security visible in order to make development projects successful.

This paper examines the food security situation and its gender dimension in one of the most backward and underdeveloped districts of India, Mewat. The specific objectives of this study are: to examine the food security of farming households in Mewat; to identify factors, including the role of gender, that affect household food security; and to determine whether individual food security varies according to gender and identify influential factors. In addition to the introduction section, the paper has three sections: *(i)* methodology, *(ii)* results and discussion, and *(iii)* major conclusions.

Methodology

This study explores the dynamics of food security in Mewat. It is based on the framework of food security chain comprising of availability, accessibility and consumption of food over time and its link with the gender theory. In specific, the study evaluates the connections between production, cropping patterns, individual-level consumption, intra-household food distribution and household gender dynamics. Initially, the food security of the household is explored through a supply-side analysis after which factors that affect the individual-level food security of women is examined through a demand side analysis. The study is conducted in the region (Mewat district of Haryana) where agricultural activity dominates the livelihoods of the people. Through purposive sampling, two group of villages were selected; one group of villages (two villages-Kotla and Uletha) of subsistence agriculture and another group (two villages-Agon and Rangala Rajpur) of commercial agriculture. In these villages, there are four major crops: *(i)* wheat, *(ii)* pearl millet, *(iii)* sorghum and *(iv)* mustard. Wheat, pearl millet and sorghum are mostly grown for household subsistence purposes while mustard is a cash crop. *Thirty* households from each village are randomly selected to participate in the survey. The questionnaire is administered on two members per household (men and women), thereby adding up to the total sample of 240 respondents. Structured questionnaires collecting both qualitative and quantitative data are prepared in the local language and administered on the participating households.

Results and Discussion

Food Security

The analysis is divided into two sections. *First,* food security indicators are compared between the commercial and subsistence region. This section is followed by an explanation of the method and reasoning used to classify households as either more or less vulnerable to food insecurity. *Finally,* characteristics of each of these groups and determinants of food security are analyzed.

Production and Consumption Pattern

Farming households procure food through own subsistence production and through market purchases. Therefore, both subsistence production and income from agriculture are necessary to ensure a household's food supply. Predictably, production of commercial crops is much lower in the subsistence region amounting to only one third to that of the commercial region (Table 7.1). Interestingly, subsistence agricultural production[1] and portion of commercial crops consumed at home is found to be noticeably higher in the commercial region. The results imply that from a holistic perspective, farming households in the commercial region could be more food secure because of their ability to earn income through the sale of commercial crops as well as a higher availability of subsistence crops, from their own farm, for personal consumption.

Table 7.1: Subsistence and Commercial Production

	Subsistence Production (in Quintals)	Commercial Production (in Quintals)
Commercial Region	1450	2699
Subsistence Region	1248	805

Though, there are found to be large differences in production in the commercial and subsistence regions, the amount of land cultivated is only slightly larger in the commercial region (average farm size is 6.77 acre and 6.55 acre respectively, in the commercial and subsistence region). This signals a greater disparity in terms of productivity of crops grown in both regions. Table 7.2 displays the average yield over the past three years for two major subsistence crops, wheat and pearl millet, and the major cash crop, mustard. For all crops, yields are higher in the commercial area, and the overall average yield for all the crops is also drastically higher.

Table 7.2: Average Yield of Major Crops (2008-10)

	Wheat (Quintal per acre)	Pearl Millet (Quintal per acre)	Mustard (Quintal per acre)	All Crops (Quintal per acre)
Commercial Region	16.02	5.86	8.21	14.08
Subsistence Region	12.52	4.21	7.29	9.13

The impact of agricultural production on food security can also be evident through the variability of yields over a period of time. A households' food security in terms of either the food made available through subsistence production or food which is purchased through the income-generated from the sale of other crops must be stable. Table 7.3 shows that yields are more variable in the subsistence region than in the commercial region. Crop diversification measured by the average number of crops grown per household can potentially be a strategy employed to ensure food availability and income in the condition of unfavorable weather condition. In the study area, it does seem to be the case that greater diversification is related to lesser yield variability since households in the commercial region grow a larger number of crops and also witness less variability in crop yields.

Table 7.3: Crop Diversification and Yield Variability

	Average Number of Crops Grown	Variability in Yield, '08-10'	Trend in Yield, '08-10'
Agon	3.70	20%	+.03
Rangala Rajpur	3.63	24%	+.00
Commercial Region	3.67	22%	+.01
Kotla	2.67	30%	+.17
Uletha	2.63	21%	-.06
Subsistence Region	2.65	26%	+.05
Overall	**3.16**	**24%**	**+.03**

Variability itself implies that yields are unstable meaning that food availability is unpredictable and food security, precarious. However, if variability overtime is accounted for by a steady increment in the yield, it cannot be treated as being detrimental to food security. Upon analysis of trends available from the study region, it is found that yields are increasing. However, these trends are divergent by village. In Uletha, crop yields vary by 21 per cent and have actually decreased by 6 per cent between 2008 and 2010, whereas yields in the other subsistence village of Kotla vary by 30 per cent but are found to have increased by 17 per cent over the same time period. The commercial region, as compared to subsistence region, though has experienced low variability in yields but the same is complemented with relatively less increase in the growth of crop yields. Overall, yields are found to have increased by 3.7 per cent over the last three years, but have varied by 24 per cent. Therefore, the rate of increase in yields accounts for little of the variability in yields. Consequently, crop production can be said to be unpredictable every year and food security is unstable.

The level of overall income can also influence food security as it provides an additional source which can be used to purchase food that is not available through subsistence production. Table 7.4 indicates that annual income is higher in the commercial region than in the subsistence region, as is annual agricultural income. As yields vary greatly every year, agricultural income also varies. The fluctuation in agricultural income is more than crop yields because it includes the effect of changes in commodity prices. Across all villages and especially in the commercial region, agricultural income is found to have risen between 2008 and 2010. The trend in agricultural income is more positive than the trend in crop yields due to steadily rising prices of major crops. This is the reason that in Uletha, where yields have actually decreased between 2008 and 2010, agricultural income has increased. The average price that farmers in these villages have received for wheat has increased by 23 per cent, pearl millet by 38 per cent, and mustard by 9 per cent over the same time period. Thus, it is not surprising to note that in commercial villages, where yields are higher for both commercial and subsistence crops, agricultural income has increased more than in the subsistence villages. With wheat and pearl millet largely being subsistence crops, price increase in these crops is favorable to households that produce a surplus and unfavorable to households that do not produce enough for their own needs. Given that households in the commercial region are able to produce 99 per cent of the cereals needed for their own consumption and subsistence households produce 88 per cent of their required cereals, increase in the price of grains is likely to have a more negative effect on the food security of households in the subsistence region.

Table 7.4: Variability in Income (2008-10)

	Average Annual Agricultural Income	Average Annual Income	Variability in Agricultural Income	Trend in Agricultural Income	Variability in Total Income	Trend in Total Income
Agon	54,267	1,46,767	36%	+.205	41%	+.169
Rangala Rajpur	60,353	1,04,120	44%	+.107	38%	+.086
Commercial Region	**57,310**	**1,25,443**	**40%**	**+.156**	**39%**	**+.127**
Kotla	50,950	70,417	44%	+.080	37%	+.056
Uletha	44,267	89,200	19%	+.060	21%	+.078
Subsistence Region	**47,608**	**79,808**	**32%**	**+.070**	**29%**	**+.067**
Overall	**52,459**	**1,02,626**	**36%**	**+.113**	**34%**	**+.097**

Determinants of Household Food Security

For the purpose of identifying the determinants of household food security, households have been divided into two groups: those that are more vulnerable to food insecurity and those who are less vulnerable to food insecurity. The indicator used to classify households is the difference between their average agricultural income over the last three years (2008-10)[2] and their consumption requirements.[3] Households for which this indicator is found to be negative (*i.e.*, agricultural income[4] alone is not enough to meet their food requirements) are more vulnerable to food insecurity and households for which this indicator is positive (*i.e.*, all food requirements are met through agriculture income) are less vulnerable to food insecurity. From the sample, seventy-five households are found to be more vulnerable to food insecurity and forty five households are found to be less vulnerable. Table 7.5 shows the distribution of more-and less-vulnerable households according to the village and region. Counter intuitively, it is found that a larger number of more vulnerable households are in the commercial villages than in the subsistence villages. Though, the commercial region is found to be more agriculturally productive as a whole, a greater number of households are not able to meet their consumption requirements through agriculture as their sole livelihood strategy.[5]

Table 7.5: Household Vulnerability to Food Insecurity

	Number of more Vulnerable Households	Number of less Vulnerable Households
Agon	19	11
Rangala Rajpur	21	9
Commercial Region	40	20
Kotla	14	16
Uletha	21	9
Subsistence Region	35	25
Overall	**75**	**45**

Logically, average production is higher in the households that are less vulnerable to food insecurity (Table 7.6). Their average landholding is more than twice the size of the average landholding of households in the more vulnerable group. Total production, both in terms of total quintals and quintals per capita is approximately 60 per cent higher in the less vulnerable group while production of subsistence crops is 40 per cent higher. Though, production of subsistence crops is higher in the less vulnerable group, the land allocated toward producing commercial crops is also found to be higher. 43 per cent land in the less vulnerable group is used to grow commercial crops as compared to 24 per cent land in the more vulnerable group. Not surprisingly, households in the less vulnerable group also have a higher annual income, that is, Rs. 143,411 compared to Rs. 78,155. (*See table on next page*)

To be food secure, farmers either prefer to allocate higher land to subsistence crops or they allocate more land to cash crops and purchase food from the market through the cash receipts earned through sale of produce. In the selected villages, farmers mostly prefer to produce subsistence crops to improve their food security levels. This is due to several reasons. *First*, small farmers face large risks if they dedicate a large portion of their land to commercial crops because if that crop fails or the price drops, they are not

Table 7.6: Production-Related Determinants of Household Food Security

	More Vulnerable Households	Less Vulnerable Households
Average Farm size (acres)**	2.59	5.96
Total Production (quintals/yr)**	42.44	67.07
Total Production/capita (kgs/yr)	670	1072
Subsistence production (quintals/yr)	19.70	27.12
Subsistence production/capita (kgs/yr)	319	452
Average yield 2008-2010 (all crops, quintals/acre)*	11.23	12.23
Percentage of land under commercial cultivation**	24%	43%
Number of crops grown**	2.80	3.76
Annual Income (Rs.)	78,155	1,43,411

*Significant at .005 level of confidence **Significant at .001 level of confidence

able to ensure production of sufficient food for their household's need and are entirely at the whim of the weather and the market. It is important to consider the strong positive correlation between commercialization and food security with the strong positive correlation between size of landholding and food security, that is, households which are less vulnerable to food insecurity (can meet their consumption requirements through agriculture alone) take less risk in growing a larger portion of commercial crops because their landholdings are bigger and their subsistence needs are covered. It is also extremely important to note the significant positive correlation between the level of diversification (number of crops grown) and food security. Households that are less vulnerable to food insecurity grow, on an average, one additional crop than those who are more vulnerable. Thus, increased commercialization is taking place with increased subsistence production through increased diversification. It is found that cash crop monoculture is not the type of commercialization that is making households more food secure. The implication here is that the size of landholding is the preeminent determinant of a household's food security. Households that have more land to farm are able to produce more, both for sale and for their own consumption and allocate a larger tract of land to cash crop production without exposing their entire livelihood to crop failure or market risks. They have access to the inputs necessary for higher mustard yields, they adjust their cropping pattern in response to market signals, and they have less need for non-farm employment.

Given that the percentage of staple foods in a household's diet is an indicator of dietary diversity and therefore food security, it is important to analyze the composition of the typical diet. In this case, the average proportion of staple foods to total consumption is found to be 86 per cent, with very little variance between villages (range of 85% to 87%). More staple foods in the diet generally signal a higher intake of starchy foods and little dietary variety implying a greater likelihood of being micronutrient deficient. Staple foods are largely starchy such as cereals and potatoes and contain a very small percentage of vegetables other than potatoes.

On the whole, a conclusion cannot be drawn as to which region is more food secure. In the first glance, it appears that the commercial region should be more food secure with higher yields, lesser yield variability, more production and higher income. However, the commercial region is also relatively plagued by higher variability in agricultural income despite a higher rate of growth in agricultural income. Consumption expenditure is only slightly lower in the subsistence region, which is more stable in terms of agricultural income.

Gender Dimension of Food Security

In this section, gender indicators are first compared between the subsistence region and the commercial region. Thereafter, the impact of role of women in household food security is assessed, which is followed by examining the determinants of food security among women.

Gender Differences in the Selected Regions

Allocation of work among men and women highlights the situation of gender in the region. Most men (heads of household) surveyed (84%) report farming as their primary activity and home-making as most of their wives' primary activity (88%). It has been reported by the men that farming is the primary activity of 10 per cent women, even though, the average number of hours per day worked in the field is found to be approximately equal for men and women (Table 7.7). This is evidence to the fact that women's work in the field is considered by men as an extension of their household duties and not as a bona fide occupation. It is only in Uletha that women are mentioned to be working more hours than men. Overall, it is reported that women work slightly fewer hours in the field than men.

Table 7.7: Distribution of Work in the Field

Village	Mens' Hours in Field	Women's Hours in Field	Ratio of Women's: Men's Hours in Field
Agon	6.15	5.37	0.87
Rangala Rajpur	5.50	5.33	0.97
Commercial Region	5.83	5.35	0.92
Kotla	5.75	4.95	0.86
Uletha	3.95	4.90	1.24
Subsistence Region	4.85	4.93	1.02
Total	**5.34**	**5.14**	**0.96**

In this region, livestock rearing makes an important contribution to food security since households with buffalo, cows or goats consume milk and sell the surplus. Women tend to livestock in nearly all cases, and it appears that a good number of women do receive the income from this activity. In households with livestock, women sell the produce in 38 per cent cases, men sell the produce in 47 per cent cases and both sell in 15 per cent households. These figures are not found to vary much by region. While land ownership by women is an important indicator of household food security (Quisumbing and McClafferty, 2003), all the land holdings belonging to the population surveyed is found to be owned by men. Yet, women's decision-making power on agricultural production issues varies greatly between households (Table 7.8). On an average, men alone make 38 per cent production related decisions, women alone make 7 per cent production related decisions and 55 per cent decisions are made by both genders together. Women alone constitute a greater portion of production related decisions in the subsistence region where they take 9 per cent of decisions than in the commercial region where they take 5 per cent decisions.

Table 7.8: Production Decisions

Village	By Men Only	By Women Only	By Both Men and Women
Commercial Region	37%	5%	58%
Subsistence Region	39%	9%	52%
All Region	**38%**	**7%**	**55%**

Another strong link between gender roles and food security is established through women's predominant role in procuring food for the household. This is not found to be the case in the sampled villages where only men buy food in 93 per cent households (Table 7.9). This may be indicative of the practice of *purdah* in the region or the confinement of women to their homesteads. In none of the cases, women mention to have gone alone to the market to purchase food. Both the genders are found to have bought food together only in 7.5 per cent households. Interestingly, it surfaces in majority of the households (52%) that it is the woman who decides what will be purchased. In a somewhat lower number of households, both genders decide what to purchase. There are found to be only a few instances (6%) in which men alone decide what to buy. According to the theory, there is a connection between increased commercialization, increased alcoholism among men, and decreased household food security (IFAD, 2010). None of the study respondents reported that anyone in their household consumes alcohol but 82 per cent of them reported that the household members consume tobacco. Women usually cook in all the surveyed households and are generally the only ones in the household who prepare food. Thus, even though, it is generally not the women who buy food, women have a strong say in what will be purchased and maintain the pivotal link to household food security in their roles as food preparers.

Table 7.9: Role of Gender in Food Purchasing and Decision-making

Percentage of Households in which...	Only Men buy Food	Only Men make Purchasing Decisions	Only Women make Purchasing Decisions	Both make Purchasing Decisions
Agon	83%	11%	46%	43%
Rangala Rajpur	97%	6%	58%	35%
Commercial Region	**90%**	**9%**	**52%**	**39%**
Kotla	97%	6%	56%	37%
Uletha	93%	2%	49%	48%
Subsistence Region	**95%**	**4%**	**53%**	**42%**
Overall	**93%**	**6%**	**52%**	**41%**

Comparison of the households that are more vulnerable to food insecurity versus those that are less vulnerable indicates some variance in the role of women. Table 7.10 shows that the average years of education completed are higher for both men and women in the less vulnerable households. On an average, women also have a slightly stronger role to play in purchasing decisions, working fewer hours in the field as compared to men, and are more likely to be earning some sort of income in the less vulnerable group. Women working outside of the homestead are found to be very rare (only three in total). In most cases, income that women are earning is from the sale of buffalo milk. Women's role in making-decisions related to purchasing food is measured on a scale of zero to one, with zero signifying that both respondents for the household report that only men decide what will be purchased. Half a point is awarded if it is reported that both genders together decide what to purchase, and a whole point is assigned when both respondents report that women only decide what will be bought (there is no intra-household divergence). Women have a slightly stronger say in purchasing decisions in the less vulnerable households. The two gender indicators that are found to be significantly correlated to household food security, are both contrary to theory. *First*, the ratio of women's to men's hours in the field is found to be inversely correlated to household food security, meaning that as women work less in the field compared to men, household food security increases. This result does not sync with the idea that women's labour in the fields is essential to household food security. *Second*, men make significantly more production-related decisions without the input of women in the less vulnerable group of households, while the theory states that household food security should be enhanced as women's power in production related decisions increases.

Table 7.10: Gender Roles in Food Security

	More Vulnerable	Less Vulnerable
Years of education-men	3.75	5.07
Years of education-women	0.53	1.29
Percentage of production decisions made by men only**	32%	44%
Strength of women's say in purchasing decisions	0.70	0.72
Households in which a woman earns income	35%	42%
Men's hours in the field*	5.15	5.66
Women's hours in the field	5.16	5.10
Ratio of women's to men's hours in the field*	1.00	0.90

*Significant at .005 level of confidence **Significant at .001 level of confidence

Women's Food Security

For the purpose of comparing the individual food security of men and women, the consumption ratio[6] has been used as an indicator. The overall ratios of women's to men's consumption are found to vary between 0.42 and 1.94. Households are categorised on the basis of this ratio which is used as an indicator of women's food security. The higher the ratio, the less vulnerable women in that household are to food insecurity. Households in which women specifically are more vulnerable to food insecurity are defined here as those having a consumption ratio of less than .90, while women living in households whose ratio is greater than or equal to .90 are less vulnerable to food insecurity. The ratio of .90 versus 1.00 is chosen as the threshold because women require less food than men if everything else is equal. Accordingly, women from 56 households are placed in the more vulnerable category and women from 64 households are found to be less vulnerable. Table 7.11 shows the spatial distribution of more vulnerable (consumption ratio <.90) and less vulnerable (consumption ratio ≥.90) women. The data implies that women in the subsistence region are more food secure relative to their spouses than their counterparts in the commercial villages.

Table 7.11: Consumption Ratios

	Consumption Ratio <.90	Consumption Ratio ≥.90
Agon	14	16
Rangala Rajpur	20	10
Commercial Region	**34**	**26**
Kotla	15	15
Uletha	7	23
Subsistence Region	**22**	**38**
Total	**56**	**64**

Analysis of the relationship between production and consumption variables and food security among women yields surprising results. Table 7.12 shows that nearly every statistical count, including size of landholding, yields, production and income, per capita consumption expenditure, is lower for the households in which women consume relatively more. All these indicators imply a lower socio-economic status, yet women in these households are able to consume nearly equal amounts or even more than men. A ratio of women's consumption relative to men's may not necessarily indicate that women with a consumption ratio less than a given amount are food insecure if the quantity of food consumed is high enough to offset any differences in consumption ratio between the two groups. However, in this case it can be used as an indicator of women's food security because available food per capita is equal between the group of women who consume relatively little and the group who consume approximately equal or greater amounts than men. Furthermore, in the previous section also, it has been mentioned that the average agricultural income minus consumption is the indicator used to evaluate a households' food security. Surprisingly, and as most of the other statistics indicate, women's individual food security does not improve as household level food security increases.

Table 7.12: Production and Consumption Variables by Consumption Ratio

	Consumption Ratio <.90	Consumption Ratio ≥.90
Land (acres)	4.00	3.73
Average yield (quintals/yr)	18.49	15.33
Production per capita (kgs/yr)	911	742
Subsistence production per capita (kgs/yr)	398	344
Percentage of land under commercial cultivation	29%	33%
Total annual income (Rs.)	116,234	90,719
Agricultural annual income (Rs.)	56,109	49,266
Annual consumption expenditure/capita (Rs.)	8610	8003
Available food per capita per month (kgs)	28	28
Average agricultural income minus consumption (Rs.)	2020	-2362

Indicators of gender relations within a household are shown in Table 7.13. While educational attainment of men is higher in the group in which women consume relatively more, the educational attainment of women is found to be lower. Years of completed education by men is found to be the only gender-related variable significantly correlated to an improved women's consumption ratio. Women have less power in purchasing decisions, working fewer hours in the field, eating last in fewer households and are more likely to be earning income in households where they consume relatively more. The presence of an income-earning woman in the household may indicate more equitable gender relations within that household, which would seem to have a positive effect on the household's food distribution practices. Since the only factor found to be significantly correlated to the relative individual food security of women is male education, it can be said that it is men who have the power to allocate food within a household and that allocation is not very equitable as the household's resources increase.

Table 7.13: Gender Related Indicators and Women's Food Security

	Consumption Ratio <.90	Consumption Ratio ≥.90
Years of education-men*	3.7	4.7
Years of education-women	1.2	0.5
Percentage of production decisions made solely by men	36%	37%
Women's power in purchasing decisions	0.77	0.66
Percentage of households in which women eat last	30%	28%
Percentage of households in which a woman earns income**	25%	48%
Men's hours in the field	5.53	5.17
Women's hours in the field	5.15	5.13
Ratio of women's:men's hours in the field	0.93	0.99

*Significantly correlated at .005 level of confidence **Significantly different at .001 level of confidence

Conclusion

The regional level investigation of food security reveals that on the whole, the commercial region, as compared to the subsistence region, have higher incomes, higher yields and total production, less yield variability, have more diversified cropping patterns and are able to spend more on food. Still, the volume of food available to households is approximately the same in both regions and the average diet is heavily dependent on staple foods. Therefore, it cannot be said that either of the regions is food secure since widespread micronutrient deficiencies are suspected based on reported food intake.

Size of landholding is found to be the most important determinant of household level food security. Households with a larger plot of land at their disposal are able to provide for their own subsistence crop needs as well as diversify into growing other crops, including the ability to allocate a larger portion of land to cash crop production. Thus, having a larger landholding allows farmers to be responsive to market signals while remaining relatively insulated to crop failures and market instability compared to farmers with less land. These households are able to purchase more food from the market, consume more food overall, and spend a smaller percentage of their income on food.

Few women in this region work outside of their household's domain. They are generally responsible for livestock rearing and food preparation. They work approximately the same number of hours in the field as men and no woman owns a land holding. It is found that gender relations are generally more equitable in the subsistence region than in the commercial region, as women there have more power in production related decisions. Households in the subsistence region generally eat together, *vs.* having women eat in the last. This study finds little support for existing gender theory as it relates to food security. Households in which men have more power in production decisions and work more in the fields are more food secure. Regarding the individual food security of women, male education is correlated with women eating more compared to their husbands, and the presence of an income-earning woman is more common in households where women consume relatively more. Most importantly, this study finds that women's status or women's food security does not improve as household income or household level food security improves.

A major implication of this research is that households need access to more land to increase their food security. This should come as no surprise. Efforts to increase yields should be concentrated in the subsistence region. Such efforts should concentrate on formulating strategies to increase farmers' access to inputs and methods that are proven to increase yields. Schemes to aid the diffusion of information surrounding these inputs and methods should also be explored. For farmers that have sufficient land, their household food security will be positively impacted if they can diversify their cropping pattern, including growing commercial crops if acreage allows without compromising subsistence production. Both regions are in need of nutrition education and schemes to increase dietary diversity through access to fruits, vegetables and legumes. *Finally*, any gender sensitivity training should include efforts to shed light on the productive contribution of women and create awareness of their actual food consumption compared to their nutritional needs.

FOOTNOTES

1. Including Crops Grown only for Home Consumption.
2. Since Agricultural is Vulnerable to Dramatic Changes in the Weather Conditions, Average Agricultural Income is Worked out using Data on the same for Three Years; 2008, 2009 and 2010 and Compared with the Average Annual Consumption Requirements at Home.
3. Food Consumption is Calculated using Disaggregated data on Major Food Items and the Same is Converted into Rupees.
4. Agricultural Income is Combining both Food Production and Income through Sale of Crops.
5. This could be due to Higher Consumption Requirements because of Bigger Family Size in the Commercial Region.

6. Due to the Difficulties of Accurately Quantifying Overall Volumes of Food Consumed in a day and Calculating Caloric and Nutrient Intakes, Food Intake has been Measured based on Items that are Easy to Quantify (Cups of Tea, Glasses of Milk, Rounds of Roti). These Three Indicators have been First made into Ratios Comparing Women's Consumption to Men's Consumption, and Thereafter, are given Equal Weights to Calculate a Consumption Index.

REFERENCES

R. Balakrishnan, Rural Women and Food Security in Asia and the Pacific: Prospects and Paradoxes. FAO (2005).

J. Coates, A. Swindale, and P. Billinsky, Household Food Insecurity Access Scale (HFIAS) for Measurement of Household Food Access: Indicator Guide. Washington, DC: Food and Nutrition Technical Assistance II Project (FANTA-2), Academy for Educational Development (AED) (2006).

J. Coates, P. Webb, and R. Houser, Measuring Food Insecurity: Going Beyond Indicators of Income and Anthropometry. Washington, DC: Food and Nutrition Technical Assistance II Project (FANTA-2), Academy for Educational Development (AED) (2003).

C. Conrood, Chronic Hunger and the Status of Women in India. New York: The Hunger Project. (1998).

D. J. Dyer, and J. Bruce, A Home Divided: Women and Income in the Third World. Stanford: Stanford University Press (1998).

FAO, FAO Thematic Brief on Food Security and Livelihoods. Rome: FAO (2008).

FAO, State of Food Insecurity in the World: Addressing Food Insecurity in Protracted Crises. Retrieved October 26, 2010, from FAO: http://www.fao.org/docrep/013/i1683e.pdf (2010).

FAO, Number of Undernourished Persons. Retrieved October 19, 2010, from Food and Agriculture Organization: http://www.fao.org/economic/ess/food-security-statistics/en (2010).

J. Hoddinott, and Y. Yohannes, Dietary Diversity as a Household Food Security Indicator. Washington, DC: Food and Nutrition Technical Assistance II Project (FANTA-2), Academy for Educational Development (AED) (2002).

IFAD, India: Impact of Market Oriented Production. Retrieved October 7, 2010, from International Fund for Agricultural Development: http://www.ifad.org/hfs/learning/in_3.htm (2010).

M. Krishnaraj, Food Security: How and for Whom? Economic and Political Weekly, (2005, June 18)

H. Melgar-Quinonez, Testing Food Security Scales for Low-cost Poverty Assessment-Draft Report. Davis, CA: Freedom from Hunger (2004).

S. Mikalista, Gender-Specific Constraints Affecting Technology use and Household Food Security in Western Province of Kenya. *African Journal of Food, Agriculture, Nutrition and Development* , 10 (4) (2010).

F. Osman Ibnouf, The Role of Women in Providing and Improving Household Food Security in Sudan: Implications for Reducing Hunger and Malnutrition. *Journal of International Women's Studies*, 10 (4) (2009).

R. Perez-Escamilla, A. M. Segall-Correa, L. Kurdian Maranha, M. D. Archanjo Sampaio, L. Marin-Leon, and G. Panigassi, An Adapted Version of the U.S. Department of Agriculture Food Insecurity Module is a Valid tool for Assessing Household Food Insecurity in Campinas, Brazil. *Journal of Nutrition*, 134 (8), 1923-1928 (2004).

A. R. Quisumbing, and B. McClafferty, Food Security in Practice: Using Gender Research in Development. Washington: International Food Policy Research Institute (IFPRI) (2003).

N. Ramachandran, Women and Food Security in South Asia: Current Issues and Emerging Concerns. Helinski: United Nations University, World Institute for Development Economics Research (UNU, WIDER) (2006).

M. T. Ruel, is Dietary Diversity an Indicator of Food Security or Dietary Quality: A Review of Measurement Issues and Research Needs. Washington: International Food Policy Research Institute (IFPRI) Food Consumption and Nutrition Division (2002).

L. C. Smith, U. Ramakrishnan, A. Ndiaye, L. Haddad, and R. Martorell, The Importance of Women's Status for Child Nutrition in Developing Countries. Washington, DC: International Food Policy Research Institute (2003).

8

Is Assurance of Healthcare a Distant Dream for the State

— Dr. Skylab Sahu

Towards the late 1980s, HIV/AIDS has emerged as an epidemic in India and has put forth several challenges; medical, developmental and socio-economic, before the state and the society at large. More importantly, HIV/AIDS has more adverse effects on women. Under the banner of national health problem, the Indian state has taken several measures to tackle the contours of the health issues. At one hand, some new socio medical institutions are set up to deal with the problem and on the other hand, already existing institutions are handed over new responsibilities of dealing with the health problem meticulously. At the policy and programme level, when the central government is intending to address the issue uniformly, implementation of the programmes and the performance of the states vary based on its prior experience, expertise, capacity and most importantly willingness. A high and a low HIV prevalence states (Karnataka and West Bengal) are selected to observe the difference in performance towards ensuring healthcare to HIV positive people, especially women. The paper has tried to identify the missing links or gaps persisting commonly and differently in the approach of the States towards assurance of healthcare to HIV positive women. HIV/AIDS is one of the major health concerns in India whereby, around 2.4 million Indians are currently living with HIV/AIDS. More importantly, the virus makes women more vulnerable and has become one of the leading causes of death of women in the reproductive age (Berer and Ray, 1993, Sibal, 2002, Chikwendu, 2004, Doyal *et al*, 1994). According to National AIDS Control Organization (NACO) estimation, in India, every minute an individual is affected by HIV, and 37 per cent out of the infected people are women. In general, women are 2.5 times more vulnerable to HIV infection than men.

The disease has gender implication as it makes women more vulnerable to the infection biologically, socio-economically and politically (MacNaughton 2004, Johnston 2003 Verma and Roy 2002). During post HIV infection period also several socio-economic factors curtail healthcare accessibility by HIV positive women (*Fried et al, 2012)*. The gender bias prevailing in healthcare, as well as gender role in society, create further hurdles for women. In such situations, general health problems like leprosy, tuberculosis, and most recently HIV affects women more adversely than men (Hartigan *et al*, 2002, Lee 1998, Michelson 1993). A study by Lichtenstein Bronwen (2006) shows how domestic violence can prevent access to healthcare by HIV positive women. Women also lack healthcare access in comparison to men in developing states of Africa, India and even in underdeveloped pockets (poor neighbourhoods in New York and Washington, DC, and rural communities of southern states of USA) of developed states like USA. Women lack access to healthcare due to economic constraints, geographical barriers and social responsibility of care on women (US Department of Health and Human Services Office on Women's Health 2011). Scholars have also indicated that prevalence of stigma in the healthcare system have emerged as a greater barrier for accessing healthcare by HIV positive women (Blanchard and Ruth Manski 2011, IPAS, 2012, Monjok *et al*, 2009, Bell *et al*, 2007). Unavailability of healthcare and persisting denial of treatment to HIV positive people in general and HIV positive women in particular has become a staggering phenomena across developing nations (MacNaughton 2004, ILO 2011).

To combat HIV and prevent its further spread in India, National AIDS Control Organization (NACO) is mandated to formulate polices and programmes to make health facilities available to all. NACO works closely with states through state-specific AIDS Cell Societies for building the required infrastructure and implement the policies at the State, district as well as grass roots levels. The major question arises whether the Indian state ensures accessibility and availability of healthcare while fulfilling the principle of 'right to health' which is recently declared as an extended part of 'right to life', (article 21).[1] Right to health is a universal right that seeks to guarantee good health to individuals irrespective of differences in terms of class, gender, caste, ethnicity, etc., and it denotes availability of health-care facilities to all and accessibility of the same without discrimination. In Indian society, disadvantaged sections, especially women face several obstacles in accessing healthcare (Sen *et al.*, 2002, Jesani, 1996). The NACO builds infrastructure for HIV patients, but the healthcare infrastructure should be accessible to patients, and this depends on many factors including geographic, social and economic. Availability and accessibility of healthcare facilities together, constitute securitisation of health rights of people.

On this backdrop, the paper analyses how far the States have made healthcare accessible and available for HIV positive women. The aim of the paper is to explore the role of state in ensuring accessibility and availability of healthcare to HIV positive women. Two States are selected *i.e.*, Karnataka as one of the high HIV prevalence states, and West Bengal as one of the low HIV prevalence states. Karnataka and West Bengal have also a different political history, Karnataka has been ruled either by centre oriented or right wing parties whereas, West Bengal has a long history of left party ruling.[2] Two vital parameters are considered *i.e.*, availability and accessibility of healthcare and treatment. It is discusseed whether availability and accessibility of healthcare varies in two states that have different prevalence rate of HIV/ AIDS.. Further, we have tried to identify the missing links or gaps that still persist in the approach of the State towards healthcare service delivery, with particular focus on violation of accessibility of healthcare through discrimination and treatment denial. The second section discusses the methodology of the study. The third section analyses timely and adequate availability of healthcare to HIV positive women and fourth section discusses accessibility of healthcare and treatment to HIV positive women in the selected States.

Methodology of the Study

The study is based on both secondary as well as primary data. For secondary literature, we have looked into existing literature, government documents, and news clippings. In order to capture the field reality, both quantitative and qualitative tools are used including interviews, observations, group discussions, and case studies. Two states were selected *i.e.*, one state with high HIV prevalence (Karnataka) and another state with low HIV prevalence (West Bengal). In absolute numbers, there were 39,491 and 6,941 HIV positive people in Karnataka and West Bengal respectively (the data are included till 31st January 2006) (Indiastat, 2009). Karnataka and West Bengal also have a different political history: Karnataka has been ruled either by centre-oriented or right wing parties whereas, West Bengal has a long history of left party ruling. It is assumed that performance of the selected states, in protecting the health rights of women would vary because of the different regimes. It is anticipated that the West Bengal government having pro-poor ideology would be redressing the issue of accessibility and availability with a greater efficacy than Karnataka, a State ruled by centre or right oriented parties. Policies and programmes carried out by the States have been analysed to understand the performance of the States towards HIV positive women. So also the opinion and perception of HIV positive women selected as sample in the particular State is considered to understand the issues of accessibility and availability.

For the selection of women, samples were taken from institutions (public, and NGO led-care centres) from both the States. This is due to inherent privacy attached with the issue and difficulty to interview HIV positive women within the family. At the outset, a list of all hospitals including, where treatment to HIV positive people was provided, was collected. From the list of hospitals, through a lottery method, three government hospitals, and two civil society organization led hospitals were selected. In the next step, from the above selected institutions, a list of the HIV positive patients were collected and from the list every 20th number woman was approached, and like wise hundred women, from each state, were selected through snow ball sampling.

For the field study, we had to undertake ethical committees' clearance in both the states, while getting permission from the Karnataka State AIDS and Prevention Society (KASAPS) and West Bengal State AIDS Control Society (WBSACS), we approached government hospital superintendents, and respective head of the departments (like VCTC, Art, PMTCT) for their consent for the interviews. Finally, a prior consent was taken from the HIV positive women before the interview. However, in all the cases their original name was changed to provide them anonymity and to preserve their privacy.

The questionnaire administered on women covered both open-ended and close-ended questions. In order to understand the issues of availability and accessibility, questionnaire was canvassed to know the HIV positive women's preference of government versus private hospital and reasons for it. In-depth interview was carried out to understand the available facilities in government hospitals in terms of existing beds as per demand, medicines, technicians, doctors to treat, and so on. In addition to probing of availability of counselling facilities, questions captured number of counselling received. Questions were framed to understand the extent of difficulty in accessing the healthcare by sampled population and its reasons. To know the HIV positive respondents' experience of discrimination, they were asked to mention their experiences; difference in treatment, any form of humiliation by any staff of the hospital and so on. In addition, the open-ended questions, and narrations collected from a few case studies of HIV positive samples helped us in understanding, capturing and analysing incidence of discrimination faced by HIV positive samples more vividly.

Availability of Healthcare Facilities

The Indian state being a signatory of the human rights has the responsibility of protecting, promoting, respecting and fulfilling these entitlements (UNFPA 2011). The state has to ensure adequate availability of healthcare facilities, which include availability of physical infrastructure, personnel including doctors, and other medical facilities like medical equipments or technologies and medicines (WHO 2009, Centre for Economic and Social Rights 2004). We have assessed the parameter of availability from three aspects;

(i) Availability of infrastructure (centres) at district, block or village level.

(ii) Availability of life saving medicines for HIV positive people including anti-opportunistic infection medicine as well as Anti Retroviral Therapy (ART)[3] medicines.

(iii) Availability of facilities for medical tests or diagnostic technologies such as, X-ray, CD4 machine, and other scanning and diagnostic facilities that may be required for the treatment.

In order to understand the availability of the centres, we looked into the secondary (government data) literature. However, the data was verified and cross checked in the light of the empirical experiences of the HIV positive women and our own observation. The performance of the centres was basically accessed on the basis of the empirical data. In both the states, VCTC (now termed as Integrated Counselling and Testing Centre (ICTC) were existing in almost all the district hospitals. However, Karnataka had more number of centres: there were 123 VCTC centres in Karnataka in contrast to 27 in West Bengal (Table 8.1). Even in case of availability of VCTC per estimated number of HIV patients, it was found that Karnataka performed fairly well as compared to West Bengal. More importantly, in Karnataka, the VCTC centres reached the block levels, while in West Bengal, VCTC centres were based at the district level. During the field work, we found that (as mentioned by respondents) in West Bengal, some of the suspected HIV positive cases or confirmed HIV positive cases were referred either to Kolkata government hospitals or to private hospitals. This was also persisting in some of the district hospitals which were situated adjacent to Kolkata (like Howrah and Hubli district hospitals) and had denied conducting HIV test for a few patients, so also they had denied admitting HIV positive people.[4] In Karnataka, the situation was found to be much better, as there was no case of denial of HIV test by the local hospitals. Although, there were cases reported from some districts of Karnataka where doctors, after coming to know the HIV positive status of the women, referred such cases to other hospitals, mainly to Bangalore based hospitals, stating that they had no technology or specialization required to handle HIV cases.

Table 8.1: Infrastructure Created by the States under National AIDS Control Programme (As on to December 2005) (In numbers)

State	VCTC Centres	ART Centres	PMTCT Centres	Community Care Centres
West Bengal	27	1	10	3
Karnataka	**123**	**4**	**59**	**12**
All India	1,114	57	485	85

Source: India statistic, Govt. of Karnataka and Govt. of West Bengal.

A study by Birungi *et al*, (2011) in Nairobi found that there was difficulty of receiving PMTCT services and skilled assistance for women in need of PMTCT services. In case of a few Indian States too, such inadequacies prevailed that in turn curtailed the accessibility of healthcare by HIV positive women.

As reported by our respondents, there was insufficient availability of PMTCT services in both the States and moreover there was significant disparity in the number of PMTCT centres established in both the States; in Karnataka, there were 59 centres as against 10 in West Bengal.

As per the health policy, these states also provided ART first regimen, free of cost, to HIV positive people. By the end of the April 2006, the number of HIV positive patients covered for ART medicine were 2,536 in Karnataka and 781 in West Bengal, which by July 2007 had increased to 8551 and 1973 people on roll for ART in Karnataka and West Bengal respectively (Indiastat, 2010). There was a growing demand for the ART medicine among HIV positive people in both the states. But, there was only one ART centre in West Bengal as against four in Karnataka. As the West Bengal ART centre[5] was situated in the School of Tropical Medicine in Kolkata, it remained extremely difficult for people from other districts to access it.

It is vital to mention here that West Bengal under the left ideology, had followed a unique policy for the distribution of ART first regimen. The state provided medicine on the basis of the socio-economic status of the patient (information shared by the officials of AIDS Cell Society). Thus, a patient in need of ART had to give the proof of her low socio- economic status in the form of a declaration by the local elected leader like *pradhan* (elected leader of the village panchayat) of the village, counsellor, or produce ration card as proof of her socio-economic status. In contrast, in Karnataka, ART was distributed without any such procedure. In West Bengal, a few women respondents reported that their medication and treatment got delayed because they could not produce proof of their low-income status. It was worth noting that obtaining income proof from the village political leader *pradhan* was not an easy task, particularly for women, as they thought that they might have to reveal their health status, *i.e.*, HIV positive status. During our field work, we came across cases where women coming from high socio-economic background, could obtain dubious declarations from the area councillor. Such reported incidents point to the corrupt practices of the local leaders. In contrast in Karnataka, a patient in need of healthcare did not depend on recommendation of local leaders for her/his treatment. When the state failed in safeguarding the health rights of people, they necessarily had to depend on the market. The medicines being very expensive, only patients with good economic background could get the medicine from private providers. For the large number of people living below poverty line, there were more chances of violations of their health rights.

Another important problem in West Bengal was the non-availability of anti-opportunistic medicines (anti-OIs) in the government hospitals. Data from the field shows that among the respondents, in West Bengal, around 64 per cent of women could not get anti-OI medicine from the government hospitals as medicines were not available (Table 8.2). In Karnataka, the position was better (81 per cent women got free anti-OI medicine); at least in a few government hospitals like Victoria Hospital, Bowring Hospital, Vani Vilas and a few more district hospitals, medicines were available. In West Bengal, even many essential drugs, required along with ART, for example, 'Septrum', were not available in the hospitals. Thus, people remained dependant on private providers or they more often had to forego medicines despite their health condition.

Table 8.2: Distribution of the Respondents on the basis of their Requirement of Medicines for Opportunistic Infections from Government Hospitals

Respondents Requirement of Medicines from Government Hospitals	Karnataka (N=80)	West Bengal (N=93)
	%	
Received free medicines from government hospitals	81.25	35.48
Did not receive free medicines from government hospitals	18.75	64.51
Total	**100**	**100**

Source: Primary Data

Apart from the short supply of the essential anti-opportunistic drugs, in West Bengal, the respondents pointed out that the user fee was charged for medical tests. According to the respondents, it was only in Calcutta Medical College where the medical tests were free. Owing to the high demand for the test in the Calcutta Medical College, people found it difficult to get test reports within the stipulated time. Often it took over two to three months to get the test report, which caused delay in commencing treatment. In case of HIV positive people suffering from some kind of illness, medical test reports were often urgently required. As a result, people were forced to depend on private medical laboratories or diagnostic centres which were costly and often unaffordable. User-fee was in vogue in a few government hospitals in Karnataka too, but, merely three or four per cent respondents complained about the user fee as others found it affordable or minimal. Recently, the state governments also have been providing CD4 test free of cost for HIV positive people which previously used to cost Rs. 500 per test.

Accessibility of Healthcare by HIV positive Women

Availability of healthcare is a necessary but not the sufficient conditions for ensuring adequate healthcare, as healthcare should also be accessible to patients. Accessibility of healthcare includes provisioning of healthcare in such a way that no person faces any difficulty in terms of healthcare accessibility within the government medical set up, in terms of geographical location, financial position and such other constraints (Black *et al* 2004, Gruskin *et al*,

2010). Right to accessibility includes accessibility of information relating diseases, cure of diseases and prevention of the disease. It also means adequate availability of counselling to HIV positive people that provides psychological healing to them. This includes provisioning of treatment of patients without denial of treatment, without discrimination, and treatment with consent. Here, we have addressed accessibility through three measures *i.e.*, treatment without geographical and economic constraints, treatment free of discrimination and denial and healthcare with adequate and proper counselling.

Treatment Accessibility beyond Economic and Regional Barriers

The state governments are implementing policies and programmes initiated by the central government, towards provisioning healthcare adequately. However, the implementation of policies have not been uniform in all the states. Therefore, there was difference in the experience and perception of HIV positive people in regard to accessibility of healthcare. In West Bengal, for instance, people faced in-accessibility due to geographical reasons as the VCTC centres were found at the district level. In addition, there were instances of some district hospitals, instead of treating HIV patients, referred HIV positive cases to Kolkata based district hospital. It was particularly problematic for poor people to access healthcare, as distance is a major hurdle for them in accessing healthcare. Constraints due to geographical distance compounded by economic constraints (as additional travel charge may be difficult to bear), prevented them from availing healthcare facilities. The secondary data shows that in Karnataka, however the VCTC centres were found at the block level, which made it little more convenient for HIV positive people to approach these centres. Also, more number of health centres in West Bengal were urban based whereas, in Karnataka centres were located across urban, semi urban and rural areas. When there were insufficient numbers of ART centres in the state, a majority of the HIV positive people, being economically powerless, failed to avail ART, or were forced to source it from near by private druggists, in order to avoid the problem of travelling long distances.

Treatment without Discrimination and Denial

Available literature carried out in diverse context indicated that discrimination prevailed across regions, countries and places (Feyissa *et al* 2012, ICRW 2007). HIV-related stigma and discrimination is a complex social process that reestablishes the power and pre-existing discrimination associated with sexuality, gender, and race (Feyissa *et al* 2012, Mahajan 2008, Parker and Aggleton 2003) .In patriarchal societies, HIV positive women[6] are expected to be victim of stigma and discrimination more than men. They face stigma at different levels, although the contours of stigma and discrimination could have the worst outcomes in hospitals or healthcare centres (Mahajan 2008, Bond *et al* 2003). In a healthcare system, if any patient, is either given less attention, treated differently (negatively), leveled or is discarded through foul words, negligence, treatment denial due to her HIV status then she or he may be considered as a victim of discrimination.

Treatment without discrimination is another major component of the right to accessibility of healthcare. Refutation of treatment directly violates the right to accessibility (Roseman *et al* 2004, CESCR 1966). In India, there were several instances, doctors denied medical treatment to people tested HIV positive[7] (Baharat *et al* 2001), and often doctors conducted the HIV test even without the patients' knowledge. In the selected states, there were cases where HIV positive people had faced discrimination and treatment denial. Incidences of discriminations were found both in private as well as public hospitals. Four respondents reported during the in-depth interview that, they were not given admittance in a few private hospitals for treatment because of their HIV positive status. In government hospitals (experience shared by HIV positive women) too, para-medical staff often had discriminated HIV positive patients, and in nine per cent cases even doctors were found mistreating HIV positive patients. Unfortunately, most such cases remained unnoticed by the state governments.

On the basis of field study, it is concluded that more number of discrimination cases (respondents faced discrimination) had taken place in West Bengal hospitals than in Karnataka hospitals (Table 8.3). In Karnataka, the number of patients who faced discrimination in government hospitals was lower (10%) than in West Bengal (25%) based government hospitals. However, discrimination rate was higher in private hospitals in Karnataka (14%) than in West Bengal (9%). In all the hospitals, doctors hesitated to carry out surgery on HIV positive patients (Baharat *et al* 2001). Recently, in Karnataka, a HIV positive woman (the respondent) was forced to deliver her baby without doctor's support, but the incidence went unreported. In a few government hospitals (like Calcutta Medical College and North Bengal Medical College) of West Bengal, in-house patients were instructed to post a sticker on their forehead indicating the diseases they suffer from. As reported by five per cent of respondents, they had to put a sticker on their forehead/ hand as HIV positive, which in turn, led to stigma and discrimination.

Table 8.3. Distribution of the Respondents by their experience with Discrimination in Hospitals

Status of Discrimination	Karnataka (N=100)	West Bengal (N=100)
Discrimination faced in Government hospitals	10	25
Discrimination faced in Private hospitals	14	9
Never faced discrimination in any hospital	76	66
Total	**100**	**100**

Source: Primary Data

In Karnataka, the incidence of discrimination persisted, and comparatively less number of respondents reported of facing discrimination. In one reported instance pertaining to Bowring hospital, (specialised hospital for HIV/AIDS treatment) in Karnataka, Sultana (name changed) an HIV positive woman, faced trouble in accessing healthcare. She reported certain disquieting facts about the hospital. The ART centre in Bowring Hospital had no lady doctor and the only doctor who did check up for patient was a virology specialist. Thus, any woman who approached the centre with gynaecology problems was referred to the gynaecologist of the hospital. During the interview Sultana said that she had been facing consistent and continuing problem of white-discharge. When we asked whether the doctor had done a medical check up, she mentioned that she had stopped going to the gynaecologists as she had been 'ill-treated thrice by the lady doctor with foul words'. She said that the doctor had abused her and did not even attend her properly, and hence she was no more interested in going to the doctor. Rather, she felt it was better to bear the infection and pain than being abused by the lady doctor in the public hospital. As Sultana was a poor woman, it was very difficult for her to go to a private gynaecologist. Sultana's plight was not the only one. However, such inhuman acts brought to the fore the paramount need to sensitising the medical profession to the need for upholding medical ethics in dealing with poor patients in order to ensure healthcare accessibility.

In certain incidences, HIV patients did not reveal their HIV positive status before the doctors and yet received treatment for some diseases. In such cases there was the possibility of HIV positive people knowingly hiding their sero-positive status, before the doctor[8] for several reasons including avoidance of the stigma and denial of treatment. Seven HIV positive women in both the states mentioned that they had visited doctors for several ailments, but because of the fear of denial of treatment, they preferred not to reveal their HIV status to the doctor.

A patient has had the right to know the disease he/she was suffering from, medicines he or she was taking and its function as well as the side effects of the medicine over the body. But, some respondents revealed that medical personal did not explain all necessary facts to patients. In three self reported cases, a few doctors had not felt it necessary to reveal the patient about their own sickness. Such witty actions often could be fatal. For instance, if a doctor did not reveal to the patient about her or his HIV positive status, it might be fatal not only to the patient but also to others. In case of, a woman named Sumi (name changed) who was treated along with her son in a private hospital of West Bengal, were given ART without having the CD4 check up done and even without the knowledge of the respondent. The respondent subsequently became bankrupt by paying for private treatment; thereafter, because of her crumbling economic condition, she approached a government hospital. It was in the government hospital where she learnt that before starting ART, a mandatory test of CD4 was most essential. Sumi's bitter experience highlighted the violation of right to accessibility of information, and also pointed to the need for regulation of private hospitals. It is quite clear that timely information and counselling could be most effective tools in preventing the spread of HIV infection. Even while treating HIV positive people, along with medications, counselling could built emotional strength of people so that they could be motivated to consume nutritious food and medicines (ART or any other) on time to prolong their life.

Accessibility of Information

Counselling to people in general and HIV positive people in particular, are a means to ensure accessibility of information, and could act as a tool to ensure right to accessibility. Adequate counselling makes people aware regarding the illness, its cure (if not permanent but at least prolonging the life span) and its prevention. Through pre HIV test counselling, the general public (who approach a health centre, blood bank) become aware of HIV and the measures to prevent the diseases. Counselling to HIV positive people helped them to manage the problem more effectively than just taking medicine. Counselling boosted psychological strength and enabled HIV positive people to live life enthusiastically despite the infection. In the selected states, there were around eleven HIV positive cases where women had been taking ART since more than 7/8 years and were still fit and had eagerness further to live like a normal person. Besides, some government hospital doctors and counsellors had positively changed their family members' attitude towards HIV positive person(s) through counselling. Counselling indeed had helped in reducing stigma at the household level.

Counselling has been often considered as a mandatory procedure as it provides awareness and information. Generally, counselling regarding HIV/ AIDS is recommended at four different stages: These are *(i)* pre-test counselling, *(ii)* post-test counselling, *(iii)* pre-ART counselling and *(iv)* post-ART or follow up counselling. The pre-test counselling is most important for all people (even for people who are not HIV positive) at least who provide consent for HIV test. Post-test counselling protects a person from a possible psychological breakdown in case that person is found HIV positive after the test.

The empirical result from our study showed that there was no adequate provisioning for counselling at the centres (Table 8.4). This had resulted in people not getting timely health information. Inadequate counselling might create socio-psychological problems that in turn might affect a person's physical health adversely. In Karnataka, in most Voluntary Counselling and Testing Centres (VCTC), or even Prevention of Mother to Child Transmission (PMTCT) centres, government hospitals or even at blood banks, consent before HIV test was not taken from individuals (this conclusion was drawn from observation as well as respondents' experience). Table 8.4 indicates that in West Bengal 84 per cent of respondents as against 95 per cent of respondents in Karnataka were not given pre-HIV test counselling. There were very few government hospitals that provided pre-test counselling in Karnataka. Even the most reputed hospitals, for example, Bowring hospital and Vanivilas, that were supposed to have integrated facilities and services, did not provide pre-test counselling to people, whereas in West Bengal, government hospitals having VCTC/PMTCT centres provided pre-test counselling. As far as post-HIV test counselling was concerned, 19 per cent in West Bengal and three per cent respondents in Karnataka had not received post-test counselling. These were clear-cut cases of violation of accessibility of healthcare as these hospitals had failed to impart awareness or information and psychological support to HIV positive women.

Table 8.4: Distribution of the Respondents on the basis of Receiving Counselling in Hospitals

Respondents who did not Receive Counselling	Karnataka (N=100)	West Bengal (N=100)
	%	
Respondents who did not received Pre-Test Counselling	95	84
Respondents who did not receive Post-Test Counselling	3	19
Respondents who had not receive pre-test or Post-test Counselling	96	87

In sum, there was a large body of evidence to show that people still faced genuine difficulties in accessing healthcare. In West Bengal, despite the historical presence of the left ideology, people faced more trouble in accessing healthcare due to improper location of health centres and their inadequate availability in number. In both the states, there were instances of treatment denial (ILO 2011). Moreover, it was also found that HIV positive people faced difficulties in a few private hospitals as well. The information relating diseases and treatment did not reach the patient, and in all such cases accessibility of healthcare remained inadequate.

Conclusion

The State governments had taken several initiatives towards ensuring healthcare to individuals. Healthcare centres, were established, personals appointed, technologies were catered to provide healthcare to HIV positive people. Despite all such initiatives, adequate availability and accessibility of healthcare remained a distant dream for many HIV positive people. In Karnataka, the VCTC centres and ART centres remained more accessible than in West Bengal. In regard to ART centres, in West Bengal, there were certain avoidable constraints for HIV positive women in accessing healthcare, such as the insistence on producing a certificate of low income for getting free treatment. In both the States, there were reports of treatment denial to HIV positive women. Similarly, many of the health centres seemed to have laid less emphasis on counselling with the result that women could not access information relating their health and psychological strength. Discrimination was found to be rampant in many medical institutions as mentioned by respondents who had faced discriminatory treatment from doctors.

The states need to retrospect on their policies and programmes for HIV eradication and take corrective measures to bridge gaps. They have to provide the required accessories/devices for adopting universal precautionary measures. In the process, the states should also regulate the role of third party players (private healthcare centres) as it impacts the right to accessibility of HIV positive women. Repeated instances of treatment denial indicate that the professed ethical conduct of the medical profession has indeed taken back seat. Several orientation and training courses have been conducted for medical and paramedical staff, yet there is need for more such courses. The administrations have to ensure that HIV positive women are not divested of accessibility to healthcare.

FOOTNOTES

1. Recently Article 21 of the Indian Constitution has been interpreted to incorporate the right to health in right to life and hence this right having now acquired a constitutional status through judicial activism. Article 21 of the constitution guarantees right to life and this court has interpreted the guarantee to cover a life with normal amenities assuring good living which include medical attention, life free from diseases and longitivity up to normal expectations" (Supra no. 20). It is also "...the constitutional obligation of the state to provide adequate medical services to the people. Whatever is necessary for this purpose has to be done (AIR 1996 SC 2426).
2. When the study was conducted, the West Bengal was led by the left government under the\ leaders hip of Buddhadeb Bhattacharya. The CPI (M) was defeated in the year 2011 Assembly Elections by the Trinamool Congress.
3. Anti Retro Viral Therapy is the life saving medicine for AIDS patients. When an infected body starts showing symptoms, ART medicine becomes a part of the daily life of people.
4. However, with the persistent effort of the Kolkata Network of Positive people, these two·district hospitals only recently have started treating HIV positive people.
5. The state government has recently proposed to set up one more ART centre in Siliguri.
6 Particularly in a society like in India where majority of the infection is led through heterosexuality contact.
7. In Kolkata, a hospital refused to touch the body of a young AIDS patient who died later. In Indore, a pregnant woman died outside a government hospital without treatment. In Lucknow , a renal failure patient (HIV positive) had to

wait for 16 hours before activists could get him a hospital bed (The Times of India, 2007).

8. The state of Karnataka as well as West Bengal have succeeded in co-opting a few dedicated and responsible counsellors for providing proper counselling to HIV positive people.

REFERENCES

Avert (2009), Overview of HIV/AIDS in India. http://www.avert.org/aidsindia.htm, Last Browsed on 5th May 2009.

Bell Emma, Mthembu,b Sue O' Sullivan and Kevin Moody (2007), Sexual and Reproductive Health Services and HIV Testing: Perspectives and Experiences of Women and Men Living with HIV and AIDS. *Reproductive Health Matters* Vol. 15(29 Supplement). pp. 113-135.

Bharat Shalini, Peter Aggleton and Paul Tyrer 2001. India: HIV and AIDS-related Discrimination, Stigmatization and Denial. UNAIDS Geneva, Switzerland, UNAIDS/01.46E. ISBN 92-9173-104-8. http://data.unaids.org/Publications/IRC-pub02/jc587-india_en.pdf, Last Browsed on 11th November 2012.

Berer, M., and Sunanda R. 1993. Women and HIV/AIDS: *An International Resource Book, Information, action, and Resources on Women and HIV/AIDS, Reproductive Health and Sexual Relationship*. Pandora Press: London.

Birungi, Harriet, Francis Obare, Anke van der Kwaak and Jane Harriet Namwebya. Maternal Healthcare Utilisation Among HIV-Positive Female Adolescents in Kenya. *International Perspectives on Sexual and Reproductive Health.* Volume 37, Number 3, pp. 143-149, http://www.guttmacher.org/pubs/journals/3714311.html. Last Browsed on 8th November 2012.

Black Michael Steeve Ebener, Patricia Najera Aguilar, Manuel Vidaurre and Zine El Morjani. 2004. Using GIS to Measure Physical Accessibility to Healthcare. *World Health Organization, RMIT University,* http://www.who.int/kms/initiatives/Ebener_et_al_2004a.pdf. Last browsed on 28th July 2011.

Blanchard Kelly and Ruth Manski. 1 December 2011. HIV-Positive Women Need Access to all Health Services, Including Abortion. RH Reality Check; http://www.rhrealitycheck.org/print/18093. Last browsed on 8th November 2012.

Bond V, Chase E, Aggelton P. 2002, Stigma, HIV/AIDS Prevention, and Mother to Child Transmission in Zambia. *Evaluation and Programme Planning*. 25:242-356.

Bronwen Lichtenstein (2006), Domestic Violence in Barriers to Healthcare for HIV-Positive Women. AIDS Patient Care and STDs; Feb 2006, Vol. 20 Issue 2, pp. 122-32.

Centre for Economic and Social Rights. 2004, The Right to Health in United States of America What Does it Mean?. http://www.cesr.org/downloads/Right%20to%20Health%20in%20USA%202004.pdf, Last browsed on 28th July 2011.

Chikwendu Eudora. 2004. When the State Fails: NGOs in Grasroots AIDS Care. In *Dilectical Anthropology,* Kluwer Academic Publishers, Vol. 28, pp. 245-259.

Doyal, Lesley. 1994. HIV and AIDS: Putting Women on the Global Agenda. In *AIDS: Setting A Feminist Agenda,* Lesley Doyal, Jenny Naidoo, and Tamsin Wilton, (eds.); Taylor and Francis: London.

Feyissa T. Garumma, Lakew Abebe, Eshetu Girma and Mirkuzie Woldie. (2012). Stigma and Discrimination against People Living with HIV by Healthcare Providers, Southwest Ethiopia. *BMC Public Health Vol.* 12:522, http://www.biomedcentral.com/content/pdf/1471-2458-12-522.pdf, Last Browsed on 7th November 2012.

Fried Susana, Brianna Harrison, Kelly Starcevich, Corinne Whitaker, Tiana O'Konek. Integrating Interventions on Maternal Mortality and Morbidity and HIV: A Human Rights-based Framework and Approach. *Health and Human Rights: An International Journal.* http://www.hhrjournal.org/index.php/hhr/article/view/512/776. Last Browsed on 11th November 2012.

Gruskin Sofia, Dina Bogecho, and Laura Ferguson. 2010, Rights-based Approaches' to Health Policies and Programmes: Articulations, Ambiguities, and Assessment. Macmillan Publishers Ltd. 0197-5897. In *Journal of Public Health Policy* Vol. 31, 2, pp. 129-145.

Hartigan Pamela, Janet Price, and Rachel Tolhurst. 2002. Communicable Diseases: Outstanding Commitments to Gender and Poverty. In Sen, Gita, Asha George and Piroska Ostlin (eds.), *Engendering International Health; The Challenge of Equity.* Cambridge, London; MIT Press.

Ipas.org. 2012, Reproductive Choice for Women Living with HIV: The S I Tuat Ion In 2 0 1 2 – And What Ne Eds To B E Done. http://www.ipas.org/~/media/Files/Ipas%20Publications/HIVPREABOE12.ashx. Last Browsed on 10th November 2012.

Johnston, Heidi Bart 2003. Safe and Accessible: Strategizing the Future. http://www.india-seminar.com/2003/532/532%20heidi%20bart%20johnston.htm. Last browsed on 1st May, 2006.

Lee Christina (1998), "Women's Health: Psychological and Social Perspective", London: Sage.

Mahajan Anish P, Jennifer N. Sayles, Vishal A. Patel, Robert H. Remien, Daniel Ortiz, Greg Szekeres, and Thomas J. Coates. 2008, Stigma in the HIV/AIDS Epidemic: A Review of the Literature and Recommendations for the way Forward. *AIDS.* Vol 22 (Suppl 2): pp. 67-79.

Michelson E H. 1993. Adam's Rib Awry? Women and Schistosomiasis. *Social Science and Medicine,* 37 (4):493-501.

MacNaughton Gillian 2004. Women's Human Rights related to Healthcare Services in the Context of HIV/AIDS. Health and Human Rights Working Paper Series No. 5. The International Centre for the Legal Protection of Human Rights, London. http://www.who.int/hhr/information/en/Series_5_womens healthcarergs_MacNaughton.pdf, Last Browsed on 11th November 2004.

Monjok Emmanuel, Andrea Smesny, and E. James Essien 2009, HIV/AIDS – Related Stigma and Discrimination in Nigeria: Review of Research Studies and Future Directions for Prevention Strategies. *African Journal of Reproductive Health* September; 13(3). pp. 21-35.

ILO 2011, Discrimination against People Living with HIV within Healthcare Settings in China. The STD and AIDS Prevention and Control Centre of the Chinese Centre for Disease Control and Prevention, The International Labour

Organization. http://www.ilo.org/wcmsp5/groups/public/—ed_protect/—protrav/—ilo_aids/documents/publication/wcms_155950.pdf. Last browsed on 11th November 2012.

International Centre for Research on Women (ICRW) 2007. Taking Action Against HIV Stigma and Discrimination: Guidance Document And Supporting Resources. http://www.icrw.org/files/publications/DFID-Taking-Action-Against-HIV-Stigma-and-Discrimination.pdf, Last browsed on 7th November 2012.

Indiastat 2009. State wise number of people infected by HIV. www.indiastat.com, last browsed on 23rd May 2009.

Indiastat, 2010. State-wise Number of AIDS Patients on Role of ART www.indiastat.com, Last browsed on 23rd December 2010.

Parker R, Aggleton P. 2003. HIV and AIDS-related Stigma and Discrimination: A Conceptual Framework and Implications for Action. *Social Science Medicine*, Vol. 57(1):13-24.

Roseman Mindy Jane and Sofia Gruskin, and Sumita Banerjee. 2004. HIV/AIDS and Human Rights in Nutshell. *The Programme on International Health and Human Rights, François-Xavier Bagnoud Centre for Health and Human Rights, Harvard School of Public Health and the International Council of AIDS Service Organizations*. http://www.hsph.harvard.edu/pihhr/files/ENGLISH.pdf Last browsed on 31st July 2011.

Sibal, Kapil. 2002. Need for a Rights Sensitive Legislation. http://www.indiaseminar.com/2002/520/520%20kapil%20sibal.htm, Last browsed on 31st July 2011

United Nations Population Fund. 2011. The Human Rights-based Approach. http://www.unfpa.org/rights/approaches.htm Last browsed on 31st July 2011.

US Department of Health and Human Services Office on Women's Health. 2011. Barriers to care for HIV/AIDS. http://www.womenshealth.gov/hiv-aids/living-with-hiv-aids/barriers-to-care-for-hiv-aids.cfm. Last browsed on 25th October 2012.

Verma, Ravi K and Tarun Kumar Roy 2002. HIV Risk Behaviour and Socio-cultural Environment. In *Living With the AIDS Virus: The Epidemic and the Response in India*. Samiran panda, Anindya Chatterjiee and Abu S. Abdul-Quader (eds.): New Delhi: Sage Publication.

World Health Organization. 2009. A Human Based Approach to Neglected Tropical Diseases. http://www.who.int/hhr/activities/NTD%20information%20sheet%20-%20English.pdf, Last browsed on 31st July 2011.

9

Prospect and Potential of Green Jobs towards Green Economy in Bangladesh

A Situation Analysis and Way Forward

— KHALID MD. BAHAUDDIN
— NAYMA IFTAKHAR

The prospects and potential of green jobs in Bangladesh are huge. There are many potential sectors such as renewable energy, buildings and construction, transportation, basic industries, agriculture and forestry etc., are the priority areas for the future green job market. In 2009, numbers of approximate green jobs were 748,701 while it increased in 2010 which was about 811,268. It is true the green jobs sector is growing in Bangladesh, but there are also challenges that need to be overcome to accelerate growth. This paper tried to investigate the outlook and potential of green jobs in Bangladesh as well as also make recommendation some ideologies, basic principles as well as reform of policy mechanism to promote and develop of green jobs in Bangladesh.

Bangladesh is a low energy-consuming though energy starved country. About 60 per cent of the population is not connected to the national grid. A large majority of the 40 per cent that do have access to the national grid live in urban areas. Although Bangladesh has made impressive gains in key human development indicators, more than 63 million people remain below the poverty line. Under employment is pervasive, unemployment levels high amongst the youth, and the informal economy estimated to account for 88 per cent of the overall employment. The Gender Empowerment Measure ranking of 76 shows continued low levels of female ownership of economic assets. To overcome this situation, green jobs can play an additional vital role to achieve green economy as there are many potential sectors in Bangladesh which can generate green jobs. In Bangladesh, green jobs create opportunities for employment for the poor in the renewable energy sector such as solar home systems and bio-gas. Other green jobs could be created in organic, plastic waste and lead acid battery recycling, or by construction projects – such as digging rivers and canals, constructing water reservoirs and building roads. It is true the green jobs sector is growing in Bangladesh, but there are also challenges that need to be overcome to accelerate growth. So to conquer the challenges, some ideologies and basic principles as well as reform of policy must be taken to develop and promote the green jobs in Bangladesh.

Concept of Green Jobs

The concept of green job is a new one. 'Green jobs' does not lend itself to a tight definition but certainly includes direct employment that contributes to the reduction of environmental impact to levels that are ultimately sustainable. This includes jobs that help to reduce the consumption of energy and raw materials, decarbonizes the economy, protect and restore ecosystem and biodiversity and minimize the production of waste and pollution. Thus green job aims to preserve the environment for both present and future generations and to be more equitable and inclusive of all people and all countries.

Environmental Dimension of Green Jobs

For a modern economy, even in the least developed countries, a complete mapping of links between the environment and economy is a major challenge given the many positive and negative feedback loops that would need to be examined.

The range of green job profiles thus defined is broad. It stretches from highly skilled research and development or management functions through technical and skilled levels to relatively low-skilled roles. In developed economies, environment related jobs tend to be concentrated in sectors/ activities directly linked to decarbonizing energy supply and improving energy efficiency, pollution control and eco-friendly services. Examples of those sectors that hold the promise of the green jobs of the future include:

- Delivering improvements in energy and resource efficiency, particularly in the building sector (new and existing built stock), but also industry and transport.
- Renewable energy (including bio-fuels and renewable technologies).
- Sustainable mobility (*i.e.,* mass transportation).
- Waste management and recycling of raw materials.
- Eco-industries related to pollution control (air, water, waste, site decontamination, noise).
- 'Eco-friendly' services (conservation, eco-tourism, etc.).

In developing economies other sectors may be at least as important, in particular:

- Those involving the sustainable use of natural resources, including agriculture, forestry and fisheries.
- Activities relating to adaptation to climate change.

Social Dimension of Green Jobs (the 'decent work' criterion)

The green job definition used here encompasses more than just the extent to which a particular job contributes to a more environmentally sustainable economy. It also captures a measure of job quality. Effectively, a job may be associated with an economic activity that is more environmentally sustainable than the norm or which contributes to such improvement in other sectors, but it cannot be considered a 'green job' if it does not meet conditions of decent work.

The decent work definition is built upon a set of social and labour rights and obligations. The eight basic Conventions of the ILO, which are recognised as defining the various aspects of socially responsible production, also apply to green jobs. 11 Indicators and criteria have been developed and endorsed at the international level through adoption of the ILO labour standards which are relevant to the further characterization of the social and labour dimension of green jobs (see box 1). Many jobs would not be considered decent. This is due to a number of factors. The so-called 'green sectors' in developing countries include sectors where achieving decent work conditions remain a challenge. Examples of 'green but not decent jobs' include low-wage jobs installing solar panels, and jobs in ship breaking or electronic waste recycling where occupational safety is inadequate or child labour is used. In many instances, these sectors are defined by their informal nature, hardship and occupational and health hazards.

The Environmental Agenda and Green Jobs in Developing Countries

International debate on global environmental issues has evolved over the last two decades since the adoption of the 1992 Rio Conventions on desertification, climate change and biodiversity. 36 more favorable conditions are being created for the development of an enlarged 'environmental economy', and the emergence of new economic sectors and services. In response, demand for jobs with new qualifications and skills has increased and other jobs have evolved. The green jobs concept highlights labour market shifts that are directly dependent on various aspects of environmental management and low carbon development, as well as climate change adaptation in accordance with the definition given by the United Nations Framework Convention on Climate Change (UNFCCC).

Box 1: The ILO Definition of Decent Work

Decent work has been defined by ILO representatives of governments and employers' and workers' organizations in over 180 countries as: "opportunities for women and men to obtain decent and productive work in conditions of freedom, equity, security and human dignity, in which women and men have access on equal terms". Decent work combines adequate income from productive work with social security, respect for worker and social rights and the opportunity to voice and defend interests collectively.

Decent work is relative and country-specific because countries differ socially and economically. None can aim for the same absolute conditions of work. Each country must set its own targets for decent work.

The following integrated agenda of policies and measures across four mutually reinforcing areas is required to achieve decent work goals:

1. Respect for and protection of basic human rights at work.
2. Promotion and creation of opportunities for full productive and remunerative employment.
3. Broad social protection.
4. Sustained social dialogue among social partners: workers, employers and private business, and government.

A universal social 'floor' applies to all countries, and includes respect for the following basic human rights:

- Freedom of association and the effective recognition of collective bargaining rights.
- Elimination of all forms of forced or compulsory labour.
- Effective abolition of child labour and the right of children to learn and develop rather than work.
- Elimination of discrimination in respect of employment and occupation.

Gaps between people's decent work aspirations and reality exist everywhere. The challenge is to reduce these gaps. Progress towards decent work should be the central goal of all economic and social policies and strategies.

A growing literature suggests that millions of green jobs already exist. The economic restructuring due to green growth will lead to changes in prices, in international trade and in the output of countries, and therefore in employment. These effects have been the subject of a number of studies seeking to quantify the net employment effects. Results show that net effects on jobs are modest but the economic structural shift can be quite substantial. Essentially, the number and nature of jobs will change as the relative importance of sectors changes, with some expanding, others contracting, and others remaining stable but with changes in processes and products. But this transition has been documented mostly in industrialized countries.

Research on developing countries is comparatively scarce. Alongside the growing need to assess the contribution of these sectors and activities to national economies, methodologies and analytical tools that integrate the complex interactions between the socio-economic and environmental fields are also required. Indeed, there is demand for a comprehensive analytical framework that can better assist policy-making in this fast-evolving field, including in developing countries.

Green growth can create new and additional employment demand. This is the case, for example, when jobs in renewable energy replace those depending on fossil fuels, or when new jobs are created by expenditure on adaptation activities.

In developing countries, which tend to have unutilised or under utilised labour, this provides opportunities to raise total employment.

Country Level Support of the Green Jobs Programme

The number of countries the Green Jobs Programme is actively collaborating with increased over the past years and the areas of work cover a great variety of issues. The map below displays the current and expected country level support of the Green Jobs Programme.

The Programme contributes to the establishment of green jobs and greener economies, among others, in the following sectors: construction and green buildings, tourism, renewable energy and energy efficiency, forestry, natural resource management, recycling and waste management and sustainable agriculture. It supports national initiatives through advocacy workshop and capacity building, assessments on green jobs potential, policy advice and strategic planning. It also supports local initiatives by promoting green entrepreneurship, the greening of enterprises and local development for adaptation to climate change.

The regional activities in Africa focus mainly on strengthening green entrepreneurship. In South Africa several studies and projects focus on the building and construction sector. The Asia and the Pacific Green Jobs Programme encourages ILO constituents to participate in social dialogue on green jobs through capacity building, promotes inclusive jobs centred and environmentally sustainable growth models and advocates for green jobs creation through demonstration projects. In 2010, two projects were initiated by the regional Programme, the Green Jobs in Asia project funded by the Australian government and the Green Business Asia funded by the Japanese government. Green Jobs Programme activities in the Arab States are at the initial stages. In Lebanon, an assessment on the green jobs potential was conducted and a Green Jobs Kick-Off Workshop was held in Beirut from 28 to 29 July. In Latin America and the Caribbean, the main focus is on waste management, renewable energy, tourism, forestry, sustainable agriculture and green social housing. Haiti receives support in the area of adaptation to climate change.

Green Jobs Initiatives and Implementation in Bangladesh

Bangladesh is a low energy-consuming though energy starved country. About 60 per cent of the population is not connected to the national grid. A large majority of the 40 per cent that do have access to the national grid live in urban areas. Although Bangladesh has made impressive gains in key human development indicators, more than 63 million people remain below the poverty line. Under employment is pervasive, unemployment levels high amongst the youth, and the informal economy estimated to account for 88 per cent of the overall employment. The Gender Empowerment Measure ranking of 76 shows continued low levels of female ownership of economic assets.

In July 2008, a national workshop on Green Jobs Initiatives (jointly organized by Ministry of Labour and Employment, Bangladesh and ILO) was held in Dhaka to raise awareness of the concept of Green Jobs and recommend steps forward. Participants at the workshop expressed support for Bangladesh as a participating country on ILO Green Jobs initiatives, noting that as a first step, there was a need to undertake an inventory of existing green jobs. A formal launching of the green jobs initiative was held on 04 December 2008, in which it was agreed, among others, that:

- A draft action plan on green jobs would be formulated following a series of regional level consultations.
- An inventory on green jobs on 'who is doing what' needs to be carried out which would support the draft action plan, and other policy interventions.

As a follow up to the initiatives mentioned above, the ILO, in consultation with the Ministry of Labour and Employment has launched two assessment studies in selected sectors: one assessment would focus on three sectors *viz.*, waste management, renewable energy and construction; the other study would focus on agriculture sector including forestry. The agriculture sector assessment on green jobs would include both an inventory and assessment of the intensive green technologies which are currently on going or are being planned in the future and those have an impact on poverty reduction, employment creation, sustainable environment and decent work.

Since 2008, the Green Jobs Programme has implemented activities in Bangladesh (first phase: 2008 to 2010). Various awareness raising activities on green jobs took place at national and regional levels. They helped to improve the effective implementation and enforcement of green jobs in the country. Baseline knowledge on green jobs was generated through a national assessment and complemented by sector based analysis and by a separate study on skills needs for green jobs.

Training in renewable energy (*i.e.*, solar home systems) and soft skills (*i.e.*, entrepreneurship capacity development) were provided to equip the project target groups (mostly women in rural areas) with adequate techniques and skills for employment opportunities. The training was provided through a Public Private Partnership (PPP) with Grameen Shakti (a non-profit company) and the Bureau for Manpower Employment and Training (BMET). The promotion of green jobs in Bangladesh provides employment opportunities through training on solar techniques and facilitates a low-carbon development by promoting renewable energy.

The lessons learned from the first phase have been successfully integrated into the Green Jobs in Asia project, under the ILO – Australian Partnership (2010-15). The Private-Public Partnership will be expanded to cover a larger market scope, not only including Grameen Shakti, BMET but also the Infrastructure Development Company Limited (IDCOL).

Potential Sectors for Green Jobs in Bangladesh

Table 9.1 showing the potential sectors for green jobs in Bangladesh.

Table 9.1: Potential Sectors for Green Jobs in Bangladesh

Sector	Scope/Field of Green Jobs
Agriculture	• Soil conservation • Water efficiency in Irrigation • Organic farming (tea cultivation already started in Bangladesh) • Reducing distance between farm and market
Forestry	• Reforestation and afforestation • Sustainable forestry management by community • Halting of deforestation
Energy	• Renewable Energy (solar, bio-gas, improved stove, biomass) • Manufacturing of energy efficient appliances such as CFL, efficient air conditions etc.
Transport	• Fuel switching in vehicles (petrol, diesel to CNG) • Use of hybrid or fuel efficient vehicles • Mass transit • Bus rapid transit (BRT)-modal shift • Car Pooling
Construction	• Cement factory (energy efficiency) • Brick Manufacturing (energy efficiency) • Concrete Blocks • Green Building/Energy efficient Buildings
Manufacturing	• Pollution control technologies such as ETP • Energy and materials efficiency
Waste Management	• Recycling of municipal organic and inorganic waste (composting, bio-gas, bio-gas to energy, RDF etc., plastic waste recycling) • Recycling of lead acid battery • Extended producer responsibility (product take back and re-manufacturing)

Sector-wise Distribution of Green Jobs in Bangladesh

There were two study conducted on number of green employments held in different sectors of Bangladesh which showing in Table 9.2 and Table 9.3.

Table 9.2: Sector-wise Distribution of Green Jobs Estimated by Waste Concern, 2009

Sector	Green Jobs (Numbers)
Agriculture and Forestry	8725
Transportation	147987
Manufacturing (energy Efficiency, Brick Kilns)	11,081
Renewable Energy	14966
Waste Recycling (compost, production, sales and distribution)	29942
Building Construction	536,000
Total	**748,701**

Table 9.3: Sector-wise Distribution of Green Jobs Estimated by GHK Consultants for ILO, 2010

Sector	Core Environment Related Jobs	Green Jobs
Sustainable agriculture	41,548	Not possible to estimate
Sustainable and participatory forestry	28,813	Not possible to estimate
Sustainable energy	18,823	18,823
Waste management and recycling	189,180	Not possible to estimate
Collection purification and distribution of water	8,441	Not possible to estimate
Climate adaptation activities	1,726,755	Not possible to estimate
Manufacturing and energy efficiency	10,934	10,934
Sustainable transportation	178,510	178,510
Sustainable construction	1,340,000	536,000 – 670,000
Total	**3,543,004**	**811,268**

Constraints and Challenges of Green Jobs in Bangladesh

It is true the green jobs sector is growing in Bangladesh, but there are also challenges that need to be overcome to accelerate growth. The burning constraints and challenges of green jobs in Bangladesh perspectives are following:

- Lack of awareness and capacity building to understand the concept of Green Jobs.
- Insufficient incentives and promotional measures.
- Inadequate research and development initiatives.
- Insufficient Public Private Partnerships.

Suggestion Towards Promoting Green Jobs In Bangladesh

Basic Principles for the Promotion of Green Employment

Green employment directly leads to increases in productivity and efficiency, helps to promote faster income growth for workers and increases the amounts of income distributed across workers. The promotion of various environmental protection measures lead to an ever-expanding green industry chain with numerous direct and indirect employment opportunities which have the potential to offset the numbers of jobs lost in conventional industries. The newly created jobs would be safer, more economical and stable. Policies in human resources, therefore, have no option but to follow the trend of green development and effectively promote green employment.

- **Promotion of Green Employment through Classification**

Different kinds of ideas and principles must be used to promote different types of green jobs, as they cannot be generalized nor standardized. For green jobs born out of demand, the government should follow market mechanisms, eliminating factors which might obstruct the proper functioning of the market and try to provide more and better employment services. For the government directed type of green jobs, policy interference needs to occur to design specific employment promotion policies.

- **Industrial/Sectoral, Environmental and Employment Policies are Equally Important and Should be Considered Concurrently**

Economic development, environmental protection and employment promotion are all bring about improvements to people's lives, all three equally important. The economy cannot be developed by ignoring the environment or employment, nor could the environment be well protected by limiting economic growth and job creation or a development model be created without employment growth be adopted.

Policy should provide leverage for integrated support, coordinating the promotion of industrial/sectoral structure optimization, the environment's continuous improvement, job increases and improvement to job quality. All these mean that, under the premise that employment goals are given full consideration, we should encourage industries/sectors in the environmental sector to promote the transformation of traditional industries towards more sustainable production and gradually improve environmental standards.

The key to realising the coordinated development of the three dimensions outlined above is to have synchronized policy making, *i.e.*, when deciding on industrial/sectoral policy and planning, there should be simultaneous drafting of employment policies and plans; when drafting employment policies and plans, the effects on economic development and the environment must be taken into account.

- **Policies that Promote Green Employment Require further Scrutiny of the Concept of Green Employment**

Further scrutiny of the green job concept is required before green policy is promoted because: some green jobs do not offer decent employment; some green jobs are good for the environment but do not promote low carbon employment, some low carbon jobs are work against environmental protection, such as the growing of biomass energy crops using of fertilizer that generates pollution; some green jobs do not meet the need for industrial development, such as photovoltaic power plants and PV power generation equipment manufacturing where over capacity is pervasive; some green jobs do not meet the characteristics of resource endowments.

Therefore, green job development should not solely involve promotion without policy constraint and control. When the government is drafting green employment promotion policies, it must take into account Bangladesh's unique position and identify the areas and levels of intervention for green employment.

- **Industry-specific Green Job Promotion Policies**

Green jobs exist in all different industries, sectors and levels and impact all kinds of workers, varying widely across different industries. Therefore, under the general guiding ideology and principles, industry/sector-specific survey and research must be conducted, and industry/sector specific green employment promotion policies must be devised.

- **Policy Suggestions for the Promotion of Green Employment**

Setting green employment promotion policies is the greening of a more active employment policy system. On the one hand the 'green' concept must be implanted into the policy system. Accelerating economic growth and expanding employment are still the government's most urgent tasks. In this scenario, the green employment promotion must give proper consideration to the following issues: *firstly*, green employment promotion should not cause great employment fluctuation, with respective employment plans well designed. *Secondly*, when it is difficult to fully transfer surplus agricultural labour to meet job demand, the government should support the greening of labour intensive employment in the agricultural. *Thirdly*, like other policies, green job promotion should focus on non-public sectors, including individual, privately-owned, and village and township enterprises etc. On one hand, these enterprises generate the majority of jobs, and on the other hand, the greening potential is quite considerable. *Fourthly*, flexible employment is still the key channel for job creation and green employment promotion must not strangle this employment channel.

In accordance with the research findings, the following policy suggestions are made:

- **Ensure Green Employment is Developed through Legal Channels**
  - *Conduct an employment evaluation of industrial/sectoral and environmental policies*: *First* of all, employment must be the centre of a social evaluation index system set up for environmental protection.

In industrial and environmental planning, employment evaluation indexes must use scientific methods, including the number of new jobs a project could possibly create, the number of lost jobs brought about by the project's existence, the impact on the local human resource supply-demand position, the impact on local income levels and the identification of potential human resources for the project, etc.

Secondly, designing of employment evaluation indexes should be followed by employment planning. This means the design of policies and measures to address the project's impacts on employment. If job losses are likely, plans must be made to counteract unemployment; if there are additional human resource needs, a supply plan must be devised. At the crux of such planning is the provision of adequate financial resources to address the project impacts.

Thirdly, employment evaluation indexes and plans should be accompanied by employment budgeting, *i.e.,* the cost benefit t of the project on employment including accounting for the cost of employment and funding.

Lastly, project evaluation should be conducted. The impacts on employment of evaluation of the industrial and environmental policies should a pre-condition for project approval.

  - *Modify and improve relevant laws and industrial and environmental policy*: *Firstly,* clear goals for green employment must be raised during the process of drafting any plan or policy. Ultimately, targets for employment and environmental protection must be clearly stated so to ensure the development of green employment in Bangladesh for future. *Secondly* respective laws and regulations should be modified.

- **Policy Measures for Promoting Green Employment**
  - *Green HR market mechanisms to promote green employment*: A green employment certification system should be set up to promote green employment. Companies or organizations in green industries and green companies in non-green industries could be acknowledged with the title of 'Green Employer', a reference for receiving related policy support. For example, Green Employers could qualify to join suppliers on the government's green procurement list.

A professional green job certification system could be set up to promote workers' transformation towards 'green collar' jobs. Improvements to the professional certification system, setting up standards for green jobs and encouraging workers to take part in certification will help to get more people to join the ranks of green employment.

The *third* point concerns the public employment service system. A green job service zone should be set up in public employment service agencies, in order to collect and advertise green job information and promote matching between demand and supply for green jobs. The labour and social security community platform should be used so that green job information can reach every worker.

- **The Greening of Existing Employment Policy to Promote Green Employment**

Jobs in those industries which were affected for institutional reasons and due to the State's industrial policies and as such they should be provided with support on employment policies, including those that promote job stabilisation and employment.

The *first* is to encourage companies to expand employment. Policy leverages such as tax benefits, social insurance subsidies, guaranteed loans and interest subsidies should be used to encourage employment of those affected in the transformation towards green economy. Policy supports such as tax benefits should be provided to those companies that use multiple channels to relocate their own affected workers by the use of their existing facilities, sites and technology for diversification.

The *second* is to help companies overcome difficulties to create as many jobs as possible. Preferential treatments such as delaying payment of social insurances, reducing social insurance rates, and providing social insurance subsidies, job subsidies, and worker training subsidies, should be given to those companies who are in the transformation towards green production and have the potential to absorb surplus workers, so that they could maintain stable employment, and eliminate or minimize redundancy.

The *third* is to encourage self-employed entrepreneurs. Entrepreneurship should be encouraged by providing free training, set tax relief and loan credit. Administrative fees and taxes could be reduced or waived for those starting their own businesses such as in small industry and privately owned businesses.

The *fourth* is to promote reemployment through public employment services and re-employment training. The government's public employment agencies should provide free employment services to people looking to be re-employed. Employees from the sunset industries should be retrained with a focus on the industries that are transforming their resource use, making it easier for those out of work to be re-employed in industries where there is growing demand.

The *fifth* is to provide employment support for those in financial difficulties. The government could create volunteer or charitable positions which have social security subsidies and job subsidies, which are open to those who are experiencing difficulty in finding reemployment. The government could provide social security subsidies to those who are expected to find re-employment relatively easily and coordinate placements for those that are finding it difficult to become re-employed.

- **Develop Green Job through Policy Support**

Some green jobs very competitive and will develop strongly without additional policy support. Environmental equipment, cleansing products and organic food are examples of such industries. However, generally speaking, green employment is an emerging phenomenon which still needs to rely on the quick set up of supportive policy. This does not necessarily refer to big investment but offers enormous potential for employment.

For example, some cities piloted waste collection and recycling stations which could not compete with private recycling operators. To build their size, jobs in waste recycling were created in communities to build up a network, using subsidies or social welfare subsidies in the early phases of growth. When green employment develops into a formal industry, it will be able to operate free from government intervention.

- **Develop Green Employment in the Process of Rural Development and Building the West**

There is broad potential for green employment in rural areas. Agriculture is the foundation of the Bangladesh economy. Building the ecological environment is the basis of Bangladesh national policy and the rural economy is a miniature national economy.

The *first* is in developing employment in eco-agriculture. Eco-agriculture combines labour with green knowledge to produce energy saving green food.

The *second* is in developing employment in specialised agriculture. Specialised agriculture based on market and regional advantages will be the development direction for modern agriculture. This would lead to the creation of groups of specialised households and villages, also helping to increase farmers' incomes. The *third* is developing employment in processing the products of specialized agriculture. This processing combines agriculture, industry and commerce, lead by an enterprise or farmer's co-operative linking farmers and the processing industry in an operational chain. The *fourth* is developing rural eco-tourism, which could achieve significant growth in production, revenue and employment. The *fifth* is developing new energy industries. Energy consumption in rural areas is undergoing a fast increase. The development of biomass energy, straw manure biogas etc., not only helps to meet countryside energy demand, but also are important areas for green employment. The *sixth* is to drive up demand for rural public services and create green public service positions on the basis of developing the rural economy.

- **Drive Employment Growth by Supporting the Development of Green Jobs in Small Business**

Small business has always played a key role in creating and absorbing employment and this is also true for green employment. Green Employer Certificates should be given out to small enterprises classified as green-jobs employers so that businesses can enjoy preferential policies. Founders of new small green businesses should be provided with micro loans; have their industrial and commercial registrations simplified. A policy to support the promotion of green technology should be made to drive the implementation and popularization of green scientific research results, and to promote green collar entrepreneurship.

- **Develop a Green Skills Development Plan for the Promotion of Green Employment**

Skills development is the key in the transformation towards green employment. All existing training should be greened, such as practical skills training in agriculture and skills training for transforming rural employment. Green skills should be incorporated into all these training programmes. A new skills development plan should also be drawn up.

- **Plan for Technical and Technological Enhancement for Green Industry**

This refers to drawing up and implementing a plan for the technical and technological enhancement of China's green industry, improving workers' overall green skills levels and supplying the necessary human resources for green development.

To achieve this, industry-specific outlines for green technology and skills and human resource planning must be drawn up. For new technologies and skills, industries and universities can work together to establish the most suitable training methods.

- ➢ *Greening Existing Corporate Training*: Greening of existing corporate training includes topics such as green entrepreneurial philosophies, green industrial skills and green entrepreneurship etc.
- ➢ *Developing Green Job Qualifications and Skills Appraisals*: Green-collar assessment and evaluation should be developed according to green job standards so to gradually develop green job practitioner qualifications and green skills appraisals.
- ➢ *Setting up a Green Skill Development System for all Workers:* As green jobs exist in every industry and involve all kinds of workers, green skills development should extend to all workers. All kinds of channels such as vocational schools, community training centres, public sector employment agencies and companies should be used to spread the concept of green employment and green skills so that the next generation of workers are aware of green jobs; to provide

green return-to-work training for the unemployed; offer up-skilling and re-training for workers in struggling companies; provide green vocational skills training for migrant workers; provide free green vocational training for demobilized soldiers; provide green entrepreneurial training for university graduates and those wanting to start their own businesses; and hold green vocational training as part of skills development for existing workers. Policies offering subsidized training could be used to encourage the scope of training. Extensions to the duration of training courses as well as improvements to training focus and effectiveness could also be made.

- **Working with Social Partners to Promote Green Employment**

Mutual understanding must be reached between the government, employers and workers. Employers must take on the social responsibility for green development, aligning green employment with economic benefits.

- **Improving Publicity and Creating an Atmosphere for the Development of Green Employment**

Different methods can be employed to promote an atmosphere where green employment is well understood, respected and developed. Awareness raising can be achieved through increasing publicity for green employment and important green projects and events, as well as road shows, activities to collect suggestions from workers, releasing news of innovative or energy efficient practices, hosting environmental knowledge contests and issuing awards to selected groups and individuals in recognition of their contribution to green employment.

- **Improving the Environment for Promoting Green Development**
    - *Improving environmental standards*: Development of the environmental standards system (industries either lacking standards or with standards partially complete) must be sped up and able to be met by the majority of businesses. The government should give thorough consideration to the position of the country when setting up the standards: *firstly* allowing companies to comply step by step and *secondly*, using funding or policy support to make it feasible for companies to implement the standards. Full consideration must be giving to the impact on society and in particular, the impact on employment when implementing environmental standards.
    - *Incentives and Punitive Measures to Encourage the Sustainable Development of Enterprise:* Refusing to fulfill environmental responsibilities equates to externalizing responsibilities for the environmental and social costs of doing business. *Firstly*, promoting a company's transformation towards green development requires incentives, putting green technology and its users in an advantageous market position such as increasing government subsidies on environmental products and

services that will not or do not yet generate financial returns. *Secondly*, law enforcement must be improved. Some enterprises are generally able to follow national environmental policies, while some small private enterprises aren't able to strictly follow the national standards. Rectification of environmental practices and environmental law enforcement should be strengthened for those enterprises.

- *Improving the Finance Mechanisms for Green Development:* The development, utilisation and popularisation of environmental technologies are critical in promoting transformation toward a green economy, and the key for the adapting environmental technology is funding. Financing facilities must be continuously improved, including the imposition of resource, environment and carbon taxes etc., to generate funding for green economic development and green job creation. International support in terms of technology and funding should also be sought.

Conclusion

The prospects and potential of green jobs in the country are huge. There are many potential sectors such as renewable energy, buildings and construction, transportation, basic industries, agriculture and forestry will be the priority areas for the future green job market. According to an ILO study, around 2.8 million people are currently involved in green or environmental jobs. The global environmental job market is projected to be doubled every year from $1,370 billion at present to $2,740 billion by 2020. More than two million people have, in recent years, found new jobs in the renewable energy sector, and the potential for job growth is huge. Being a new concept in Bangladesh, green jobs need not only be defined in our country's context but it also needs to identify the areas and sectors where green jobs can be promoted and the specific measures to be adopted. In this perspective, it is high time for Bangladesh to explore the alternative areas of co-operation in creating job opportunities.

REFERENCES

Apollo Alliance. (2008), Green-Collar Jobs in America's Cities, United States.

Anker, R. *et al.* (2002), Measuring Decent Work with Statistical Indicators, Working Paper No. 2, Policy Integration Department, Statistical Development and Analysis Group (Geneva, ILO).

BBS (Bangladesh Bureau of Statistics). 2005. Yearbook of Agricultural Statistics of Bangladesh. pp. 186. Ministry of Planning Government of Bangladesh.

Briggs C., *et al.*, 2007. Going with the Grain? Skills and Sustainable Business Development: Project Report, Workplace Research Centre, University of Sydney, Australia.

Connection Research. (2009). Who are the Green Collar Workers?, Department of Environment and Climate Change NSW and the Environment Institute of

Australia and New Zealand, Australia, available at: www.eianz.org/sb/modules/news/attachments/71/Green%20Collar%20Worker%20reportper cent20Final.pdf, accessed 26 October 2009.

Esty, Daniel C., and Winston, Andrew S. 2009. Green to Gold: How Smart Companies are using Environmental Strategy to Innovate, Create Value, and Build Competitive Advantage. Hoboken, NJ: John Wiley and Sons.

GED (General Economics Division), 2008. Moving Ahead-National Strategy for Acceleration Poverty Reduction II (FY 2009-11), Planning Commission, Government of Bangladesh.

Green Jobs: Towards Decent Work in a Sustainable, Low-carbon World. Source http:/www.ilo.org/global/About_the ILO/Mainpillars/what is Decentwork/index.htm.

ILO. (International Labour Organization). 2008. Global Challenges for Sustainable Development: Strategies for Green Jobs in ILO Background Note of G8 Labour and Employment Ministers Conference, Niigata, Japan, 11-13 May 2008.

ILO. (International Labour Organization). 2009. Green Job Assessment In Agriculture and Forestry Sector of Bangladesh, p. 37-38.

ILO. (International Labour Organization). 2011. Assessing Green Jobs Potential in Developing Countries: A practitioner's Guide, p. 5-13.

Institute of Labour Studies, Ministry of Human Resources and Social Security. 2010. Study on Green Employment in China, p. 63-72.

Islam, M S, M S Khan, R Sen, K M Hossain, S Noor and M S Islam. 2008. Effect of Grameen Shakti Jaibo sar on the Yield and Yield Component of Tomato. Bangladesh J. Agric. and Enviro. 4(2): 1-9.

Jones, Van. 2008. The Green Collar Economy: How one Solution can fix our two Biggest Problems. New York: Harper Collins Publishers.

Kammen D., K. Kapadia, and M. Fripp. 2004. "Putting Renewables to Work: How many Jobs can the Clean Energy Industry Generate?", Energy Resources Group, Goldman School of Public Policy, University of California, Berkley.

Mujeri, M. J. 2004. Bangladesh Decent Work Statistical Indicators: A Fact-finding Study (Dhaka, ILO).

OECD. 2004. Environment and Employment: An Assessment, Working Party on National Environmental Policy, Environment Policy Committee, May 2004, OECD, Paris.

Pollin, R. and J. Wicks-Lim. 2008. Job Opportunities for the Green Economy: A State-by-State Picture of Occupations that Gain from Green Investments, Political Economy Research Institute, University of Massachusetts, Amherst.

Ong, Paul M., and Patraporn, Rita Varisa. 2006. The Economic Development Potential of the Green Sector. Retrieved June 2, 2013, from http://repositories.cdlib.org/lewis/pb/Policy_Brief_06-06/.

UNEP. 2008. Green Jobs – Towards Decent Work in a Sustainable, Low-Carbon World, Report Produced by Worldwatch Institute and Commissioned by UNEP, ILO, IOE, ITUC, Nairobi.

Waste Concern. 2011. Options for Green Jobs in Bangladesh: Overview of Sectors, p. 9-13.

10

Construction of Identity and Sustainable Development in Socio-Cultural Landscapes

— Motaleb Azari
— Nanjunda

For the purpose of this study, construction of personal identity is understood to be a state of social stability, influenced by relationships with outside 'others' as well as how such relationships transform or inform each culture's understanding of its own being. Focusing on plural societies, this paper addresses the nature of such social identities and the consequences of the social comparison process, as a selective application of the accentuation effect, primarily to those dimensions that will result in self-enhancing of each individual culture in plural societies. Understanding identity in this way enables us to seriously talk about 'interweaving' or 'communing' of various cultural practices which is the very process of dialectical investigation and the possibility of discourse in a social context. The word 'identity' is an umbrella term and cannot be defined simplistically. Literally it comes from the French word 'identite' which finds its linguistic roots in the Latin noun 'identitas', – 'tatis', itself a derivation of the Latin adjective 'idem', meaning 'the same'. The term is comparative in nature, as it emphasizes the sharing of a degree of sameness or oneness with others in a particular area and it takes on different connotations depending on the field of study (Rummens, *Canadian Identities* 3).

In general, identity makes an entity definable and recognisable, in terms of possessing certain qualities or characteristics that distinguish it from entities of a different type. In philosophy, the personal idiosyncrasies that distinguish one individual from the next, are commonly recognised as personal identities and they may be used to refer to the result of an identification of self, by self, with respect to an other. In sociology, identity may be defined as the distinctive character belonging to any given individual, or shared by all members of a particular social category or group. In other words, social identity may be used to refer to the outcome of an identification of self by other. Thus it is identification, accorded or assigned an individual by another social actor (Rummens, *Personal Identity* 1993).

Sociologists, such as Cerulo, focus primarily on the formation of the 'me', exploring the ways in which interpersonal interactions mold an individual's sense of self (386). And for Howard, the study of identity forms a critical cornerstone within modern sociological thought which carries the full weight of the need for a sense of 'who', together with an often overwhelming pace of change in the surrounding social environment (367).

In his research on 'identity studies', Keough brings Stuart Hall's strategic method of describing identity. In his theory, Hall suggested that identity does not evolve linearly throughout history and it does not emerge only from within an individual. Instead, identity is an ever-changing process with various branches that emerge at different periods of time, and these branches are all linked back to the same individual, or group of people. Hall believed that identities are about questions of applying the resources of history, language and especially culture in the process of becoming rather than being (170 - 172). Considering the construction of identity, Hall made two assertions; the first is that identities are constructed through discourse, not outside it, because identities emerge by verbalizing differences rather than unity. It was Hall's opinion that without discourse, differences would not surface, and specific identities would remain unspoken.

Hall's first assertion is directly related to his second; that identities are constructed through, and not outside difference. Identities are constructed around uniqueness and without interacting with 'the other', or individuals with different characteristics and traits would never realise their identities (170). Therefore, individuals who are able to cope themselves with such differences, can take a huge step for the well-being of their community members and act as fully responsible individuals in sustaining positive developments in their plural societies.

For Michael Foucault (*The Archeology of Knowledge* 1972), knowledge about identity, society and social life is part of a continual process of becoming. According to him, offering an answer to the question 'Who am I?' is to locate an identity that is specific to a certain time and place, and that is always temporary and fleeting. In other words, there is no authentic 'I', to which Foucault can refer, and there is no one fundamental identity that constitutes his experience as a human being.

Hier and Bolaria believe that for Foucault, there are only complex sets of social relations that configure to neutralize and normalise what are always temporary historical forms of knowledge about who we think we really are.

Therefore, a clear comprehension of this knowledge demands that we explore human identity – especially in a social context – according to its unique features (2). That uniqueness results from the combination of various specifically identifying characteristics. And to explore the true nature of such characteristics, we may start with Plato's metaphysical vision on 'Identity as a Form'.

Among the concepts central to Plato's metaphysical vision are those of identity, sameness and difference. It is on the basis of this theory that Plato postulates the existence of separate forms and in reflecting on the forms and their relations among themselves, it is their self-identity that is to be compromised. Plato evidently sees the need to incorporate principles of identity and difference into the soul's fabric. In this regard, two forms are alike because they each have a property that is like the other. In other words, one form is different from another precisely because of its own nature (Gerson[1]). Accordingly, the form of acceptance of socio-cultural differences is different from the form of resistance because of its having a contrary nature.

Gerson believes that the form of 'self' is not the same as other concepts defined in Plato's metaphysical vision.[2] Each self has an identity but that identity is not because of the nature of that particular self, rather it is entirely expressed in the essence or nature of which it partakes. In other words, the determination of the formal identity of the self is just what results from the analysis in dialectic of the essence of which it partakes. Consequently, if self is a set of dependent traits, its existence entails 'weak unity' unless these traits within, are identical or differentiated from other traits of a different self.

When it comes to 'social identity', the self becomes reflexive in that it can take itself as an object and can name, categorise or classify itself in particular ways in relation to other social categories or classifications.[3] Therefore, a group of individuals who hold a common social identification or view themselves as members of the same social category, consist a social group with a set of defined characteristics. And through a social comparison process, individuals who are similar to this self are categorised with the self and are labeled the 'in-group'; individuals who differ from the self are categorised as the 'out-group' (Dominic Abrams and Michael A. Hogg 20).

In early work, social identity included the emotional, evaluative, and other psychological correlates of in-group classification (Turner *et al.* 20). Later researchers often separated the self-categorisation component from the self-esteem and commitment components in order to empirically investigate the relationships among them.[4] This self categorisation along with social comparison, produced different cultural identities within a society with multiple in-groups. Therefore, the consequence of self-categorisation in a multicultural community becomes an accentuation of the perceived similarities between the self and other in-group members, and an accentuation of the perceived differences between the self and out-group members. This accentuation occurs for all the beliefs, attitudes, affective reactions, behavioural norms, styles of speech and other properties that are believed to be correlated with the relevant inter-group categorisation (Stets and Burke 225). Accordingly, if we refer back to Hall's models of identity construction, we perceive that identities are formed around differences and through interaction but his models did not account for the fact that an individual or group can experience multiple identities.

Grossberg (*Identity and Cultural Studies* 87 - 107) believes that when more than one difference such as difference in race, class and gender is experienced, an individual or group can experience multiple identities. Because Grossberg believed in the existence of multiple, simultaneous identities, he saw identities as fragments or categories of a dominant identity (87 - 107). Of course, we need more seminal research to examine the challenges that such a dominant identity may create for minor ethnic groups in a multicultural society. On the whole, the most important factor in creating sustainable development in socio-cultural landscapes, especially in plural societies, is mutual understanding of each individual with his/her social surroundings. Consequently, the whole society is transcended to fully responsible individuals.

FOOTNOTES

1. This Paper is Drawn from: Azari, Motaleb. (The Present Scholar). Canadian Intellect and Cultural Identity: A Study of John Ralston Saul's Fictional Works. A Thesis Submitted to The University of Mysore, India for the Award of Doctor of Philosophy in English Literature.
2. For more Dimensions on these Concepts See; Lloyd P. Gerson, *Plato on Identity, Sameness and Difference* (Philosophy Education Society, Inc. 2004) 1.
3. For more Information on Identity Theory, See: John C. Turner, *et al.*, *Rediscovering the Social Group: A Self-Categorisation Theory* (New York: Basil Blackwell, 1987).
4. These Researches are Done by Noami Ellmers and van Knippenberg", Stereotyping in Social Context", 1997, pp. 208-235.Web. 07. 09. 2008.

Works Cited

Cerulo, Karen A. 'Identity Constructions: New Issues, New Directions". *Annual Reviews New Jersey Rutgers University.* (1997): 385- 409. Web. 07. 05. 2008.

Dominic, Abrams and Michael A. Hogg. *Social Identifications: A Social Psychology of Intergroup Relations and Group Processes*. London: Rotledge, 1988. 20. Print.

Foucault, Michael. *The Archeology of Knowledge*. New York: Pantheon, 1972. Print.

Gerson, Lloyd P. "Plato on Identity, Sameness and Difference". *Philosophy and Education Society.* (December 1, 2004): 1. Web. 01. 10. 2008.

Grossberg, L. "Identity and Cultural Studies: Is that all there is?" In; Hall, S. and Gay, P. Eds. *Questions of Cultural Identity*. London: Sage Publications, 1996. 87-107. Print.

Hall, Stuart. "Introduction: Who Needs 'Identity'?" In Hall, S. and Gay, P. eds. *Questions of Cultural Identity*. London: Sage Publications. 1996, 1-17. Print.

Hier, Sean P. and B. Singh Bolaria. Eds. *Identity and Belonging: Rethinking Race and Ethnicity in Canadian Society*. Toronto: Canadian Scholars Inc. 2006. 2. Print.

Howard, Judith A. "Social Psychology of Identities". *Annual Review of Psychology* 26. (2000): 367-393. Web. 05. 06. 2009.

Keough, Sara Beth. *Canada's Cultural Media Policy and Newfoundland Music on the Radio: Local Identities and Global Implications*. A Dissertation Presented for the Doctor of Philosophy Degree. University of Tennessee, Knoxville, May 2007. 170 - 172. Web. 03. 05. 2009.

Rummens, Joanna (Anneke). "Canadian Identities: An Interdisciplinary Overview of Canadian Research on Identity". Halifax, Nova Scotia: Department of Canadian Heritage. (2001): 3. Web. 09. 11. 2009.

—. "Personal Identity and Social Structure in Sint Maaritn/Saint Martin: A Plural Identities Approach." N. P. York University. (1993). Web. 09. 01. 2009.

Stets, Jan E. and Peter J. Burke. "Identity Theory and Social Identity Theory." *Social Psychology Quarterly*. 63. 3 (September 2000): 224-225. Web. 09. 08. 2008.

Turner, John C., Michael A. Hogg, Penelope J. Oakes, Stephen D. Reicher, and Margaret S. Wetherell. *Rediscovering the Social Group: A Self-Categorisation Theory*. New York: Basil Blackwell, 1987. 20. p.

11

The Impact of Financial Crisis on Developing Countries

— Roohollah Arab

ABSTRACT

The paper analyses the impact of the global economic crisis of 2007-09 on the developing countries of a sample of 4 counties (South Africa, India, Brazil and China). Within the context of globalisation, the evolution of the financial crisis is outlined and its impact on the global economy identified, and the main transmission mechanisms by which the crisis spread to the developing world discussed. By contrast, although developing countries didn't make this crisis, it has become all too clear that they are in the firing line when it comes to suffering its effects and the current financial crisis had a significant effect on economic developments in developing economies.

Keywords: Financial crisis, integration, recession, trade, financial inflow, imports earning.

Introduction

The global economic crisis of 2007-09 has been unprecedented since the Great Depression of 1929-1932.[1] The crises originated in the US mortgage market and quickly spread to a number of other countries. By the time of the bankruptcy of Lehman Brothers in September 2008, the financial crisis had become a more general banking crisis which in turn rapidly impacted on the real economy and turned into a global recession. The global financial system is in crisis, and that crisis is hitting developing countries hard. But the system has never served developing countries well. Those that opened their doors to global finance have seen huge increases in their vulnerability to shocks like the one we are living through now, but little more in the way of improved human development than countries which took a more cautious approach. And the poorest countries have not got the financing they so desperately need. It is becoming increasingly clear that we need a system that actually serves development without the huge risks that are now all too apparent. Considering that the pre-crisis forecast was that earning from trade and private sector flows should actually rise between 2007 and 2009, the crisis has clearly hit hard and hit quickly. For countries that based all or part of their development strategies on attracting funds from abroad, and for the companies and individuals that were dependent on these flows, this fall is likely to be calamitous.

To see which countries are most affected, and why, we've calculated the estimated financial inflows and export earnings in 2008, and the inflows that are now predicted for 2009, for middle-income countries.[2] We then compared them to the inflows in 2007, before the crisis hit, to get an indication of the impact of the crisis so far. The results are in Table 11.1 below. Every single country in our sample is predicted to see a real drop in inflows between 2007 and 2009.

Table 11.1: Financial Inflows and Export Earnings, 2007-09 (current US$, millions)

Country	Total Inflows 2007	Total Inflows 2008	% Change 2007-08	Predicted Inflows 2009	% Change 2007-09
South Africa	118,022	95,203	-19	62,307	-47
India	247,932	222,825	-10	175,344	-29
China	1,372,763	1,446,750	5	1,075,844	-22
Brazil	255,005	219,845	-14	176,816	-31

Source: Calculated from Data Available from WTO, UNCTAD, Bank of International Settlements, IMF, World Bank, IIF.

The crisis is really two crises – a financial crisis and a recession – and although they are of course connected, it is possible to untangle the effects and assess the impact of each. The financial crisis will affect factors such as bank lending, equities and foreign direct investment, and changes in interest rates will impact on countries and companies that raise money by issuing bonds. While the recession will have the biggest impact on trade flows, it is also likely to affect aid levels and money sent home by relatives working in rich countries.

The Impact of the Crisis in South Africa, India, Brazil and China

The impact of policy on vulnerability to both financial crisis and recession is starkly illustrated in the differing fortunes of South Africa, India, China and Brazil. All members of the G20, different policy choices in the 1990s and early 21st century mean that the crisis will have a very different impact on each of these four countries. The crucial difference lies in how countries are integrated into the global economy. China and India have historically been less open to the global economy than many other developing countries, and both have retained capital controls. Brazil is more open and South Africa more open still. While its financial system is relatively closed, China is the most dependent on external trade of all four countries. As a consequence, the total drop in Chinese export earnings between 2007 and the end of 2009 is predicted to be around 18 per cent – an amount equivalent to nearly 7 per cent of China's 2007 (*i.e.*, pre-crisis) GDP.[3] The long-term consequences are likely to be dire – and most likely include unemployment, reduced state spending, increased poverty and, eventually, more deaths. The immediate threat in China is real. A large part of China's economic success over the last 10 years has been based on a strategy of export-led growth. In 2007, earnings from exports accounted for 37 per cent of China's GDP. The financial crisis shows that this was a risky strategy – but it is one that has been key to providing jobs for millions of migrants moving to the cities from urban areas, and has brought China many billions of dollars of export revenue over the years.

But the prediction of hundreds of millions of dollars of lost export revenue is not a death sentence. Export-led growth in China was accompanied by highly controlled engagement with international finance. China's exposure to international financial markets is the lowest in this group of four, and it has been holding steady over the last 10 years. While international inflows are small, the domestic financial sector is moderately large, and most financing for development in China (including for its very high rates of investment) comes from domestic sources. Losses to China's financial system between 2007 and 2009 are predicted to be just over 2 per cent of the country's pre-crisis GDP.[4] So it's likely that China's financial system will be resilient enough to provide the capital to allow Chinese companies to switch their focus to domestic and regional markets – and China's sheer size means that there is more of a prospect of developing a domestic market, providing the huge and growing inequalities in Chinese society can be tackled. As mentioned above, recent IMF research indicates those recessions that follow banking crises tend to last longer and cut deeper than other recessions. Whether this general conclusion can predict different countries' experiences of this crisis remains to be seen, but it's a possibility that since the crisis in China is predominantly a trade rather than a banking or financial crisis, the impact will be correspondingly shallower than in countries such as South Africa where the crisis is both a trade and a banking crisis.

If this turns out to be the case, the dire predictions for 2009 and beyond may not come to pass. Already the stimulus package announced by the Chinese government in November seems to be having some effect, for example December saw a five-year high in new bank loans.[5] China is by no means definitively in recovery yet, but it is clear that the government, by virtue of its sheer size and of its relative financial isolation, has choices that others might well envy. South Africa is at the opposite end of the spectrum. Since 1994, the government has adopted a strategy of extreme openness to the global economy, a strategy that now looks highly questionable – and which, according to recent research, has not been particularly effective in stimulating economic growth.[6] South Africa's financial sector is relatively big compared to other similar emerging economies such as Brazil and India, and particularly dependent on foreign flows. In particular, dependence on foreign buyers in the equities market and in the banking sector has made the country especially vulnerable to the immediate effects of the current crisis. The value of shares in the South African stock market held by foreign investors, referred to as equities, rose from being equivalent to less than 2 per cent of GDP in 1995, to nearly 20 per cent 10 years later. In 2007, foreign lending accounted for around 20 per cent of total bank credit in South Africa. By 2009, it's predicted that export earnings in South Africa will be down just under 7 per cent from their 2007 levels, an amount equivalent to just under 9 per cent of pre-crisis GDP, but the fall in flows due to the financial crisis – mainly accounted for by dramatic drops in bank lending and the value of equities – is predicted to be more than 15 per cent of pre-crisis GDP. Of the four countries, South Africa and China offer the most contrasting experiences of globalisation, and correspondingly are likely to have very different experiences of the financial crisis. While China is already being hit by the recession, its financial system looks resilient enough to survive more or less intact.[7]

However South Africa, more integrated into precisely those global financial markets most affected by the crisis, is likely to be hit by both the recession and even more by the financial crisis, as those external sources of development finance on which it is most dependent dry up. The long-term consequences are likely to be dire – and most likely include unemployment, reduced state spending, increased poverty and, eventually, more deaths. India and Brazil sit somewhere between China and South Africa, though they are quite different to each other. Both are more or less equally exposed to international trade flows. But while Brazil is highly dependent on foreign investment, India funds most of its investment domestically. By contrast, India's banking system is more dependent than Brazil's on foreign loans, and its stock market more dependent on foreign buyers. The losses in the two countries will be similar: a fall in financial flows equivalent to around 5 per cent of pre-crisis GDP, and a fall in export earnings equivalent to around 2 per cent of pre-crisis GDP. However, in the long run India may prove to be more resilient, having a much higher rate of investment, most of which is funded domestically.[8]

Table 11.2: Patterns of Integration into the Global Economy

Country	Integrationin Financial Markets	Dependenceon Foreign Investment	Dependence on Rich Country Economies for Aid, Trade, Remittances
China	low	low	high
South Africa	high	high	medium
Brazil	medium	high	medium
India	medium	medium	medium

Source: Calculated from Data Available from IMF, World Bank, WTO, UNCTAD, Bank of International Settlements, Bloomberg.

These four countries show different patterns of integration into the global economy, and how the impact of the crisis will play out through all the different channels of connectedness. The key difference between them is in how dependent they are on foreign capital in their financial sectors and for investment, and how sizeable their earnings from exports. The higher the dependence on external flows, particularly financial flows, the bigger the losses that will result.

However, though there are differences, the crisis will be severe in every country, both for people immediately affected, and for long-term development prospects – the comparisons here are all about degrees of disaster, and capacity to bounce back from disaster, and don't imply that any country can escape the shocks all together.

Conclusion

The comparison between the developing countries in our survey shows how financial markets have failed developing countries on two fronts. Countries like South Africa have bought into the rhetoric of financial liberalisation and the promises of untapped wealth that could be mobilised for development.

These countries opened up their markets and now face the consequences – a possible serious reversal in development. This small survey indicates that there was no great pay-off in development terms for the risks countries took in opening up – South Africa's development performance was any better than that of countries that took a more cautious approach – and that openness, which brought dubious rewards, now puts any development gains at risk. But other countries never had this choice – a financial system organized purely around short term returns simply didn't register the existence of the poorest countries. At the moment, this might seem like a lucky escape. But in the long run, countries with little domestic capital will need to get money for development from somewhere. Evidence suggests that domestic capital is the most stable and has the biggest pay-off in development terms. All countries, even the poorest, would be well-advised to look to how they can mobilise more domestic resources through, for example, increasing tax revenues from foreign investors and encouraging citizens to keep their money in local banks. But the very poorest countries face absolute limits on how much domestic capital they can mobilise for development. For them, as for all countries, the question should be how they can engage with international markets to get the development benefits of more capital, without the risks of that capital being of the footloose, extractive and nonproductive variety that much foreign investment and financial flows have proved to be.

It is this question that should be at the heart of the attempt to create a better international financial system out of the wreckage of this crisis.

Implications for Policy

The development of the vulnerability index over time, and the link to what we know about policy changes, tells a few harsh truths about how global and national economies have been managed over the last 20 years, as this crisis has been slowly building. At the moment, financial globalisation for developing countries is all risk and little benefit. The countries that have done best have primarily used their own resources for development, supplemented with foreign capital as needed, while those whose strategy or circumstances relied on opening up to international markets as a source of resources for development did not see benefits sufficient to compensate for the huge costs they are now experiencing. Others have been left on the sidelines. This has some important lessons for development.

1. The importance of domestically generated development. It's clear that both from poverty and a vulnerability perspective, it's better to have a solid domestic base from which to build financial institutions. This means that the ongoing commitment of many rich countries to continued financial liberalization in poor countries under the guise of 'free trade' agreements needs to be challenged.
2. The importance of diversified financial flows. Shocks can and will happen, however the economy is designed. It's important that financial flows are as diversified, and as predictable, as possible. A mix of domestically generated and foreign flows is crucial. To raise domestic flows, governments need to increase their tax revenues.
3. The importance of controlling risk in the global economy. Anyone interested in development should be interested in controlling risk. This means a global economy that is managed to reduce the risks of sudden shocks – to private flows, government flows, and short and long term-flows. The regulatory net needs to be spread very wide if the range of shocks that can derail development is to be contained, and both source and recipient countries need to have access to the full array of capital controls needed to control these risks.

4. The importance of transparency. Those countries that opened themselves up to international financial markets in the 1990s did not have full information about how those markets worked or what the risks were of exposure to them. Like developed countries, they were at the mercy of the ever-more complex financial instruments devised by banks to conceal the functioning of the markets and ensure that they had the upper hand in every transaction.
5. The importance of regulating financial markets so that it becomes thinkable to provide funds in the poorest countries. At the same time as managing risk, financial markets need to be organized to encourage more long-term investments and investment in countries that lack their own domestic capital but at the moment are ignored by international capital altogether.
6. The importance of involving even the poorest countries in decisions about global financial markets.

The data shows that all countries are affected by the financial crisis, so all countries have a stake in improving the system. It's essential that all countries have a say in how the system is reformed, not just the G20.

Recommendations

Tinkering around the edges won't help. The extent of global integration, and the way that this crisis has reached deep into the economies of many poor countries, means that anyone interested in reducing poverty needs to be calling for a broad agenda at the G20, where the many and varied sources of risk and vulnerability in the global economy can be addressed. Top of the agenda should be: Changing how financial markets operate so that they:

1. Control risk, so that countries with little option but to build their financial markets from external sources can do so with confidence.
2. Improve transparency: on the government side by reforming tax havens to ensure that information is automatically exchanged between them and on the company side by requiring that companies report their profits and financial transactions on a country-by country basis.
3. Encourage the development of regionally based financial markets in developing countries, to maximize the possibilities of local resource mobilisation and to increase their global weight with other financial institutions.

Supporting development by:

4. Helping in the development of domestic financing. Reducing capital flight, through greater transparency in company accounting and in a reduction in banking secrecy would be an important start.
5. Providing assistance to countries affected by the crisis, to ensure that poor people do not suffer the consequences of badly managed markets.

In particular, those countries suffering from either the crisis or the recession, but who cannot afford their own stimulus packages, will need extra assistance to cope with the short-term impact of the crisis and to restart their economies on a more stable footing in the medium term.

6. Ensuring that additional financing is provided in a way that supports longer term, more resilient development, by ensuring that foreign assistance is geared toward developing domestic capacity and resource mobilisation rather than assuming that foreign flows must hold the key to development.

REFERENCES

1. UNIDO. (2009), Impact of the Global Economic Crisis on LDCs' Productive Capacities and Trade Prospects: Threats and Opportunities, November, Vienna.
2. Data sources as follows: Export Earnings, WTO; FDI and Remittances, UNCTAD; Bank Lending, Bank of International Settlements; Equities, IMF, overseas Development Assistance, World Bank World Development Indicators.
3. Wad, P. (2009), "Impact of the Global Economic and Financial Crisis over the Automotive Industry in Developing Countries", *Working Paper 16/2009*, United Nations Industrial Development Organization.
4. UNCTAD. (2005), *Economic Development in Africa: Rethinking the Role of Foreign Direct Investment.* United Nations Publication, Sales No. E.05.II.D12. New York and Geneva.
5. Figures on 2007 Flows from UNCTAD the Bank of International Settlements and the IMF. Forecasts from the IIF, for all Countries.
6. Impact of Financial on the Developing Countries; Action Aid. Registered Charity No. 2744, March 2009 and IIF, 'Recent Developments in Asia', February 12 2009.
7. Tswamuno, D., Pardee, S., and Wunnava, P. (2007), Financial Liberalisation and Economic Growth: Lessons from the South African Experience. *International Journal of Applied Economics*, 4, 2, 75-89.
8. Devarajan, S. (2009), A Sub-Prime Crisis on the US and Infant Deaths in Africa, Africa Can Blog, World Bank http://africacan.worldbank.org/a-sub-prime-crisis-in-the-us-and-infant-deaths-in-africa.

12

The Effect of Financial Market in New Zealand's Economic Development

— Dariyoush Jamshidi
— Neda Pouradeli

Introduction

New Zealand is an island country in the sought – western Pacific Ocean with 4,315,800 populations in year 2009. The life expectancy at birth is 80 years in last 5 years. New Zealand has e modern, prosperous and developed market economy with an estimate gross domestic product (GDP) at purchasing power party (PPP) per capital. The income level in New Zealand is high. The New Zealand dollar is known as the kiwi dollar. New Zealand was ranked the 3rd most developed country in continue development programs, 4th in the 2011 index of economic freedom published by the Heritage foundation. New Zealand's economic freedom score is 82.3 making its economy the 4th freest in the 2011 index. New Zealand continues to be a global leader in economic freedom performing well on most of the components measured in the index. The economy is diversified and modern, with high level of property rights and an efficient legal framework with transparent and stable business climate. New Zealand has created a dynamic entrepreneurial environment. The average tariff rate is low and commercial operations are aided by a flexible labor market and efficient regulations. Inflationary pressures are under control, and foreign investment is welcome. The entrepreneurial environment of New Zealand, reflecting the country's enduring commitment to economic freedom is the most efficient and competitive among the economies graded in the index. New Zealand does not discriminate against foreign investor but it does limit foreign ownership in certain state-owned sector. There is no restriction on currency transfer repatriation of profit or access to foreign exchange. New Zealand financial sector is well developed and competitive, offering a full range of financing instrument for entrepreneurial activity. New Zealand's financial sector is well developed and competitive, offering a full range of financing instrument: regulation is efficient and transparent in accordance with international standards.

New Zealand has three main markets:

1. The premier market (stock market).
2. Smaller and growing companies (alternative market).
3. For corporate and government bond and fixed income securities.

New Zealand gross domestic product is worth 125 billion dollars. New Zealand's GDP was 39.48 billion dollars, over past 20 years.

This dynamic growth has boosted real incomes. In New Zealand a net 27 per cent of 690 companies survived in first quarter of 2011. New Zealand reported a trade surplus equivalent to 11 million$ in January 2011 and New Zealand is greatly dependent on international trade.

Background of the Study

Financial Market Factors

Interest rate

The amount charged, expressed as a percentage of principal, by a lender to a borrower for the use of assets. Interest rates are typically noted on an annual basis, known as the annual percentage rate (APR). When the borrower is a low risk party, they will usually be charged a low interest rate; if the borrower is considered high risk, the interest rate that they are charged will be higher.. In general, interest rates rise in times of inflation, greater demand for credit, tight money supply, or due to higher reserve requirements for banks. A rise in interest rates for any reason tends to dampen business activity (because credit becomes more expensive) and the stock market (because investors can get better returns from bank deposits or newly issued bonds than from buying shares).

Interest rate ↑ → save ↑ → aggressive spending ↓ → investment ↓ → GDP ↓

Interest rate ↓ → save ↓ → aggressive spending ↑ → investment ↑ → GDP ↑

Exchange Rate

The price of one country's currency expressed in another country's currency. In other words, the rate at which one currency can be exchanged for another. For example, the higher the exchange rate for one euro in terms of one kiwi (New Zealand dollar), the lower relative value of kiwi.

Exchange rate ↑ → country's currency ↑ → price of foreign good ↓ → import ↓ → GDP ↓

Example: New Zealand Exchange in 4 Years

Trading Hours

- Pre-Market Session: 08:00 - 10:00
- Normal Trading Session: 10:00 - 17:00
- Post-Market Session: 17:00 - 17:30

	2004	2005	2006	2007
Number of Listed Companies	200	185	182	178
Domestic Market Capitalisation (in $ million)	43,731	40,593	44,817	47,486
Value of Shares Traded (in $ million)	17,034	20,892	22,241	24,161
Average Daily Turnover (in $ million)	67	83	89	96
Average Value of Trades (in $ thousands)	28.6	34.5	41.0	41.9
New Capital Raised from Initial Public Offerings (in $ million)	823	429	179	317
New Capital Raised from Secondary Public Offerings (in $ million)	723	988	830	1,774
Number of Trading Days	253	251	250	251

Bond Yield

The bond yield is the rate of return on the bond, which takes into account the sum of the interest payment, the redemption value at the bond's maturity, and the initial purchase price of the bond. Yield on the bond relates to the return on the capital you invest in the bond. You will hear the term yield a lot as it relates to investing in bonds. There are many types of yields you'll need to be aware of listed below.

Bond yield ↑ ⟶ save ↑ ⟶ aggressive spending ↓ ⟶ investment ↓ ⟶ GDP ↓

Stock Market Index

An aggregate value produced by combining several stocks or other investment vehicles together and expressing their total values against a base value from a specific date. Market indexes are intended to represent an entire stock market market's changes over and thus track the time.

Index values are useful for investors to track changes in market values over long periods of time. For example, the widely used Standard and Poor's 500 Index is computed by combining 500 large-cap U.S., stocks together into one index value. Investors can track changes in the index's value over time and use it as a benchmark against which to compare their own portfolio returns. Stock indexes are useful for benchmarking portfolios, for generalising the experience of all investors, and for determining the market return used in the Capital Asset Pricing Model (CAPM).

Stock index ↑ ⟶ wealth ↑ ⟶ aggressive spending ↓ ⟶ GDP ↑

Economics Factor

Gross Domestic Product - GDP

The monetary value of all the finished goods and services produced within a country's borders in a specific time period, though GDP is usually calculated on an annual basis. It includes all of private and public consumption, government outlays, investments and exports less imports that occur within a defined territory.

GDP = C + G + I + NX

where:

'C' is equal to all private consumption, or consumer spending, in a nation's economy.

'G' is the sum of government spending.

'I' is the sum of all the country's businesses spending on capital.

'NX' is the nation's total net exports, calculated as total exports minus total imports. (NX = Exports - Imports).

Methodology

For investigate the effect of financial market in the New Zealand economic growth especially in GDP we gather data from year 1990-2009. The data are real interest rate, exchange rate, stock index and bond yield. Data for exchange rate gather form World Bank, the stock index from yahoo finance for New Zealand and bond yield and interest rate from New Zealand central bank. In the second part the trend curve for these four data drawn and at the third part we use SPSS to analysis of data for this part we have to write Hypothesis that we want to test.

Hypothesis

H01: There is any relationship between interest rate and GDP.

HA1: There isn' trelationship between interest rate and GDP.

H02: There is any relationship between exchange rate and GDP.

HA2: There isn't relationship between exchange rate and GDP.

H03: There is any relationship between bond yield and GDP.

HA3: There isn't relationship between bond yield and GDP.

H04: There is any relationship between stock index and GDP.

HA4: There isn't relationship between stock index and GDP.

The model written is:

$$Y = \square_0 + \square_1 X_1 + \square_2 X_2 + \square_3 X_3 + \dots\dots\dots\dots \square_k X_k + \square$$

Year	Interest Rate	Exchange Rate	Bond Yield	Stock Index	GDP
1990	13.4	1.71	13.5	240.800	44,503,568,894
1991	9.9	1.73	9.8	276.987	41,820,222,974
1992	6.6	1.86	6.8	266.330	40,744,409,331
1993	6.25	1.85	6.4	305.980	45,827,934,439
1994	6.12	1.69	7	278.870	54,263,384,779
1995	8.9	1.52	8.6	252.980	62,795,370,404
1996	9.37	1.45	8.5	302.876	68,801,785,257
1997	7.3	1.51	7.3	301.874	64,839,303,347
1998	6.8	1.87	7.2	252.190	55,075,444,076
1999	4.3	1.89	4.9	289.880	57,554,501,687
2000	6.12	2.20	6.6	311.980	51,449,284,416
2001	5.7	2.38	5.4	283.240	52,688,033,651
2002	5.4	2.16	5.4	260.878	65,269,401,794
2003	5.3	1.72	5.2	313.465	86,540,742,763
2004	5.7	1.51	5.8	314.933	102,210,420,168
2005	6.7	1.42	6.4	248.554	110,977,261,732
2006	7.2	1.54	7.3	298.822	110,562,438,545
2007	7.9	1.36	7.2	343.248	138,316,764,059
2008	7.5	1.42	6.5	279.437	117,816,507,937
2009	2.8	1.60	3.8	251.350	126,679,258,010

GDP = $\square_0$ + real interest rate X_1 + Exchange rate X_2 + stock indexX_3 +$\square$

We can see in the above graph that the correlation between GDP and interest rate, stock index and bond yieldare not liner but for stock index it looks linear and they have negative correlation with each other.

We can see that the correlation between interest rate and bond yield is high and near to zero because the bond yield contain of interest rate and redemption value at the bond's maturity so if one of them increase the other one increase also.

Table of Data

Trend Curves

Interest Rate 1990-2009

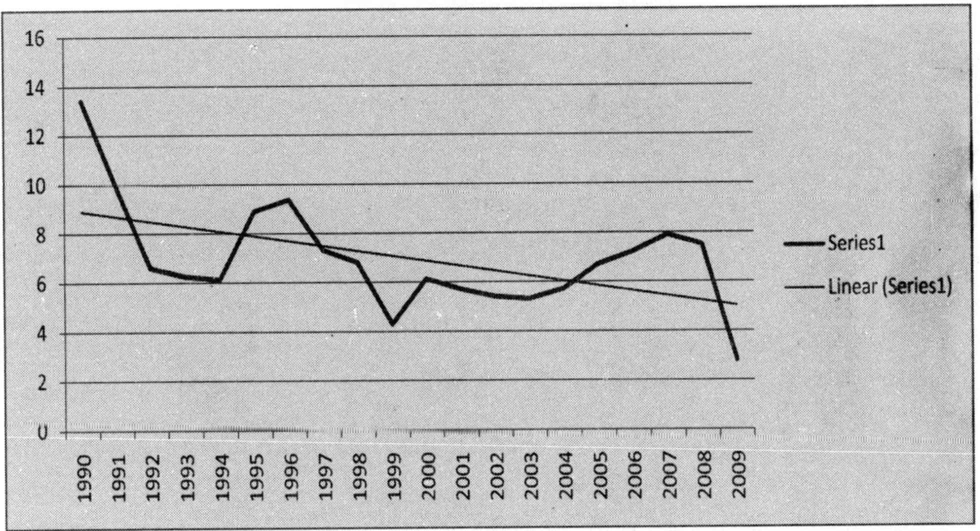

Exchange Rate 1990-2009

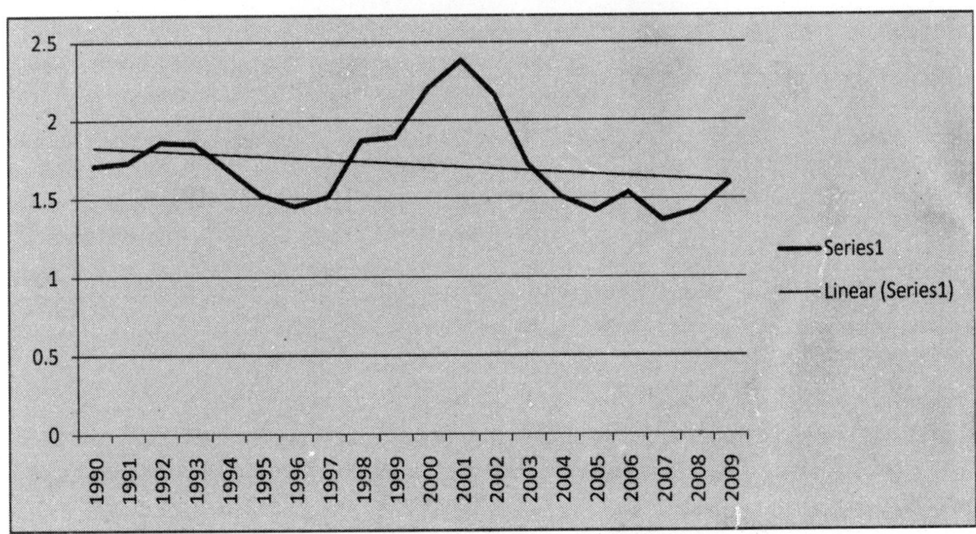

When we look at the correlation table we can see the correlation of real interest rate and GDP is -0.269 so the relation is lightly negative but near to zero so we can say no linear relationship between GDP and real interest rate. It doesn't show any significant correlation with GDP (p-value 0.251> =0.05).

Stock Index 1990-2009

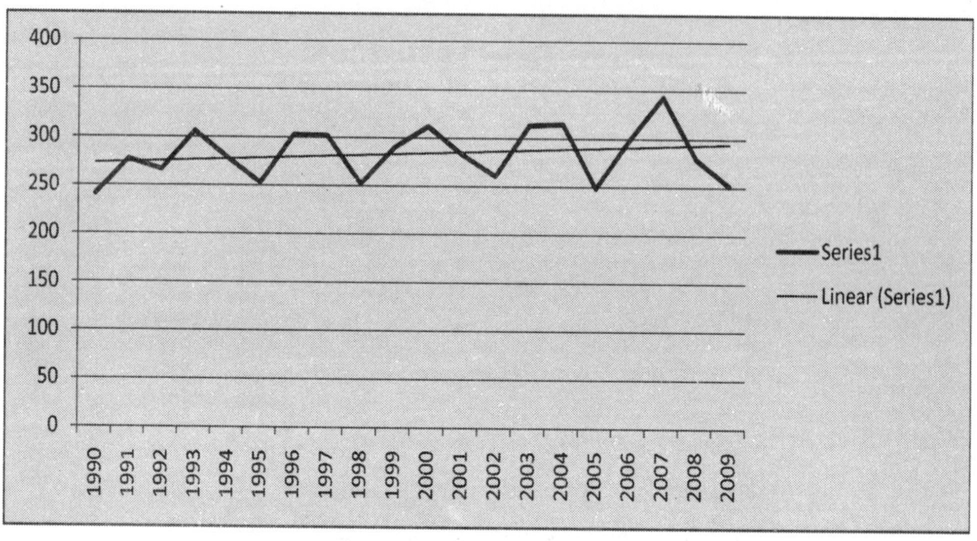

Bond Yield 1990-2009

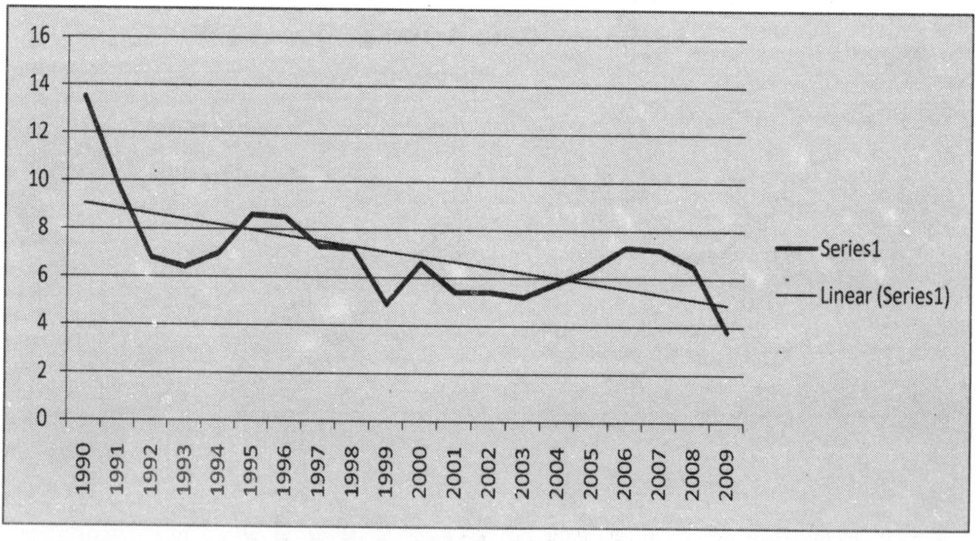

The correlation of Exchange rate is -0.614 is near to -1so we can say perfect negative relationship. That is mean if one of them goes up the other come down. It shows significant correlation with GDP (p-value 0.004<=0.05).

The correlation of bond yield is -0.362 is near to zero and we can say that there isn't linear relationship between them. It doesn't show any significant correlation with GDP (p-value 0.116>=0.05).

GDP Current $, from 1990-2009

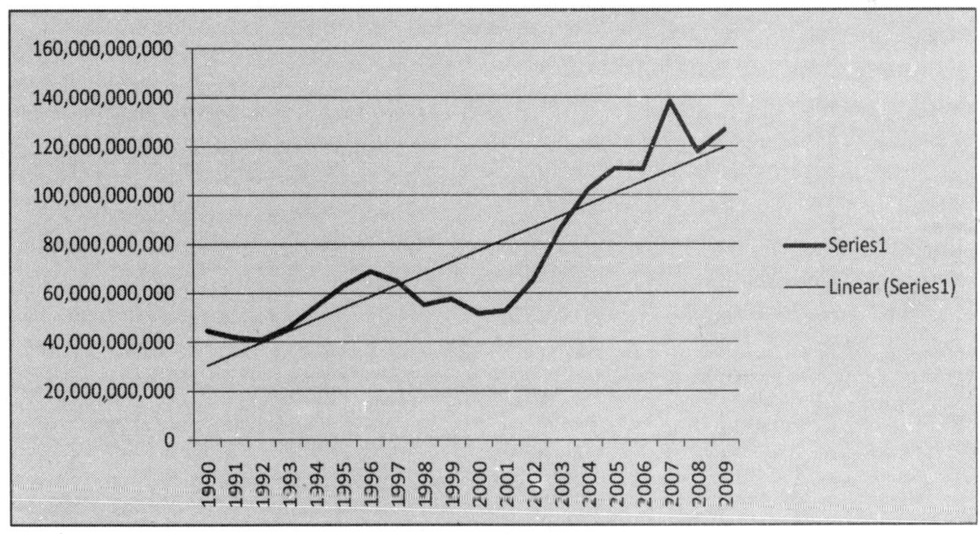

SPSS Analysis

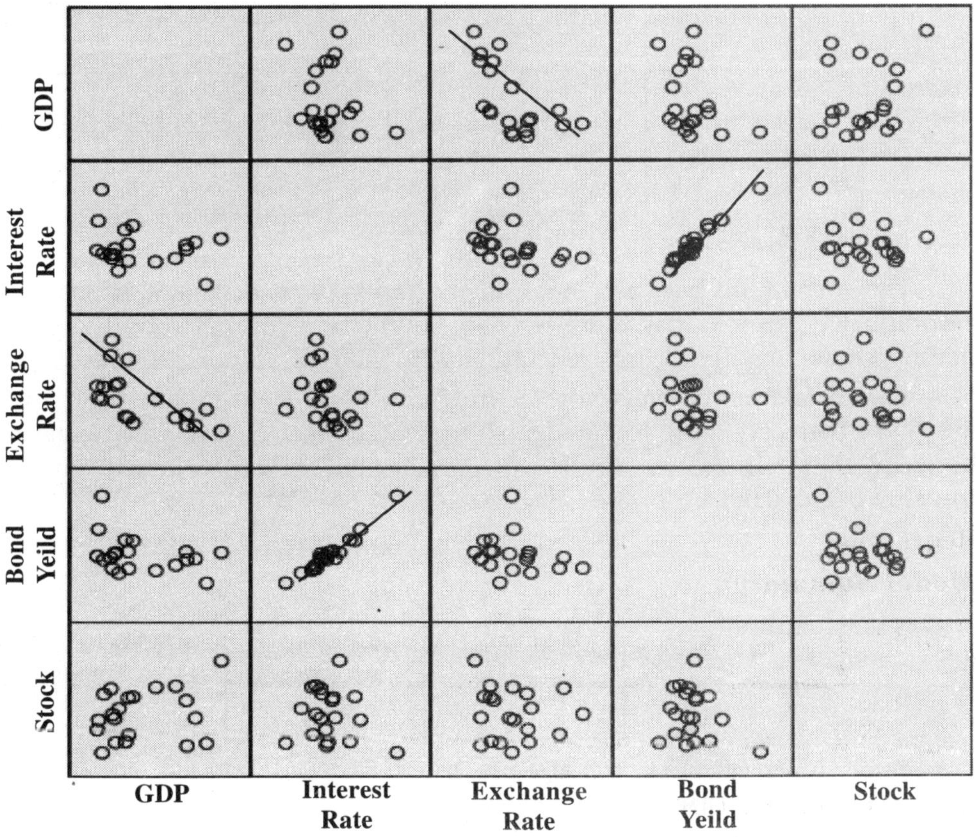

GDP

Interest Rate

Exchange Rate

Bond Yeild

Stock

GDP | Interest Rate | Exchange Rate | Bond Yeild | Stock

Correlations

		GDP	Interset Rate	Exchange Rate	Bond Yeild	Stock
GDP	Pearson Correlation	1	-.269	-.614**	-.362	.250
	Sig. (2-tailed).		.251	.004	.116	.288
	N	20	20	20	20	20
Interset Rate	Pearson Correlation	-.269	1	-.280.	974**	-.165
	Sig. (2-tailed)	.251		.232	.000	.487
	N	20	20	20	20	20
Exchange Rate	Pearson Correlation	-.614**	-.280	1	-.215-.	117
	Sig. (2-tailed)	.004.	232.		363	.624
	N	20	20	20	20	20
Bond Yeild	Pearson Correlation	-.362	.974**	-.215	1	-.243
	Sig. (2-tailed)	.116	.000	.363		.303
	N	20	20	20	20	20
Stock	Pearson Correlation	.250	-.165	-.117	-.243	1
	Sig. (2-tailed)	.288	.487	.624	.303	
	N	20	20	20	20	20

**. Correlation is significant at the 0.01 level (2-tailed).

The correlation between stock index and GDP is 0.25 that is near to zero and we can say that there isn't linear relationship between them. It doesn't show any significant correlation with GDP (p-value 0.288>=0.05).

The correlation between interest rate and bond yield is very high and it is 0.974 that very close to 1 and it shows the perfect positive relationship between them .It shows significant correlation between them because (p-value 0.00<=0.05).

Regression

Model Summary[b]

Model	R	R Square	Adjusted R Square	Std. Error of the Estimate
1	.811[a]	.658	.566	2.059E10

a. Predictors: (Constant), stock, exchange rate, interset rate, bond yeild.

b. Dependent Variable: GDP.

For R-square value =0.811. This means 811 per cent of the variance in GDP can be explained by the variation in real interest rate , Exchange rate, bond yield and stock index.

ANOVA[b]

Model	Sum of Squares	df	Mean Squares	F	Sig.
1. **Regression**	**1.221E22**	**4**	**3.053E21**	**7.200**	**.002[a]**
Residual	6.360E21	15	4.240E20		
Total	1.857E22	19			

a. Predictors: (Constant), stock, exchange rate, interset rate, bond yeild.

b. Dependent Variable: GDP.

In the ANOVA Table we can see that the P-Value is 0.002, which is less than 0.05. This means at list one of the four predictor variable model can be use for the model GDP.

Co-efficients

Model	Unstandardized Co-efficients		Standardized Co-efficients	t	Sig.
	B	Std. Error	Beta		
1. (Constant)	2.630E11	7.194E10		3.656	.002
Interset rate	1.013E10	1.033E10	.728	.982	.342
Exchange rate	-7.472E10	1.820E10	-.673	-4.106	.001
Bond yeild	-1.846E10	1.126E10	-1.218	-1.640	.022
Stock	-4538911.189	1.863E8	-.004	-.024	.981

a. Dependent Variable: GDP.

From the table we can write the formula:

GDP = 36703 + 2.5 X_1-325524355X_2-357 X_3-4538911 X_4

GDP = 36703 + 2.5 interest rate - 325524355 Exchange rate - 357 bond yield _4538911 stock index

But we have to mention that p-value of interest rate =0.342>= 0.05, stock index p-value is =.981>= 0.05 and these are too high, so the first and fourth hypothesis ($H_0$1, $H_0$2) are not supported and rejected and we have to resolve it by SPSS.

Residuals Statistics[a]

	Minimum	Maximum	Mean	Std. Deviation	N
Predicted Value	2.07E10	1.12E11	7.49E10	2.535E10	20
Residual	-2.342E10	3.135E10	.000	1.830E10	20
Std. Predicted Value	-2.140	1.448	.000	1.000	20
Std. Residual	-1.137	1.523	.000	.889	20

a. Dependent Variable: GDP.

Residuals are the differences between the observed values and the predicted values (obtained from the regression equation). For the residuals we have four assumptions that are:

1. The residuals must be linearly related.
2. The residuals must be independent.
3. The residuals must be normally distributed.
4. The residuals must have an equal variance across the range of X.

For the first third assumption we have to look at Residual Statistics and Residual Plot as attached above and for normality we have to check normality of residual that attach below.

In the graph we can see all the standard residual value is whit in -3 to + 3s so the equal variance fulfilled.

The dots are scattered randomly so they are independent. There isn't any non-linear or quadratic pattern. So the first third assumptions fulfilled.

Normality

	Kolmogorov-Smirnov[a]			Shapiro-Wilk		
	Statistic	df	Sig.	Statistic	df	Sig.
Unstandardized Residual	.128	20	.200*	.925	20	.126

The test of normality table shows us that the p-value in the both model (kolmogorov and Shapiro) are more than 0.05 so they are normality distributed.

The p-value in kolmogorov is 0.20>= 0.05 and in Shiparo is 0.126>= 0.05 so we accept the assumption for normal distributed. So assumption for residual fulfilled.

So we resolve SPSS and we get:

Model Summary[c]

Model	R	R Square	Adjusted R Square	Std. Error of the Estimate
1.	.614a	.378	.343	2.534E10
2.	.796b	.634	.591	2.000E10

a. Predictors: (Constant), exchange rate.

b. Predictors: (Constant), exchange rate, bond yeild.

c. Dependent Variable: GDP.

Co-efficients[a]

Model	Unstandardized Co-efficients		Standardized Co-efficients	t	Sig.
	B	Std. Error	Beta		
1. (Constant)	1.923E11	3.595E10		5.347	.000
exchange rate	-6.823E10	2.065E10	-.614	-3.304	.004
2. (Constant)	2.684E11	3.595E10		7.466	.000
exchange rate	-8.060E10	1.669E10	-.726	-4.830	.000
bond yield	-7.860E9	2.279E9	-.518	-3.449	.003

a. Dependent Variable: GDP.

So in this table we can see that the model is:

$Y = 51225\text{-}1073741824\ X_1\text{-}106868920\ X_2$

GDP = 51225-1073741824 Exchange rate – 106868920 bond yield

By consider to the above formula we can see that the bond yield and exchange rate have negative effect on GDP.

We can see that interest rate and stock index don't have direct relationship whit GDP in New Zealand, we have to consider it doesn't mean that these factors don't have any effect on GDP but actually the effect of them are not directly on the GDP.

Conclusion

In this paper we try investigate the effect of New Zealand stock index, interest rate, exchange rate and bong yield in the GDP, from 1990-2009. For this purpose we investigate two parts. *First* we investigate the correlation between them and second the liner line between them. Actually in the first part we find that Exchange rate and GDP are near to -1 that's mean if the Exchange rate increase the GDP decrease and reverse, so when in New Zealand Exchange rate trend decrease the GDP increase. For other factors we don't find significant relation between them and GDP although the bond yield correlation with GDP is higher than others.

For the *second* part we write the line linear and we can see that in this formula the bond yield and exchange rate are affect on GDP, so in this part we reject first and fourth hypostasis and accept second and third hypostasis. Actually the trend line for Exchange rate and Bond yield are is negative and these cause the trend for GDP increase.

As a conclusion we can say that New Zealand is successful in its economic growth because of high amount increase in GDP.

REFERENCES

Http://data.worldbank.org/country/new-zealand

13

Growth of Public Expenditure on Education in India

— M. James Antony
— S.Saravanan

Introduction

Education is a critical input for human capital. Education is sought not only as it confers higher earning capacity on people but also for its other highly valued benefits. It provides knowledge to understand changes in the society and scientific advancements and thus facilitates invention and innovations. Investment in education is considered as one of the main sources of human capital. Economically, expanding educational opportunities in a nation accelerates the development process. Economic growth means increase in real national income of a country and naturally the contribution of an educated person to economic growth is more that of an illiterate person.

Educational influences and is also influenced by rapid economic growth and the social changes that accompany it. Education by itself is not sufficient for economic growth that preceded the take off by India was built on the foundation of educational achievement. Human capital acquired through education influences economic growth by increasing adoption of new technologies and the productivity of the labour force. It also influences the evolution of politico economic institution and the anticipation of future economic growth and affects enrollment decisions and attainment through changes in the rate of return to education.

Expanding access to education, especially at lower levels is a common objective of governments in developing countries and it has met with considerable success over the last two decades. Developing countries have been quite successful at expanding enrolments in education, especially at the lower levels. But for any given level of efficiency, increased enrollments required increased resources to maintain quality and the countries have to take this account in their educational plans. Developing countries also increased their investment in education, particularly primary education. Becasue these efforts, many school aged children who did not attend school are now attending school. The World Bank estimates show that 125 million school-aged children in developing countries were out of school in 1995. In India alone, the school-aged children out of school were 30 million in 1995.

With increasing recognition of the role of education in development, broadening of educational opportunities has been given due importance since independence. In 1990, India endorsed the Jomtien Commitment of providing Education for All (EFA) through a strategy of basic education. The Constitutional (93rd Amendment) Bill has been passed by both the houses of parliament and has received the President's Assent on December 12, 2002. This was a significant measure for achieving the goal of Education for All by making free and compulsory education a fundamental right for all children in the age group of 6-14 years. In order to fulfill this constitutional obligation Sarva Shiksha Abhiyan (SSA) has been launched in partnership with the states. Increase in the level of education raises earnings, reduces poverty and improves child health. Educational policy makers have responded to the continuing high rate of non-enrolment in primary education by adopting policies to raise school quality.

A well developed and equitable system of education promotes quality learning and is central for success in the emerging knowledge economy. It is widely acknowledged that education contributes significantly to economic development. The developed world understood the fact much earlier that individuals with higher education have an edge over their counterparts. They are the ones who always believed that any amount of investment in education was justifiable. So, developing countries also give due importance to both the quantitative and qualitative expansion of education.

In this paper, an attempt is made to analyse the broad trend in the public expenditure on education of India. This analysis was done using 17 years data over the period from 1990-91 to 2006-07 fro each variable depending on the availability of data. For the period from 2007-08 to 2011-12 relevant data are not available.

Classification

In order to analyse the growth of different components of public expenditure on education, the variables are classified into four items.

1. Elementary level.
2. High/Higher secondary level.
3. Adult education level.
4. University and High level.

Table 13.1: Growth of Public Expenditure on Education in India during 1990-91 to 2006-07

(Rs. in Crores)

Year	Expenditure on Education	Index No.	Annual Growth Rate
1990-91	17193.66	100.00	–
1991-92	18757.61	109.09	9.09
1992-93	20952.97	121.86	11.70
1993-94	23413.1	136.17	11.74
1994-95	27232.15	158.38	16.31
1995-96	31516.59	183.30	15.73
1996-97	36371.64	211.15	15.40
1997-98	41109.32	239.09	13.03
1998-99	51225.26	297.93	24.61
1999-2000	61281.46	356.42	19.63
2000-01	62498.09	363.49	1.98
2001-02	64847.7	377.16	3.76
2002-03	68561.55	398.76	5.73
2003-04	73044.93	424.84	6.54
2004-05	81280.85	472.74	11.28
2005-06	97224.19	565.47	19.62
2006-07	111888.6	650.75	15.08

Source: Educational statistics of India.

The public expenditure on education in India, during the period from 1990-91 to 2006-07 has increased sizably. The value of public expenditure on education has increased from Rs. 17,193.66 crores in 1990-91 to Rs. 111888.6 crores in 2006-07. The index number has increased from 100 in 1990-91 to 650.75 in 2006-07 with fluctuations. The linear growth rate is 34.42 per cent. The lowest annual growth rate was 3.76 in 2001-02 and the highest annual growth rate was 24.61 per cent in 1998-99. (Table 13.1)

The public expenditure on elementary level education in India, during the period from 1990-91 to 2006-07 has increased sizably. The value of public expenditure on elementary level education has increased from Rs. 9076.28 crores in 1990-91 to Rs. 62112.56 crores in 2006-07. The index number has increased from 100 in 1990-91 to 684.34 in 2006-07 with fluctuations.

Table 13.2: Growth of Public Expenditure on Elementary Level Education in India during 1990-91 to 2006-07

(Rs. in Crores)

Year	Expenditure on Elementary Level Education	Index No.	Annual Growth Rate
1990-91	9076.28	100.00	–
1991-92	10367.22	114.22	14.22
1992-93	11321.50	124.74	9.20
1993-94	13071.14	144.01	15.45
1994-95	15133.05	166.73	15.77
1995-96	18433.93	203.10	21.81
1996-97	21543.63	237.36	16.87
1997-98	24083.17	265.34	11.79
1998-99	30191.07	332.64	25.36
1999-2000	34068.78	375.36	12.84
2000-01	39274.60	432.72	15.28
2001-02	40019.36	440.92	1.89
2002-03	43403.45	478.21	8.46
2003-04	47409.51	522.35	9.23
2004-05	52123.42	574.28	9.94
2005-06	59561.84	656.28	14.27
2006-07	62112.56	684.34	4.28

Source: Educational statistics of India.

The linear growth rate is 36.52 per cent. The lowest annual growth rate was 1.89 in 2001-02 and the highest annual growth rate was 25.36 in 1998-99. (Table 13.2)

The public expenditure on high/higher secondary level education in India, during the period from 1990-91 to 2006-07 has increased sizably. The value of public expenditure on high/higher secondary level education has increased from Rs. 6310.33 crores in 1990-91 to Rs. 39859.45 crores in 2006-07. The index number has increased from 100 in 1990-91 to 631.65 in 2006-07 with fluctuations. The linear growth rate is 33.23 per cent. The lowest annual growth rate was -3.43 in 2001-02 and the highest annual growth rate was 28.33 in 1998-99. (*See table 13.2 on next page*)

Table 13.3: Growth of Public Expenditure on High/Higher Secondary Level Education in India during 1990-91 to 2006-07

(Rs. in Crores)

Year	Expenditure on High /Higher Secondary Level Education	Index No.	Annual Growth Rate
1990-91	6310.33	100.00	–
1991-92	7400.56	117.28	17.28
1992-93	8574.97	135.88	15.87
1993-94	9371.34	148.51	9.29
1994-95	10835.33	171.71	15.62
1995-96	12530.38	198.57	15.64
1996-97	14164.01	224.46	13.04
1997-98	15663.5	248.22	10.59
1998-99	20100.97	318.54	28.3
1999-2000	25447.89	403.27	26.60
2000-01	26057.5	412.93	2.39
2001-02	25163.47	398.77	-3.43
2002-03	28301.35	448.49	12.47
2003-04	31251.41	495.24	10.42
2004-05	33284.65	527.46	6.51
2005-06	36588.98	579.83	9.93
2006-07	39859.45	631.65	8.94

Source: Educational statistics of India.

Table 13.4: Growth of Public Expenditure on Adult Education in India during 1990-91 to 2006-07

(Rs. in Crores)

Year	Expenditure on Adult Education	Index No.	Annual Growth Rate
1	2	3	4
1990-91	273.15	100.00	–
1991-92	228.52	83.66	-16.34
1992-93	210.97	77.24	-7.68
1993-94	280.01	102.51	32.73
1994-95	338.31	123.86	20.82

Condt...

1	2	3	4
1995-96	259.71	95.08	-23.23
1996-97	205.74	75.32	-20.78
1997-98	209.8	76.81	1.97
1998-99	189.45	69.39	-9.69
1999-2000	186.53	68.30	-1.54
2000-01	226.12	82.78	21.22
2001-02	359.56	131.63	59.01
2002-03	415.77	152.21	15.63
2003-04	485.42	177.71	16.75
2004-05	515.86	188.86	6.27
2005-06	546.78	200.18	5.99
2006-07	601.58	220.24	10.02

Source: Educational statistics of India.

The public expenditure on adult education in India, during the period from 1990-91 to 2006-07 has increased sizably. The value of public expenditure on adult education has increased from Rs. 273.15 crores in 1990-91 to Rs. 601.58 crores in 2006-07. The index number has increased from 100 in 1990-91 to 220.24 in 2006-07 with fluctuations. The linear growth rate is 75.15 per cent. The lowest annual growth rate was -23.23 in 1995-96 and the highest annual growth rate was 59.01 in 2001-02. (Table 13.4)

The public expenditure on university/high education in India, during the period from 1990-91 to 2006-07 has a witnessed a sizable increase. The value of public expenditure on university/high education has increased from Rs. 3956.09 crores in 1990-91 to Rs. 26878.81 crores in 2006-07. The index number has increased from 100 in 1990-91 to 679.43 in 2006-07 with fluctuations. The linear growth rate is 36.21 per cent. The lowest annual growth rate was -15.39 in 2001-02 and the highest annual growth rate was 36.18 in 1999-2000. *(See table 13.5 on next page)*

Conclusion

In India, the priority has been on secondary and higher education. In most Indian states the share of secondary education is higher than that in Latin American middle income countries although they have secondary enrolments higher than those in most Indian states. Due to the public subsidization of secondary and higher education, the children coming from poor socio-economic backgrounds not benefited, and they constitute the bulk of school students who do not pursue higher education in India. They are in no position to gain anything from the public spending on secondary and higher education.

Table 13.5: Growth of Public Expenditure on University/High Level Education in India during 1990-91 to 2006-07

(Rs. in Crores)

Year	Expenditure on University/High Level Education	Index No.	Annual Growth Rate
1990-91	3956.09	100.00	–
1991-92	4396.78	111.4	11.14
1992-93	4922.91	124.44	11.97
1993-94	5557.2	140.47	12.88
1994-95	6299.53	159.24	13.36
1995-96	6954.07	175.78	10.39
1996-97	7983.11	201.18	14.79
1997-98	8595.67	217.28	7.67
1998-99	11097.42	280.51	29.10
1999-2000	15112.89	382.02	36.18
2000-01	16928.21	427.90	12.01
2001-02	14323.32	362.06	-15.39
2002-03	17099.87	432.24	19.38
2003-04	17114.54	457.89	5.93
2004-05	20174.23	509.95	11.37
2005-06	23588.78	596.26	16.93
2006-07	26878.81	679.43	13.95

Source: Educational statistics of India.

Every country which has achieved universal elementary education has done so through public intervention; the experiences of the developed and high achieving developing countries were markedly similar; and the private sector's role was limited at the elementary level. It is concluded that additional public spending should concentrate mainly on elementary rather than secondary education and should go to government schools.

REFERENCES

Aggarwal, Ya. (2000), Public and Private Partnership in Primary Education in India - A Study of Unrecognised Schools in Haryana. Operations Research and System Management Unit, NIEPA.

Bashir, S. (2000), *Ggovernment Expenditure on Elementary Education in the Nineties.* New Delhi: European Commission.

Cordella, T.and G. D. Ariccia (1988), Budget Support *vs.* Project Aid. (IMF Working Paper, WP/03/88). Washington: International Monetary Fund.

Dev, M.and Mooij, J (2002), Social Sector Expenditures in The 1990s: Analysis of Centre and State Budgets. *Economic and Political Weekly,* Vol. No. 27 (9), 2002.

Prakash, V. (2007), Trends in Growth and Financing of Higher Education in India. *Economic and Political Weekly,* Vol. No. 39.6, 2007.

Ramji, V., Sujatha, S.and V.K. Srinivasan (2001), A Study on Management of Public Expenditure by State Governments in India, Indian Institute of Economics, New Delhi.

14

Unirrigated Agriculture in Tamil Nadu – India
Problems and Prospects

— Gayathri
— P. Veerachamy

This paper explores problems and prospects of unirrigated agriculture in Tamil Nadu. The paper gives the details of district wise unirrigated agriculture in Tamil Nadu. Besides, the study identifies the major problems in production, cropping pattern and crop diversification, availability of institutional credit and crop insurance schemes. The paper suggests that effective implementation of watershed development projects, ease in access to credit and modernisation in crop insurance policies for achieving sustainable production in unirrigated agriculture.

Introduction

This paper examines the problems and prospects of unirrigated agriculture in Tamil Nadu. Agriculture continues to be the main economic activity in rural areas of the developing world in spite of a steady diversification of their economic base during the preceding decades. Likewise, agriculture is the backbone of the rural India and the largest industry in the country. The role of agriculture is important in terms of food security, international trade and economic development. India ranks first among the countries that practice unirrigated agriculture both in terms of extent and value of production. India has 143 million hectares of agricultural land and about 108 million hectares are unirrigated area, which constitutes nearly 75 per cent of the total land (Kumar *et al.* 2009). Unirrigated agriculture is largely practiced in arid, semi-arid and subhumid regions of our country. With about 68 per cent of rural population, these regions are also home to 81 per cent of rural poor (Rao *et al.* 2005). In such areas, crop production has become difficult as the intensity and frequency of rainfall is low.

The unirrigated agriculture refers to crop production in a farming system which depends entirely on rainfall but may include supplementary irrigation from small dams or tanks fed from rainfall and associated run-off on a particular land holding. However, all unirrigated areas are not of the same characteristics. Unirrigated areas are highly diverse, ranging from assured rainfall and resource-rich areas with good agricultural potential to erratic rainfall and resource-poor areas with much more restricted potential. Some resource-rich unirrigated areas potentially are highly productive and already have experienced widespread adoption of improved seeds. In drier, less favorable areas, on the other hand, productivity growth has lagged behind, and there is widespread poverty and degradation of natural resources (Bhatia, 2005). However, nearly 50 per cent of the total food grains are grown under unirrigated agriculture and millions of rural poor depend on unirrigated agriculture. In addition, 85 per cent of the cereals, 83 per cent of the pulses, 70 per cent of the oilseeds and 65 per cent of the cotton are predominant unirrigated crops grown in India. Nearly 50 per cent of the total rural workforce and 60 per cent of livestock in the country depend on unirrigated agriculture (CRIDA 2011). It emphasises the crucial role played by unirrigated agriculture in food security and livelihood of the rural households.

By considering the above facts, the policy makers give much importance to the unirrigated agriculture in order to meet the rising demand for food, basic staples, non-food grains, and exports. At the same time, the productivity of irrigated land is being utilised at the maximum level. The growth in total factor productivity in irrigated agriculture has declined slightly in major crops (Singh and Rathore, 2010). As a result, the opportunity for continued expansion of irrigated agriculture is limited and the need for Unirrigated agriculture has always been an important part of the agricultural sector. However, the state of unirrigated agriculture is precarious and the problems associated with it are multifarious. To name the more striking ones: low cropping intensity, high cost of cultivation, poor adoption of modern technology, uncertainty in output, low productivity, increasing number of suicides among farmers, lack of institutional credit, inadequate public investment and high incidence of rural poverty (Anon, 2009).

With this background, this paper explores and identifies the major problems of unirrigated agriculture and opportunities for stimulating agricultural growth in Tamil Nadu.

Unirrigated Agriculture in Tamil Nadu

Agriculture continues to be the mainstay of livelihood for more than 50 per cent of the population in Tamil Nadu. It contributes 12 per cent of the Net State Domestic Product. Agriculture is the single largest sector providing job opportunities for rural people, besides being the source of supply of food grains and other dietary staples and serving as the chief source of raw material for industries. In Tamil Nadu, out of 7 million hectares of cultivable area, around 3.1 million hectares comes under unirrigated agriculture. The major segment of the pulses and oilseeds are produced by the unirrigated agriculture (Season and Crop Report 2010).

The existing studies in the area of unirrigated agriculture have used the gross cropped area under irrigation as an indicator to identify unirrigated agricultural areas. They consider that the predominant rainfed agriculture as 'unirrigated areas' and predominant irrigated agriculture as 'irrigated area'. However, several previous studies have faced this conceptual issue in categorising unirrigated agriculture. Therefore, the studies in the area of unirrigated agriculture have followed both average rain fall and gross cropped area under irrigation (Rangaswamy, 1981; Bapna *et al.* 1984; Jodha, 1985; Subbarao, 1985; Shah and Sah and 1993; Thorat, 1993).

As a result, the Statistical Hand Book of the Tamil Nadu has classified the districts according to the range of actual rain fall (see Table 14.1). The average actual rain fall is categorised as below 800 mm, 801 to 1000 mm, 1001 to 1200 mm, 1201 to 1400 mm, 1401 to 1800 mm and above the 1800 mm. This categorization may be useful to identify the gross cropped area under irrigation and unirrigated districts of Tamil Nadu state.

Table 14.1: Distribution of Districts by Range of Average Actual Rainfall 2009-10

Sl. No.	Range of Rainfall	Distribution of Districts by Range of Rainfall
1.	Below 800 mm	Namakkal, Erode, Tiruchirapalli, Karur, Perambalur, Madurai, Virudhunagar and Thoothukudi.
2.	801 to 1000 mm	Vellore, Salem, Dharmapuri, Krishnagiri, Thiruvannamalai, Pudukkottai, Dindugul, Theni, Ramanathapuram, Sivagangai, Tirunelveli and Ariyaliur.
3.	1001 to 1200 mm	Kancheepuram, Thiruvallur, Villupuram, Coimbatore and Kanniyakumari.
4.	1201 to 1400 mm	Chennai, Cuddalore, Thanjavur and Thiruvarur.
5.	1401 to 1800 mm	Nagapattinam.
6.	1801mm and above	The Nilgiris.

Source: Tamil Nadu Statistical Hand Book 2010, Department of Economics and Statistics, Chennai.

As mentioned above, the average actual rain fall and gross cropped area under irrigation are considered for identifying the unirrigated agricultural districts. In Tamil Nadu, Namakkal, Erode, Tiruchirappalli, Karur, Perambalur, Madurai and Virudhunagar districts are identified as low rain fall district and their actual rain fall is below 800 mm. Among the low rain fall districts, percentage of gross cropped area under irrigation is relatively lower in Thoothukudi (24.94), Perambalur (30.99) and Virudhunagar (46.64) districts.

Table 14.2: Details of Percentage of Gross Cropped Area under Irrigation and Annual Actual Rain Fall in Districts of Tamil Nadu State

Sl. No.	Districts	Percentage of Gross Cropped Area under Irrigation	Total Annual Rain Fall (Actual in mm.)
1.	Kancheepuram	88.42	1156.80
2.	Thiruvallur	85.59	1062.00
3.	Cuddalore	59.03	1351.40
4.	Villupuram	72.02	1096.90
5.	Vellore	53.89	814.80
6.	Thiruvannamalai	74.75	957.70
7.	Salem	50.29	860.20
8.	Namakkal	48.59	592.30
9.	Dharmapuri	43.83	812.70
10.	Krishnagiri	28.65	920.50
11.	Coimbatore	61.53	1177.80
12.	Thiruppur	61.27	–
13.	Erode	69.52	708.60
14.	Tiruchirappalli	59.19	757.30
15.	Karur	60.31	637.10
16.	Perambalur	30.99	760.20
17.	Ariyalur	31.98	823.70
18.	Pudukottai	74.27	813.70
19.	Thanjavur	82.21	1217.00
20.	Thiruvarur	68.42	1325.80
21.	Nagapattinam	57.00	1666.90
22.	Madurai	63.68	713.30
23.	Theni	57.46	821.40
24.	Dindigul	48.44	820.00
25.	Ramanathapuram	35.56	866.40
26.	Virudhunagar	46.64	503.20
27.	Sivagangai	73.81	892.50
28.	Tirunelveli	77.38	901.10
29.	Thoothukudi	24.94	634.70
30.	The Nilgiris	0.52	2368.60
31.	Kanyakumari	41.70	1142.40
	Tamil Nadu	**58.12**	**937.80**

Source: Tamil Nadu Statistical Hand Book 2010, Department of Economics and Statistics, Chennai.

In general, unirrigated agriculture is considered as a gamble with monsoon. In this context, Government of Tamil Nadu has initiated a Mission on Rain fed Farming to increase the productivity and income of the farmers in unirrigated agricultural areas by adopting integrated watershed approaches of International Crop Research Institute for Semi-Arid Tropics (ICRISAT) with the assistance from TNAU and Central Research Institute for Dry land Agriculture (CRIDA). However, the problems of unirrigated are unresolved and those are discussed in the forthcoming sections.

Cropping Pattern and Crop Diversification in Unirrigated Agriculture

Historically unirrigated farmers practice high diversity in cropping systems with livestock integration which is an inbuilt risk management strategy. The cropping patterns have evolved based on the rainfall, length of the growing season and soil types. However, due to changed consumer preferences and market demand, farmers are now rapidly shifting to crops and cropping patterns which are more remunerative. But the change in cropping pattern not towards the food crops to commercial crops and other high remunerative crop. The change in cropping pattern shows sharp increase in area under maize and cotton took place in few years at the cost of coarse cereals like sorghum and pearl millet mainly due to higher returns. Such changes will have implications on fodder availability to livestock. However, it is viable only in unirrigate where the miner irrigation sources are possible.

The change in cropping pattern will have implications on the resource use. Continuous mono-cropping increases vulnerability of farmers to weather risks depletes soil fertility, ground water and leads to build up of pests and diseases. This issue has to be dealt both through technology and policy. In general, the Indian agrarian structure is dominated by marginal and small farmers not only in terms of number but also in terms of area cultivated. In this context, the type of crop diversification and extent of crop diversification may differ among the different land holders (Gupta and Tewari, 1985; Kalpana., *et al*, 2009). The cost of cultivation in Unirrigated agriculture includes plough, manure and harvesting. Hence, the cost and return of the Unirrigated agriculture may differ according to farm character, farmer character, type of crop and other factors.

The Problems of Unirrigated Agriculture

The important problems in unirigated agricultural are explored by reviewing the relevant literature of the subject. In addition, it examines the role of economic and social policies, area development programmes, infrastructural investments and provides the measures for promoting sustainable unirrigated agricultural development.

Unstable Production

Unirrigated agriculture is often characterized by high variability of production outcomes or, production risk. Unlike most other farming systems, farmers are not able to predict with certainty the amount of output that the production process will yield due to external factors such as weather, pests, and diseases. Farmers can also be hindered by adverse events during harvesting or threshing that may result in production losses. However, unirrigate agricultural farmers have developed various coping strategies to insulate themselves from income risk, at least to a certain degree. As a result, even if individual crop yields vary greatly across years, farmers' incomes may not, so increased yield variability of HYVs is not necessarily a deterrent to adoption. Due to the frequent crop failure, the farmers in unirrigated agriculture need to involve plough, seeding and manure practices within the single season.

Unstable Market

Input and output price volatility is important source of market risk in agriculture. Prices of agricultural commodities are extremely volatile. Output price variability originates It causes increase in cost of cultivation in the mid of great fluctuations on crops yield at from both endogenous and exogenous market shocks. Segmented agricultural markets will be influenced mainly by local supply and demand conditions, while more globally integrated markets will be significantly affected by international production dynamics. In local markets, price risk is sometimes mitigated by the 'natural hedge' effect in which an increase (decrease) in annual production tends to decrease (increase) output price (though not necessarily farmers' revenues). In integrated markets, a reduction in prices is generally not correlated with local supply conditions and therefore price shocks may affect producers in a more significant way. Another kind of market risk arises in the process of delivering production to the marketplace.

Lack of Infrastructure

The inability to deliver perishable products to the right market at the right time can impair the efforts of producers. Lack of infrastructure and well-developed markets make this a significant source of risk in one hand, and the large fluctuations in input and output prices which restrict the reliability on price predictions on the other hand. Unstable farm income resulting from business and financial risk coupled with lack of infrastructure in the area may affect production decisions, delay adoption of the new technology, prohibit long-term investment in agriculture and hence delay the agricultural development in this sector (Hazal and Ramasamy, 1991).

Lack of Drought Management of Strategies

Implementations of farmers' drought management strategies fail, however, in the event that widespread drought causes crop failure over a wide area and depresses the rural economy so much that all sources of income are affected. Such aggregate level, covariate risk calls for government intervention to help stabilize incomes and prevent famine. In this context, the effective implementation of rural employment and food subsidy programmes deserve credit for reducing drought-related hunger in India in the last two decades. On the other hand, government-sponsored rainfall insurance schemes have probably not contributed to incrased adoption of improved seeds, but they have done a great deal to drain public funds.

Failure of Institutional Finance

Credit is well known to play an important role in facilitating investment in improved agricultural technology. Commercial Banks, Regional Rural Banks (RRBs) and Co-operatives are the three main rural financial institutions that provide credit to the agricultural sector at the village level. In most of India, weak formal banking and cooperative systems provide subsidized credit, but defaults are extremely high and funds are provided disproportionately to relatively large farmers. In addition, occasional interference by politicians to forgive farmers' debts only serves to weaken the banking system. In addition, some of the studies estimates that the excluding Kerala, the ratio of credit supply to farmers' short-term credit requirements in India is about 1:10. Meanwhile, informal village moneylenders provide coverage to a wider range of clients but at very high rates of interest (Desai, 1988). Whereas, many village moneylenders borrow from the formal sector at concessional rates in order to relend to their poorer neighbors at higher rates (Hanumantha Rao and Gulati, 1994). These phenomenons are frequent and problems are acute in unirrigated agriculture. In some extreme cases, these unfavorable events become one of the factors leading to farmers' suicides which are now assuming serious proportions (Raju and Chand, 2007).

Lack of Crop Insurance

As stated earlier, production process in unirrigated agriculture is entirely different than in other kind of farming. It has been observed through the variability and instability in production and productivity and high cost of cultivation. These factors lead severe impact negatively on most rural households simultaneously and are therefore difficult to manage through traditional risk sharing and coping strategies. However, the risk bearing capacity of the average farmer in the unirrigated agriculture is very limited. As a result, government policy may sometimes play an important role in helping farmers manage risk. In this context, the Government Police of Crop Insurance was established to manage risks in agriculture (Walker and Jodha 1986; Rao *et al.* 1988).

Conclusion and Policy Suggestions

In Tamil Nadu, low rainfall districts are Namakkal, Erode, Tiruchirappalli, Karur, Perambalur, Madurai and Virudhunagar. Therefore, the authorities need to evolve management practices for farmers' of the districts. Besides, choice of remunerative crops without degradation of the natural resource base has to be suggested and also to define agro-ecological zones where such cropping systems can be adopted sustainably. Simultaneously, need based policy incentives are required to encourage farmers adopt agro-ecology compatible cropping systems so that the farmers' income is maintained and the natural resource base of the country is not degraded.

Financial assistance to the farmers in the low rainfall area is highly imperative. But, formal sector funds often are not available due to rationing and bureaucratic hassles. The neediest farmers would be made better off if concessional lending were abandoned and bank managers were given more autonomy and protection against political interference. Banking operations could be made simpler and more decentralised in order to reduce transactions costs of both banks and their clients. Higher interest rates would help banks become viable credit institutions rather than merely a means for channeling concessional funds. Under these circumstances, banks could attract deposits, and they would have more incentive to develop better loan portfolios. In short, this step would help develop greater professionalism in the banking sector (Hanumantha Rao and Gulati, 1994).

Crop insurance is provided by the public sector in many countries. However, it fails to reach its target in unirrigated agricultural areas. The primary reasons are follows: Majority of the unirrigated holdings is in small and marginal farm categories and these farms have poor access to institutional credit. Since Crop insurance was linked to crop loans, many small and marginal farmers could not participate in the crop insurance scheme. The threshold yield was fixed on the basis of the average of the preceeding 10 years whereas the trend in the growth of yield levels for most of the crops was positive. Further, the threshold yield or level of non-indemnifiable yield was very high even for low risk areas and the high risk areas in unirrigated agriculture are exclusion of from crop insurance scheme. As a result, the farmers in unirrigated agriculture not prefer to adopt the crop insurance policies. In particular, unawareness among the farmers about the crop insurance scheme and non-availability of insurance coverage for the major commercial crops like cotton and others were excluded from the crop insurance scheme. Therefore, the agencies for crop insurance need reform the policies and insurance coverage to include the different type of farmers and crops for managing the uncertainty and risks in unirrigated agriculture (Bhende, 2005).

As a whole, the policy makers have to look into the above mentioned problems and suggestions thereby to improve the agricultural production, farmer's livelihood and sustainable agricultural development.

REFERENCES

Anon. 2009. "Agricultural Statistics at a Glance." Ministry of Agriculture, New Delhi.

Bapna, S. L., H. Binswanger, and J. Quizon. 1984. "Systems of Output Supply and Factor Demand Equations for Semi-arid Tropical India." *Indian Journal of Agricultural Economics*, 39 (2): 179-202.

Bhatia, M.S. 2005. "Viability of Rainfed Agriculture in Semi-Arid Regions." NABARD Occasional Paper No. 40, Mumbai.

Bhende, M.J. 2005. "Agricultural Insurance in India: Problems and Prospects." NABARD Occasional Paper No. 44, Mumbai.

CRIDA. 2011. Vision 2030. Central Research Institute for Dry land Agriculture, Hyderabad, Andhra Pradesh.

Desai, D. K. 1988, Institutional Credit Requirements for Agricultural Production-2000 AD, *Indian Journal of Agricultural Economics,* 43 (3).

Government of Tamil Nadu. 2010. Tamil Statistical Hand Book 2010. Department of Economics and Statistics, Chennai, Tamil Nadu.

Gupta, R. P. and Tewari, S. K. 1985. "Factors Affecting Crop Diversification: A Critical Analysis." *Indian Journal of Agricultural Economics,* 40 (3): 304-309.

Hanumantha Rao, C. H., and Ashok Gulati. 1994. "Indian Agriculture: Emerging Perspectives and Policy Issues." New Delhi: ICAR and Washington, DC: IFPRI.

Hazell, Peter B.R., and C. Ramasamy. 1991. *"The Green Revolution Reconsidered: The Impact of High Yielding Rice Varieties in South India."* Baltimore: Johns Hopkins University Press.

Jodha. N.S. 1985. *Development Strategy for Rainfed Agriculture: Possibilities and Constraints.* Economics Programme, ICRISAT.

Kalpana R., P. Devasenapathy and R.K. Kaleeswari. 2009. "Crop Diversification for Increasing Productivity and Profitability in Irrigated Uplands of Tamil Nadu." *Indian J. Agricultural Research,* 43 (1): 73-76.

Kumar P., Joshi P.K. and Birthal P. S. 2009. "Demand Projections for Food Grains in India." *Agricultural Economics Research Review,* 22(2): 237-243.

Raju, S.S and Ramesh Chand. 2007. "Progress and Problems in Agricultural Insurance in India." *Economic and Political Weekly,* May 26, pp. 1905-1908.

Rangaswamy, P. 1981. "Economics of Dry Farming in Drought Prone Areas: A Case Study of Hissar in Haryana." Research Study No. 81/1. Agricultural Econcomics Research Centre, University of Delhi.

Rao K.P.C., Bantilan M.C.S., Singh K., Subrahmanyam S., Deshingkar P., Rao P. Parthasarathy and Shiferaw B. 2005. "Overcoming Poverty in Rural India: Focus on Rainfed Semi-Arid Tropics." Patancheru 502 324, Andhra Pradesh, India: International Crops Research Institute for the Semi-Arid Tropics, 96 pp.

Rao, C.H. H., S. K. Ray and K. Subbarao. 1988. "Unstable Agriculture and Droughts-Implications for Policy." New Delhi: Vikas Publishing House Pvt. Ltd.

Shah, Amita, and D.C. Sah. 1993. "Dry Land Farming under the Changing Source Environment: A Case Study of Gujarat." *Artha Vijnana* 35 (3) (September).

Singh, S. and Rathore, M. S. 2010. Rain-fed Agriculture in India – Perspectives and Challenges, Rawat Publications, Jaipur.

Subbarao, K. 1985. "Institutions, Infrastructure and Regional Variations in India's Input Delivery System." In Agricultural Markets in the Semi-Arid Tropics: Proceedings of the International Workshop, October 24-28, 198. Patancheru, India: ICRISAT.

Thorat, S. K. 1993. *"Technological Change and Regional Differentiation."* Khama Publishers. New Delhi.

15

Impact of Self-Help Groups on Economic Development of Empowered Rural Women

— T. R. Gurumoorthy
— AR. Annadurai

Micro-finance through women Self-Help Groups (SHGs) is a considerable medium of poverty mitigation and empowerment of women. SHGs formed by women in different places have proved that they could certainly bring about a change in the mindset of the very conservative and tradition-bound illiterate women in rural areas. The concept of group formation is the best strategy to enlighten women and provide necessary mental courage for self-employment. This article makes a strong case for SHGs as a new development paradigm for bringing about economic development and gender equity among rural women in India by creating self-employment opportunities through micro credit. The study is based on the premise that poor women can internalise production possibilities in groups only. They are better-equipped to conquer the harmful social stress and gender biases operating against them through group identity and movement. Conversely, the relationship of credit admittance to self-employment is not involuntary but depends on different factors.

Introduction

In India micro-credit groups are being recognised by the Government as an effective tool for achieving the distributional objectives of monetary policy. In the recent period, considerable emphasis has been placed on promotion of micro-credit enterprises in view of perceived inadequacies of existing agencies in providing productive credit to those with little or no previous access to formal credit facilities.

Self-Help Group

A SHG is a registered or unregistered group of micro-entrepreneurs with a homogenous social and economic background, voluntarily coming together to save small amount regularly and mutually agreeing to contribute to a common fund to meet their needs on mutual help basis.

The group members use collective wisdom and peer pressure to ensure proper end-use of credit and timely repayment thereof. In fact, peer pressure has been recognised as an effective substitute for collaterals. Besides, financing through SHGs reduce transaction costs for both lenders and borrowers.

"Self-help group is a homogeneous group consisting of 10 to 20 women. These women may select their own leader and also fix the tenure for such leadership". The SHGs are being linked with the banks for the external credit under the projects of rural development. The joint appraisal teams consisting of bank managers, rural development officers, and NGOs, visit the groups and select the beneficiaries proposed by the women groups for providing financial assistance to the respective entrepreneurial activities. Banks provides financial assistance for various entrepreneurial activities such as setting up of petty shops, vegetable shops, tailoring units, charcoal – making units, dairy units etc.

The borrowers repay the bank loans properly. They remit the loan dues to the animators at group meetings and the animators repay the same to the bank. The SHGs repay more than 90 per cent loans of the banks on time in contrast to less than 35 per cent of repayment under IRDP. Beside focusing on entrepreneurial development and empowering women, SHGs concentrate on all round development of the beneficiaries and their village as a whole. The group undertakes the responsibility of delivering non credit services such as literacy, health and environmental issues. The concept of SHG moulds women as responsible citizens of the country achieving economic status.

Self-Help Groups are important vehicles for credit delivery to women in rural and semi-urban areas. Issues relating to structure and sustainability, fundings, regulations and capacity building for SHGs are engaging attention of Reserve Bank of India. The objective has been to accelerate the flow of bank credit to micro-finance institutions while maintaining their decentralised, voluntary and non-bureaucratic character, particularly in rural and semi-urban areas.

The number of SHGs linked to banks aggregated 12.94 lakh as on March 31, 2010 with almost 40 per cent concentrated in Andhra Pradesh. More than 90 per cent of the groups linked with banks are exclusive women groups and the scheme has more than 95 per cent on-time repayment record. Cumulative disbursement of bank loans to women SHGs stood at Rs. 12429 crore as on March 31, 2010, with an average loan of Rs. 57795 per SHG and Rs. 4128 per family. There are at present, 49 commercial banks, 192 RRBs and 264 Co-operative Banks associated with the SHG-bank linkage programme.

Statement of the Problem

The Self-Help Group (SHG) is a viable organized set up to disburse micro-credit to the rural women for the purpose of making them enterprising women and encouraging them to enter into entrepreneurial activities. Credit needs of the rural women can be fulfilled totally through the SHG. The women led SHGs have successfully demonstrated how to mobilise and manage thrift, appraise credit needs, maintain linkages with the banks and enforce financial self-discipline.

The process of economic development would be incomplete and lopsided unless women are fully involved in it. Emancipation of women is an essential prerequisite for economic development progress of the nation. The SHGs empower women and train them to take active part in economic progress of the nation and make them sensitised, self-made and self-disciplined. SHG paves the way for availing credit from the financial institutions and creating entrepreneurial culture in rural area. Studying functioning of SHGs in selected villages and the contribution of SHGs towards economic development of the rural women become essential to the planners and financial institutions for further creation and sponsoring SHGs in rural areas.

It is planned to undertake this study in the Sivagangai District, Tamil Nadu State. It is a backward district. One of the objectives of SHGs is to improve economic independence of women. This study will help to measure economic independence of women in a backward district and suggest measures for improving economic independence that will make this district a developed one. Hence this study.

Objectives of the Study

The objectives of the study are given below:

1. To study the economic development of rural women through self-help groups in Sivagangai District.
2. To study financial assistance provided to SHGs under micro-credit system Commercial Banks, Co-operative Banks and NABARD.

Methodology

The present study is an empirical research based on survey method. This study is based on both primary and secondary data. The primary data are collected from the members of the SHGs though questionnaire. Secondary data are collected from the published sources *i.e.*, books, journals, websites, and other reports of Government agencies, NABARD and banks.

SHG-Bank Linkage Models

The three basic groups of banks which are involved in SHG linkage with banks are Commercial Banks, Regional Rural Banks and Co-operative Banks. It is interesting to note that while considering the average amount of disbursement per SHG by the banking sector as a whole commercial banks stand in the first place (50.34%) followed by RRBs (38.66%) and Co-operative Banks (11%) in the second and third places respectively. Average per SHG loan disbursement as micro-finance by commercial banks was Rs. 31,836 and the same by RRBs was Rs. 26,220 and by Co-operative Banks was Rs. 21,703.

In Tamil Nadu 2,09,197 SHGs have linkage with banks as on end of March 2009-10. In line with the national trend, the SHGs had linkage with banks in all the three sectors namely, *(i)* Commercial banks in the private and public sector, *(ii)* the Regional Rural Banks and *(iii)* the Co-operative Banks. The linkage of SHGs with PACBs takes place through District Central Co-operative Banks of the Districts. In Tamil Nadu out of 56126 SHGs, 1,18,497 are assisted by Commercial Banks, 58,743 and 32,953 SHGs are assisted by RRBs and PACBs respectively.

Models of Financing SHG

Model – 1

The bank branch finances directly to SHG by opening the loan account in the name of SHG. Bank loan disbursed in the ratio of savings in the common fund of SHG. The maximum permissible ratio between savings in the common fund and bank loan is from 1:1 to 1:4. The NGO does not play any role in the formation of SHG.

Model – 2

The bank branch finances SHG which is formed at the instance of NGO. The maximum permissible ratio between savings in the common fund and credit is 1:4 for concerned NGO which acts as facilitator, but the responsibility of repayment solely lies with SHG.

Model – 3

In case, the local bank branch does not have adequate confidence in lending to SHG promoted by NGO, or in SHG for various reasons and is not willing to be linked directly with the bank, the bank can finance such SHG through the agency that promotes to the group, provided the agency is willing to borrow from the bank and the bank is also prepared to lend bulk to the agency. The NGO may act as a financial intermediary and is responsible for loan repayment.

Benefits of Linkage

- Fulfill concept of priority sector lending.
- Higher rate of repayment.
- Reduction in lending and monitoring cost and work load.
- SHG members become permanent financial partners to the Bankers helps in recovering other overdue accounts.
- SHG linkage is a profitable business and in future, it will improve the advance portfolio, with good recovery.
- 100 per cent refinance is available from NABARD.
- In simple words SHG is a concept not a programme.
- It actually teachers Banking to the poor.

Managers are advised to form and link as much as possible the Self-Help Groups in their branches for the benefit of both.

Hypotheses

1. "There is no significant relationship between monthly income before and after joining Self-Help Groups".
2. "There is no significant relationship between monthly savings before and after joining Self-Help Groups".

(i) Average Monthly Income of SHG Members

The researcher has interviewed one thousand (1000) members belong to hundred (100) SHGs to collect data related to monthly income before and after joining SHGs. One group consists of ten (10) members. The total numbers of group members are classified into Six Taluks of Sivagangai District. Random Sampling is used to identify sample respondents.

Table 15.1: Average Monthly Income of the Respondents before and after Joining Self-Help Groups

Taluk	Average Monthly Income		D(X-Y)	D^2
	Before Joining SHG Rs.	After Joining SHG Rs.		
Tirupathur	2100	3800	-1700	2890000
Karaikudi	2400	4500	-2100	4410000
Sivagangai	2500	4300	-1800	3240000
Devakottai	2100	4200	-2100	4410000
Manamadurai	2300	3700	-1400	1960000
Ilayangudi	2200	3500	-1300	1690000
	Total		-10400(ΣD)	18600000$(\Sigma D)^2$

This hypothesis is tested by using't' test.

Table 15.2: Average Monthly Income of the Respondents before and after Joining Self-Help Groups

Variable	Calculated Value	Table Value	Degrees of Freedom	Result
Income	12.533	2.132	5	Rejected

The calculated value is more than the Table 15.2 value. The null hypothesis is rejected. It is concluded that there is a significant difference in the average monthly income of SHG members before and after joining SHGs.

(ii) Average Monthly Savings of SHG Members

The researcher has interviewed one thousand (1000) members belong to hundred (100) SHGs to collect data related to monthly savings before and after joining SHGs.

Table 15.3: Average Monthly Savings of the Respondents before and after Joining Self-Help Groups

Taluk	Average Monthly Saving		D(X-Y)	D^2
	Before Joining SHG Rs.	After Joining SHG Rs.		
Tirupathur	350	750	-400	160000
Karaikudi	370	850	-480	230400
Sivagangai	360	820	-460	211600
Devakottai	350	720	-370	136900
Manamadurai	320	670	-350	122500
Ilayangudi	300	650	-350	122500
	Total		**-2410 (ΣD)**	**983900 $(\Sigma D)^2$**

This hypothesis is tested by using't' test.

Table 15.4: Average Monthly Savings of the Respondents before and after Joining Self-Help Groups

Variable	Calculated Value	Table Value	Degrees of Freedom	Result
Savings	18.42	2.132	5	Rejected

The calculated value is more than the Table 15.4 value. The null hypothesis is rejected. It is calculated that there is a significant difference in the average monthly savings of SHG members before and after joining SHGs.

Average Monthly Income of Before Joining SHG Members

This hypothesis is tested by using'F' test.

Table 15.5:

Source of Variation	Sum of Squares	Degrees of Freedom	Mean Square
Between samples	**136**	**5**	**27.20**
Within samples	**947**	**94**	**10.07**
Total	**1083**	**99**	

Table 15.6:

Variable	Calculated Value	Table Value	Degrees of Freedom	Result
Income	2.70	2.29	99	Rejected

The calculated value is more than the Table 15.6 value. The null hypothesis is rejected. It is calculated that there is a significant difference in the average monthly income of SHG members before joining SHGs.

Average Monthly Income of After Joining SHG Members

This hypothesis is tested by using'F' test.

Table 15.7:

Source of Variation	Sum of Squares	Degrees of Freedom	Mean Square
Between samples	184	5	36.8
Within samples	713	94	7.59
Total	**897**	**99**	

Table 15.8:

Variable	Calculated Value	Table Value	Degrees of Freedom	Result
Income	4.848	2.29	99	Rejected

The calculated value is more than the Table 15.8 value. The null hypothesis is rejected. It is calculated that there is a significant difference in the average monthly income of SHG members after joining SHGs.

Average Monthly Savings of Before Joining SHG Members

This hypothesis is tested by using'F' test.

Table 15.9:

Source of Variation	Sum of Squares	Degrees of Freedom	Mean Square
Between samples	184	5	36.80
Within samples	937	94	9.97
Total	**1121**	**99**	

Table 15.10:

Variable	Calculated Value	Table Value	Degrees of Freedom	Result
Savings	3.69	2.29	99	Rejected

The calculated value is more than the Table 15.10 value. The null hypothesis is rejected. It is calculated that there is a significant difference in the average monthly savings of SHG members before joining SHGs.

Average Monthly Savings of After Joining SHG Members

This hypothesis is tested by using'F' test.

The calculated value is more than the Table 15.12 value. The null hypothesis is rejected. It is calculated that there is a significant difference in the average monthly savings of SHG members after joining SHGs. (*See table on next page*)

Table 15.11:

Source of Variation	Sum of Squares	Degrees of Freedom	Mean Square
Between samples	292	5	58.40
Within samples	625	94	6.64
Total	917	99	

Table 15.12:

Variable	Calculated Value	Table Value	Degrees of Freedom	Result
Savings	8.79	2.29	99	Rejected

Borrowings and Repayment of Loans by SHG Members

The researcher attempts to study borrowings and repayment of loans by SHG members in selected villages.

(i) Loan Received from SHGs

SHG members get loan from their groups for meeting their financial requirements arise from time to time. Generally they get loans from SHGs to meet the expenses relating to Children education, Medical expenses, Fulfillment of basic needs, Marriage expenses and other incidental expenses. The following Table 15.13 shows purposes for which loans are received by members from SHGs.

Table 15.13: Purpose of Loan Received from SHGs

Purpose	No. of Respondents
Children education	210
Medical expenses	230
Fulfillment of basic needs	180
Marriage expenses	160
Other incidental expenses	220
Total	**1000**

It is revealed in Table 15.13 that all the respondents have received loan from the SHGs. Out of 1000 respondents, 210 have received loan from the SHG to meet expenses of their children education, 290 respondents received loan for medical expenses, 160 respondents received loan for fulfilling their basic needs, 150 respondents received loan for marriage expenses and 190 respondents have received loan for meeting their incidental expenses.

The rate of interest charged for the loan will vary from one SHG to another. It varies 12 per cent to 36 per cent.

(ii) Loan Received from Banks

Banks provide loans to SHG members for the various entrepreneurial activities, such as, tailoring business, pickle and appalam business, handloom business and other small scale businesses. Rate of interest is decided by bankers. Financial assistance will be provided by banks to the SHGs after ascertaining their satisfactory performance in managing SHGs.

The purposes of loans received by members from the banks are given in the following Table 15.14.

Table 15.14: Purpose of Loan Received from Banks

Purpose	No. of Respondents
Textiles and Tailoring business	280
Pickle and Appalam business	260
Handlooms	250
Other small scale business	210
Total	**1000**

It is revealed in Table 15.14 that all the respondents have received loans from the banks. Out of 1000 respondents, 280 respondents have received loan from banks for textiles and tailoring business, 260 respondents have received loan for pickle and appalam business, 250 respondents have received loan for handloom business and 210 respondents have received loan for other small scale businesses.

Suggestions

In this study it has been attempted to analyze income and savings of members before and after joining SHGs, loan borrowed and repaid by them and economic development of Self-Help Group members. It is suggested that the members of SHGs should identify viable and feasible income generating entrepreneurial activities in order to enhance and strength their economic empowerment. It is suggested that they should raise their monthly contribution and savings. This becomes possible when their standard of living and economic status are improved. The Commercial Banks/Co-operative Banks should establish a separate branch to serve SHGs. The bank should appraise viability of entrepreneurial projects SHGs members and monitor their ongoing projects. The Government machineries and NGOs should sponsor and organize periodical meetings to explain economic issues to SHGs members. This will help them to get economic development. The encouraging performance of SHGs in the recent past prompted our Finance Minister to create a 'Women's SHGs Development Fund' with a corpus of 500 crore to protect the interest of small borrowers is a welcoming phenomenon.

REFERENCES

Mukundhan. N., Soundari, .M.H. (2008), Emerging Dimensions in Self-Help Groups, Dominant Publishers and Distributors, New Delhi.

EDA and APMAS Self-Help Groups in India: A Study of the Lights and Shades, CARE, CRS, USAID and GTZ, 2006, p. 11.

Narayanaswamy , Micro-credit and Rural Enterprises" , *Journal of Rural Development*, 2005.

Misra,I. (2004), Micro-credit for Macro Impact on Poverty. National Publishing House, New Delhi.

Krishnan. C. (2000), Role of Rural Banks in the Rural Development, Printwell Publishers, Jaipur.

Stuart Rutherford. Self-Help Groups as Micro-finance Providers: How good can they get? mimeo, 1999, p. 9.

K.G. Karmakar, 1999, 'Rural Credit and Self-Help Groups: Micro-finance Needs and Concepts in India', Sage Publications.

Micro-finance for SHGs – Kurukshetra Volume 48 and Volume 58.

'Women SHGs Fewer in Western India: Expert', The Financial Express, Jan 21, 2006.

'Micro-credit: Looking beyond group Lending', The Hindu Business Line, April 14, 2006.

16

Tribal Development

A Critical Analysis of Development Programme Focusing Vulnerable Tribal Groups in the Mayurbhanj District, Odisha – India

— MADHULIKA SAHOO

'Odisha' in India, which is known for one of the largest tribal dominated state, off late the Economic Survey 2010-11 at the state assembly claims that, Odisha has achieved 9.57 per cent against the national average of 7.79 per cent, at the same time the state has witnessed wide range of regional and social disparities in development, failing to address economic circumstances of the underprivileged and marginalized group of KBK and Mayurbhanj district of Odisha.

Although the state and central Government has introduces immense number of tribal development programmes and schemes but in real it has failed to reach the targeted population in many ways. The question remains whether there are flaws in the scheme or lack of proper implementation of the tribal development policies or lack of awareness. The reasons may be numerous but there are less effective actions undertaken at the grass root level to curb the crisis. The Mankirdia who are particularly vulnerable Tribal groups of Mayurbhanj are the nomadic tribal groups, the Government in recent time has tried to settle the tribal groups by providing various tribal developmental schemes and programmes. The present case study has tried to critically analyze the impact of development programmes on Mankirdia's on their transit phase from nomadic to settled living in Mayurbhanj district of Odisha.

Introduction

The term development indicates the overall improvement in the quality of life. However, development in tribal region has remained a challenge since time in memorial. The anthropological school of thought in reference to tribal development says any development for tribal communities should be along the lines of their genius and the programmes to be implemented in the tribal areas should have a 'tribal touch' or 'tribal bias' (Taradatt 2001). Nevertheless, the battle of isolation and assimilation has leaded the tribal communities affected and obstructing the implementation of the tribal development programmes. It was understood that the progress of social development can be observed in the form of empowerment, equitable distribution of income and wealth or in broader context of socialisation of natural resources, which can be possible only with the involvement of the tribals in the project formulation and implementation by working through their traditional system. The present tribal development process gives a complete different scenario; instead of involving the tribals in the process of planning and implementation of the development programmes, they are rather blamed for the failure of the developmental schemes and programmes. The concern remains within the administrative system itself, the multiplicity and complexity of the administrative machinery helps only in confusing the innocent tribals. For example the tribal development schemes and poverty alleviation projects which are certainly implemented by the Integrated Tribal Development Agencies (ITDA) and the District Rural Development Agencies (DRDA) having common beneficiaries has frequently fails to pool resources together for drawing integrated action plans, both agencies tend to work parallel to each other and in isolation (Taradat 2001). The needy tribal communities who fail to have access to the development programmes gives a open space for the non-tribal communities to dominate the government machinery in the tribal area and not only feel bitter about the various welfare programmes designed for tribals, but also get into an exploitative relationship with the local traders, contractors and police. This results in benefitting the handful of people than actually reaching the mass population. While tribals preserve the natural resources as life sustaining forces, the non-tribals outlook is one of utilitarian and short term commercial exploitation. This disregard for tribal – nature symbiosis is causing not only a threat to tribal survival but is also leading to depletion of resources in the tribal regions and affecting the nature and environment. In the current paper I have tried to study the impact of development programmes and schemes implemented by the Hill Kharia and Mankirdia Development Agency (HKMDA) in two Mankirdia settlements *i.e.,* Kendumundi and Durdura at Mayurbhanj district, I have also tried to trace the upshot of the developmental programmes and schemes on Mankiridia's livelihood and culture. The findings are based on the field work done with the Mankirdia's in the community.

About Mankirdia Particularly Vulnerable Tribal Groups

The Mankirdia's are the most primitive nomadic tribal groups of Odisha. Mankirdia are known for their monkey eating habit. However, the term *Brihor or Mankirdia* was originated from Austro-Asiatic language group, *Bir* means 'forest' and *Hor* means 'Men'. The Brihor are nomadic tribal communities majorly located in northern parts of Odisha. They are hunting and food gathering group which has reciprocal economic relations with their neighboring peasants. The Brihor are addressed in various names such as in places like Kalahandi and Sundergarh are called as *Mankidi*, where as in Mayrubhanj and Sambalpur they are called as *Mankirdia*. There are two types of Birhors, 'the Uthal' who are nomadic and the other type of Birhor is 'the Jagi' who are settled Birhors. The Birhors are called as Mankedi or Mankirdia because they are known to be as skilled monkey catchers.[1] The Birhors (Mankirdia) in Simlipal are mainly seen in Sirrampur, Thakurmunda, Thungudihi, Podadiha, Kendumundi, Durdura, Banlabasa, Uthania, Chatani, Malibasa village. As per 1971 census the total Mankirdia population was 3, 464 in Odisha, in 1991 the population drastically decreased to 825 and further 702 in 2001.[2] The worrying population figures shows from the five decadal census years (1961-2001) that the male population is higher than the female. The decadal growth rate of the population is variable. In comparison to 1961 and 1971 population there was -64.10 per cent sharp decline of population growth. In the census year 1981 the population 44.90 per cent increases.

The reason for decrease population could be the remarkable features of the Birhors who are constantly shifting in groups from one place to another and staying in camps known as *'Tanda*. The camps are usually done close by the market and peasant village. The Mankirdia (Brihor) make their houses in leave and wooden twigs popularly known as *'Khumba'* which is conical in shape having an oval shaped base, the *Khumba* usually constructed like any modern house having a bedroom, kitchen and a place for storing things. In every temporary Tanda there has to be a *'Mukhia'* or headman, a *'Dehiri'* or priest and Shaman has to be nominated through rituals, the selected leaders are there to take decision during ritual hunting, change of Tanda and selecting new site, selecting village sacred and secular functionaries. However the leadership changes along with the change of the Tanda.[3] The Birhors are mostly nuclear families, multi clan in nature having inter-clan marriages.

The Brihors are known for making ropes out of the bark of Siali creepers (Lama Bayers) which are used for different purposes like making net for hunting monkey and making tupa (small basket). They are also aware of weeding, transplanting and harvesting of paddy which helps them to substitute their income. They also collect roots and tubers, fruits (kendu, jackfruit, mango etc.) and flowers from the forest for consumption purposes. The Birhors are technically sound in extracting oil from *Kususm* and *Mahua* seeds by using traditional wooden oil press. They use nets made of Siali creepers for catching monkeys. They eat the flesh of the monkey and sell the skin.

The major celebration observed by the Birhors are Karma Naukhia (first eating of maize), Dasai parab and Dak Bonga, Sohrai, Makara, Magh Parab, Sendra Bonga (for hunting). In Pana Sankranti during mid April the Birhor set camps for ritual hunting known as 'Akhanda Sikar' the mass hunting is known to be as sign of manhood *i.e.,* if an adult boy doesn't kill a wild animal he is not accepted as reaching manhood.[4]

In the year 1986-87 the Hill Kharia and Mankirdia Development Agency (HKMDA) established at Jashipur was given an order by the state government to endow with special emphasis to improve the quality of life of the Hill Kharia and Mankirdia tribes through the developmental activities. At present there are many Mankirdia colonies in various parts of Jashipur, Karanjia and Thakurmunda block of Mayurbhanj Distirct, such as in Durdura, Kendumunundi, Kiajhari, Podagarh etc. As per 1990s census the total Mankirdia population in Jashipur and Karanjia block was 203 surrounding Mayurbhanj district. The Mankirdia communities are still considered to be as the monkey eater's primitive tribal group in the district. The population is numerically low in comparison to other primitive tribal groups of Odisha.

Mankirdia Colony at Kendumundi

The colony is located 10-15km from the Karanjia town. The Mankirdia community people were brought to the Kendumundi colony 20-25 years back. The Mankirdia colony has total 31 households, along with 3 khadia household who had built their own houses in the colony. The colony is provided with 31 cemented houses, school building, aganwadi, tube well, Job and BPL card to each Mankedia family by the HKMDA.

The Developmental Programme vs. Mankirdia Traditional Practices

Though the Mankirdia's have started living in the cemented houses provided by the Government under *Mon Kudia* scheme but the pity condition of the houses has compelled the Mankirdia to construct Khumba (traditional houses) next to each house. Many villagers confessed that the modern houses do not give enough shelter to the family during summer they prefer to sleep inside the Khumba. To many women Khumba has still remained a sacred sign of giving birth to the baby inside it. At the time of labour pain the women is taken to Khumba for the delivery, once the baby is born the umbilical cord is cut with sharp snail. The Mankirdia people are spiritual in nature, they believe in various god and goddess, for them when a baby is born in a household, one of the ancestors has taken rebirth and therefore the family fortune and well-being have come back with greater potency and vitality.[5] Early marriages are majorly seen amongst the Mankirdia community. The marriage is mostly inter-clan (endogamy) in practice. However, at present due to frequent seasonal migration by the Mankirdia male groups are seen having partner outside the clan (exogamy). According to them malevolent who create trouble and cause illness and death. Although the government has tried to fetch the Mankirdia's with modern houses but the strong believe in tradition and culture has made the tribals not to accept the modern housing and technology yet.

Government Interventions

The Government has taken painstaking effort to provide settled colony and livelihood options to the Mankirdia community which will enable the tribals from nomadic to settled life; the concept might be appearing splendid but the evolution for Mankirdias is not an easy state of affairs. The Mankirdia who have lived a nomadic life for long could never able to assimilate with the urban kind of living. The Government has provided homestead land of 0.97ac with constructed cemented houses to the Mankirdia's, which certainly not the cure to poverty for the nomadic tribes. The Government had taken initiative to provide livelihood training on honey brewing, jute rope making, leaf plate stitching, poultry farm, goats for gotary but capturing the skills and leading a market economy is not the cup of tea for the Mankirdia's. The villagers in Kendumuni were seen with unused poultry farm, rolling empty honey brewing boxes on the floor which were saying loud and clearly about the failed government livelihood schemes. However, the failed government schemes have made many young boys to migrate outside the district to earn there living and allowing many to get married from different community. From all the above factors, one can say that though the settled life style amongst the Mankirdia's has started prevailing at the same time many yearn for old life style of hunting and gathering. The older generation people are trying there best to preserve traditional practices of catching monkey and sacredness in the community. On the similar note the Durdura Mankirdia settlement was no different than the Kendumunidi.

Mankirdia Colony at Durdura

The Mankirdia colony at Durdura is situated 12-15 km from Jashipur town. The Mankirdia population is the smaller group amongst the rest of the PVTGs in Odisha. The Makirdia of Durdura who used to have their temporary shelter near Durdura hata (Durdura Market) was provided with a resettlement colony popularly known as 'Mankirdia sahi' the Mankirdia colony now have 25 households where 5.56 ac homestead land with construct houses has been given to each Mankirdia family.

Government Intervention

The Government wanted to settle this nomadic community in various parts of Karanjia, Jashipur and Thakurmunda in the Mayurbhanj district. A colony with construct houses along with basic facilities such as tube well, school building, community hall, cemented houses, road, goats to each household, poultry farm for livelihood was provided by the Hill Kharia and Mankirdia Development agency. Although Government has provided all basic developmental facilities for minimum income to the Mankirdia but the usage of those facilities has remained unsuccessful. Various flaws in the government schemes and programmes were identified which are described below.

Gaps in Government Plan and Practices

- *Lack of Knowledge on Tribal Culture:* The Government has provided cemented houses to every Mankirdia family but the houses could barely provide them shelter during summer. Also the spiritual connection they have with the leaf houses (Khumba) are still under practice by the Mankirdia's. The livelihood skills provided to the Mankirdia has remained a big failure. None in the community were seen making proper usage of the skills for generating livelihood options. This gives a clear indication that the government officers has less knowledge on tribal culture and have not taken the Mankirdia traditional practices and culture into consideration, especially whilst designing the livelihood plans and schemes. The consequences of the failure of the developmental schemes have certainly created unconstructive impact on Mankirdia tribe livelihood and culture.
- *Lack of Knowledge on Tribal Livelihood Practices:* Mankirdias are hunter and gatherer by nature and having no agricultural practices, many rely on collecting Siali bark as major livelihood by making rope from the Siali bark. The Government didn't allot agricultural land to the Mankrrdia's in which case their livelihood remained unsustainable. Rather the Government tried its best to restore their livelihood in the form of providing advanced mode of livelihood options such as honey brewing boxes, poultry farm, gottary, and fishery, leaf plates stitching machines, jute and murga training. However, those equipments have remained unused by the tribals. Mainly due to lack of planning on tribal development schemes, its implementation procedure, follow up on the market linkage has deliberately put a question mark on sustainable livelihood of the tribals.
- *Lack of Market Linkage and Unsustainable Livelihood Programmes:* Mankirdia's are nature friendly by practice, getting acquainted with modern equipment like honey brewing boxes, leaf plate machine is a difficult task for the nomadic tribes. The lack of market linkage is also compelling many not to use the skills. Rather obtaining self livelihood option like use of Ambeda fruit could be better source of income *i.e.*, processing of Ambeda fruit and using the seed which is further processed used for making crock, such excellent livelihood option was self obtaining method by the Mankirdias in Kendumundi which gained them an income of (Rs. 20 per Kg). If those self livelihood options can be further enhanced by the Government then the Mankerida's can have better living.
- *Lack of Awareness on Tribal Development Schemes:* Due to lack of awareness on development programmes and other benefit schemes many Mankirdia's are unable to have access to the benefits which they are entitled for. The Government or the local NGOs should take initiative

to educate and bring awareness on Government provisions to the Mankirdia's. Although the Multi Purpose Coordinator who live in the community try its best to equip the villagers and train them, but a constant effort and cooperation from the line department along with the existing civil society is required for the successful implementation of the development programmes.

- *Lack of Data Base on Mankirdia Community Population:* Due to nomadic life style of the Mankirdia's the government took initiative to provide settled lifestyle through HKMDA but there are Mankirdia's in many other places which are still not coming in the purview of the micro project. This is mainly because of lack of data available base with the Government on demographic detail of the Mankirdias.

Impact of Faulty Development Programmes on Mankirdia's

- *Seasonal Migration:* Due to faulty intervention of the livelihood programmes at Mankirdia colony many young Mankirdia's are migrating out of district for work, many old people and women groups are moving to different place for agricultural work on the lands of the host villagers. Since this has become an alternative livelihood options for the Mankirdia's many have realised agriculture could be the main source of income. However, if land and plough is provided by the Government for the agricultural work then there can be sustainable livelihood options for the Mankirdia.
- *Community Conflict:* Mankirdia being the small group and most primitive tribals in the district, their monkey eating habits has made them elope from integrating with other host communities. This is somewhere leading to community conflict, where the Santal's are trying to invade the Mankirdia's area for their purpose. However, the separate colony premises and separate gate to the Mankirdia colony will always prevent the Mankirdia to get integrate with other communities and portray a weaker primitive group.
- *Lost Tribal Culture:* The Mankirdia's might have stepped to modern civilization but they still long for their traditional practices somewhere within their heart. The freedom of free access to the forest to collect Siali bark, catching monkey for food and leading a nomadic life has always given them immense pleasure. The present life in the settlement colony is literally suffocating the older Mankirdia's who always desire to go to the forest. Although settled lifestyle has been injected but many young boys and girls are migrating to the nearby city for better livelihood options. The situation at a snail's pace affecting the tribal culture and this will further sweep away the traditional practices perpetually.

- *Faulty Forest Right Act Procedure:* In order to bring fairness on historical injustice done to SC and ST, the Forest Right Act was introduced by the Government in the year 2006, Mankirdia being known for nomadic lifestyle and due to no agricultural practices which have never permitted them to encroach lands for agricultural work, they are legally not viable for individual rights. However, the forest they access for their dependency could have been given community rights, where the HKMDA took initiative to facilitate the process erroneously. The Mankerdia community is provided with a small patch of sal forest on road side *i.e.* 42.67 Ha under community rights, Kendumundi colony at Tataa village (Tataa Jungle) where they could barely get anything for their livelihood. But the central question is how far the Mankirdia's been benefitted out of this act and other development programmes?

Conclusion

The necessity of development has driven the Mankirdia tribals to such an extent that many young masses are becoming seasonal migrants to earn there living; it was observed that many young men and women are migrating to near by urban areas for work. Although government has introduced large number of schemes and plans under 'Conservation-cum-development' for development of the Mankirdia but little is being done to promote and integrate the traditional life style of Mankirdia. Rather, they are being continuously persuaded to give up their traditional and indigenous way of life and assimilate in the main stream. The result is the older generations are constantly fighting with the contemporary lifestyle imposed on them by the Government and losing the original wilderness they have as hunter and gatherer. Lack of traditional way of educating the Mankirdia has made the tribal development plans paralyzed.

The development programme should be planned and implemented in such a way that maximum benefit should be going to the community need. So, they can easily accept the programme and accommodate themselves within it. Lately, there has been agreement with the Panchayat Raj department and SC and ST development department for the effective implementation of the development plans and programmes.[6] However, to visualize this practically, if the Government would make larger effort to consult the villagers for linking up such development plans with the traditional practices of the Mankirrdia then they would be more benefited from the skills. Nonetheless the present scenario of the Birhor is that they can neither lead a modern life nor follow the traditional one it is more sort of as if they are caught in a confluence.

FOOTNOTES

1. Patnaik, N., "Primitive Tribes of Orissa and their Development Strategies" D. K. Printworld Pvt. Ltd., New Delhi, 2005.
2. Census of India 201.

3. Dash, J, "Human Ecology of Foragers" Common Wealth, New Delhi, 1998.
4. Wright, B. and Mohanty, B., "Simlipal Tiger Reserve: Assessment of Recent Elephant Poaching and Protection Initiatives" National Tiger Reserve Authority, June 2010.
5. Patnaik, N., "Primitive Tribes of Orissa and their Development Strategies" D. K. Printworld Pvt. Ltd., New Delhi, 2005.
6. Government of Odisha, Panchayat Raj Department.

REFERENCES

Dash, J, 1998 *"Human Ecology of Foragers"* Common Wealth, New Delhi.

Mahapatra, L.K. 1956 'From Shifting Cultivation to Agriculturists – The Paurl Bhuiyan in Transition, Adivasi.

Mishra, S.N., 1998 'Antiquity to Modernity in Tribal India' Ownership and Control of Resources among Indian Tribes, Vol. III, Inter-India Publications, New Delhi.

Patnaik, N., 2005 *"Primitive Tribes of Orissa and their Development Strategies"* D. K. Printworld Pvt. Ltd., New Delhi.

Pragada, R. R. Unrest in Tribal areas and Impact of Extremism on Tribal Development, Unpublished Paper Presented in for Panel Discussion on Unrest in Tribal Areas and Impact of Extremism on Development of Tribal Areas, at Dr. MCR Institute of Administration.

Pratheep, P.S. 2010 'Globalisation, Identity and Culture: Tribal Issues in India' Catholic College, Mahatma Gandhi University. LASCAC Proceedings.

Reddy, M.G. and Kumar, K.A. 2010, 'Political Economy of Tribal Development: A Case Study of Andhra Pradesh' Working Paper No. 85 Centre for Economic and Social Studies, Hyderabad.

Roy, S.C., 1925, The Birhor: A Little Known Jungle Tribe of Chotanagpur Man in India Office, Church Road, Ranchi.

Sachidananda 1964, 'Culture Change in Tribal Bihar, Book land Pvt. Ltd., Calcutta.

Sachidananda and Mandal, B.B. 1985, 'Industrialization and Social Disorganization: A Study of Tribes in Bihar Concept Publishing Company, New Delhi.

Taradatt, 2001, 'Tribal Development in India with Special Reference to Orissa' Gyan Publishing House, New Delhi.

Upadhyay, V.S. and Pandey, G. 2003, Tribal Development in India (A Critical Appraisal) Crown Publication, Ranchi.

Vidyarthi, L.P. 1980, 'Tribal Development and Its Administration' Concept Publishing Company, New Delhi.

Vidyarthi, L.P. 1968 'Applied Anthropology in India' Kitab Mahal, Allahabad.

Vidyarthi, L.P. 1960, 'Anthropology and Tribal Welfare in India' Council of Social-cultural Research, Ranchi.

Wright, B. and Mohanty, B., 2010, *"Simlipal Tiger Reserve: Assessment of Recent Elephant Poaching and Protection Initiatives"* National Tiger Reserve Authority, June.

17

Profile Characteristics of Female Headed Households in Small-Scale Dairying
A Gender Perspective

— Jyoti Yadav
— Hema Tripathi

The present study has been carried out purposively in the Bareilly district of Uttar Pradesh. Final data were collected personally through interview schedule from 100 distinct households (50 female headed + 50 male headed) from 05 different clusters from 05 different block comprising 10 villages in each of Bareilly district. The study revealed that majority of female headed households (70%) were found in middle age group. Ninety eight per cent of the females were Hindus and majority belonged to the backward caste category. Sixty six per cent females had medium family size and 70 per cent were widowed. Sixty two per cent respondents in female headed households had marginal (<2.5 acres) land holding and 34 per cent were landless. Livestock rearing was the major occupation found among 30 per cent female against 20 per cent male headed households. Eighty two per cent of females had small herd size, followed by 18 per cent owned medium number of livestock. In contrast, 52 per cent male respondents owned medium size of herd followed by 26 per cent, who had large herd size. Majority of females were not using extension services as information sources, thus had low access to extension personnel. Private agency staff and NGOs were not at all used by females. Neighbors were the major information sources of female respondents (86%) followed by friends and relatives (64%).

In India, dairying is recognised as an instrument for social and economic development. Dairying provides women with a regular daily income, vital to household food security and family well being. The responsibility in this sector further increases in female headed household because in such households female is the major provider and/or protecter, carrier, bearer, decision maker and assumes all the responsibilities in the household. In some conditions like; death of husband, divorce, separation or desertion, migration of males for employment, female remain alone in the house hence they become head of the house. Along with households work, they go for agriculture and animal husbandry or both for income generation and to fulfill the household's requirements. In such households, she is more likely to be considered the owners of small stock compared to larger livestock, and have a say in the disposal and sale of small stock and its products and in the use of income from this. Small stock provide an important resource for women being cheaper to acquire, require little labor, space, feed and fewer inputs for survival. In India 10.35 per cent households are female headed and their average size of family is 4 whereas the average household size for male headed household is 5.4 (Census, 2001). A woman faces many challenges in the rearing of livestock because livestock rearing is a culturally male dominated sector, where man owns a disproportionately large number of the livestock, mainly cattle and buffalo. Although women provide the main source of labor for livestock related activities, they own few animals and these are mostly small ruminants. Study of profile of female headed households engaged in small scale dairying is very much important as it may affect their involvement in rearing of dairy animals in a given family which ultimately generate the income and employment for family members thus profile characteristics may help in sustaining the income generating activity and economically empowered them.

Methodology

The present study has been carried out purposively in the Bareilly district of Uttar Pradesh. Final data were collected personally through interview schedule from 100 distinct households (50 female headed + 50 male headed) from 05 different clusters comprising 10 villages in each cluster from 05 different blocks of Bareilly district. Socio-personal and economic characteristics of respondents such as age, religion, caste, family size, marital status, land holding, major occupation and annual household income etc., were categorised into groups on the basis of equal class intervals between the minimum and maximum values obtained. Family education status of respondents was measured with the help of Ray's scale (1967) and herd size was measured with the help of cattle equivalent score using method of Gadgil (1947), National Accounts Statistics (1961) and Lalwani (1981). Communication profile of respondents included institutional, non institutional and mass media information seeking sources, for which data were collected on three point continuum scale *viz.*, always, sometimes and never with respective scores of 3, 2 and 1, among the sampled households.

Results and Discussion

Socio-personal Profile

A perusal of Table 17.1 indicates that majority of the respondents from female headed households (70%) were found in middle age group followed by 24 per cent in old age group. Rest fell in young age category. In male headed households, also 72 per cent were found in middle age group followed by 14 per cent in both young and old age groups. Ninety nine per cent of the respondents were Hindus, except the one per cent, who was Muslims. Table 17.1 further shows that the majority of both female and male headed households belonged to the backward caste category. In female headed households, six per cent respondents were found in general category and 2 per cent came from schedule castes. Majority of female and male headed households belonged to medium family size comprised of 3-6 members. Majority of the females heading the households (70%) were widowed followed by 30 per cent, who were married, but their husband's have been migrated to the cities for work. All the male respondents under study were married and living with their spouse within the village. Findings of the present study are consonance with the findings of Khin Mar Oo (2005), Subba (2010) and Rathod *et al.* (2011). They also observed that the majority of the dairy farmers (about 55%) belonged to 30-50 years age group, 53.33 per cent were literates while 46.67 per cent of women were illiterates. According to Duku (2011) male headed households had significantly bigger households size than female headed households. (*See table on next page*)

Socio-economic Profile

Table 17.2 indicates that 62 per cent of respondents in female headed households had marginal (<2.5 acres) land holding, 34 per cent were landless and 4 per cent owned between 2.5-5 acres land as compared to respondents of male headed households wherein 80 per cent had marginal (<2.5 acres) land holding, 12 per cent comprised no land and 8 per cent owned small (2.5-5 acres) land holding. Dominance of agriculture followed by animal husbandry as their main occupation in both the respondents categories. Livestock rearing was the major occupation found among 30 per cent female and 20 per cent male headed households. Fourteen per cent female and 6 per cent male were also working as labors in building constructions. Table 17.2 further reveals that 96 per cent females heading the households had low annual income because of less resources and less accessibility of inputs and other facilities as compared to male, heading the households, wherein 44 per cent had medium and high (44%) level of annual income. Eighty two per cent of females, heading the households had small herd size, followed by 18 per cent owned medium number of livestock. In contrast, 52 per cent male respondents, heading households were owning medium size of herd followed by 26 per cent, who had large and the rest 22 per cent owned small number of livestock.

Table 17.1: Socio-personal Profile of Sampled Households

Socio-personal Variables	Households		Overall
	Female Headed (n=50)	Male Headed (n=50)	
Age			
Young (<25years)	03(6.00)	07(14.00)	10(10.00)
Middle (25-50 years)	35(70.00)	36(72.00)	71(71.00)
Old (>50 years)	12(24.00)	07(14.00)	19(19.00)
Religion			
Hindu	49(98.00)	50(100.00)	99(99.00)
Muslim	01(2.00)	–	01(1.00)
Caste			
Schedule caste	01(2.00)	05(10.00)	06(6.00)
Other backward class	46(92.00)	40(80.00)	86(86.00)
General	03(6.00)	05(10.00)	08(8.00)
Family size			
Small (upto 3 members)	17(34.00)	02(4.00)	19(19.00)
Medium (4-6 members)	33(66.S00)	37(74.00)	70(70.00)
Large (>6 members)	–	11(22.00)	11(11.00)
Marital status			
Unmarried	–	–	–
Widowed	35(70.00)	–	35(35.00)
Divorced	–	–	–
Married	15(30.00)	50(100.00)	65(65.00)
Family education status (Scores)			
Low (1-2.75)	31(62.00)	14(28.00)	45(45.00)
Medium (2.75-4.5)	14(28.00)	28(56.00)	42(42.00)
High (>4.5)	5(10.00)	08(16.00)	13(13.00)

Figures in parentheses indicate percentage.

Majority of females, heading the households (58%) were depended on single animals either cattle, buffalo or goats. Rao *et al.* (2003) reported that about 50 per cent families were earning 50-75 per cent of their income from dairying. There was no single family which was deriving less than 25 per cent of its income from dairying. Rathod *et al.* (2011) also revealed that 60.83 per cent of the women families had low followed by medium (35.83%) and high income (3.34%) and about 80 per cent families had medium and 12 per cent had smaller livestock holding. Waldie and Ramkumar (2002) reported in their study that the approximate contribution of dairying to the total income ranged from 50 to 80 per cent.

Table 17.2: Socio-economic Profile of Sampled Households

Socio-economic Variables	Households		Overall
	Female Headed (n=50)	Male Headed (n=50)	
1	2	3	4
Land holdings			
Landless (no land)	17(34.00)	06(12.00)	23(23.00)
Marginal (upto 2.5 acres)	31(62.00)	40(80.00)	71(71.00)
Small (2.5-5 acres)	02(4.00)	04(8.00)	06(6.00)
Major occupation			
Laborer	07 (14.00)	03(6.00)	10 (10.00)
Govt. service	01(2.00)	01(2.00)	02(2.00)
Livestock farming	15 (30.00)	10(20.00)	25 (25.00)
Crop farming	27 (54.00)	35 (70.00)	62 (62.00)
Private service	–	01(2.00)	01(1.00)
Annual household income (Rs.)			
Low (8000-30334)	48(96.00)	06(12.00)	54(54.00)
Medium (30334- 52668)	02(4.00)	22(44.00)	24(24.00)
High (52668-75000)	–	22(44.00)	22(22.00)
Herd size (cattle equivalent score)			
Small (0.4-3.25)	41 (82.00)	11 (22.00)	52(52.00)
Medium (3.25-6.10)	09 (18.00)	26 (52.00)	35(35.00)
Large (6.10-8.94)	–	13 (26.00)	13(13.00)
Herd structure			
Single animal			
Cattle only	12(24.00)	03(6.00)	15(15.00)
Buffalo only	13(26.00)	10(20.00)	23(23.00)
Goat only	04(8.00)	–	04(4.00)
Combination of two animals			
Cattle + Buffaloes	08(16.00)	16(32.00)	24(24.00)

Contd...

1	2	3	4
Buffalo + Goats	06(12.00)	–	06(6.00)
Cattle + Goats	06(12.00)	–	06(6.00)
Cattle + Draft animals	–	02(4.00)	02(2.00)
Buffalo + Draft animals	–	04(8.00)	04(4.00)
Combination of three animals			
Cattle + Buffalo + Goats	01(2.00)	04(8.00)	05(5.00)
Cattle + Buffalo + Draft animals	–	10(20.00)	10(10.00)
Cattle + Goat + Draft animals	–	01(2.00)	01(1.00)

Figures in parentheses indicate percentage.

Communication Profile

Speedy and effective transfer of information is basic to livestock development. Thus frequency of extension contact and participation in extension activities assumed greater significance. Data presented in Table 17.3 indicates that the majority of females were not using extension personnel as information sources, thus had low access to them. Private agency staff and NGOs were not at all used by females. Neighbors were found to be major information sources of female respondents (86%) followed by friends and relatives (64%). Fifty two per cent female respondents were sometimes taking information about livestock management from local leaders as compared to 62 per cent male respondents. Statistically significant differences were observed in information seeking sources at 1 per cent level of significance between the female and male respondents, heading their households with respect to all the sources except for local leaders and extension personnel, which did not yield significant difference. (*See table on next page*)

Table 17.4 indicates that both set of respondents (72% females and 82% males) had mobile phones followed by 36 per cent and 48 per cent female and male headed households owned the radio. Ownership of male headed households regarding television as a mass media source was comparatively higher (30%) than female headed households. Radio used daily by majority of both the sampled respondents. Mobile phone however, was used by the respondents as and when required. According to Rezvanfar *et al.* (2007) significant number of respondents used radio and television (17.6%), to seek information in respect of dairy farming. Subba (2010) also observed that radio remains the major source of mass media information utilised by most of the farm women in both districts followed by television utilising it as a mass media sources of information. (*See table on next page*)

Table 17.3: Institutional and Non-institutional Information Seeking Sources of Sampled Households

Information Seeking Sources	Female Headed (n=50)			Male Headed (n=50)			χ^2 Value
	Always	Some Times	Never	Always	Some Times	Never	
Institutional							
Extension personnel	–	09(18)	41(82)	–	40(80)	10(20)	0.040
Development dept. officers (BDO, DDO, VDO, VO etc.)	–	10(20)	40(80)	6(12)	30(60)	14(28)	36.560**
University/Institute personnel	–	07(14)	43(86)	–	24(48)	26(52)	14.440**
Private agency staff.	–		50(100)	–	07(14)	43(86)	73.960**
NGOs	–		50(100)	–	04(8)	46(92)	84.640**
Non-institutional							
Friends and relatives	32(64)	16(32)	02(4)	40(80)	07(14)	03(6)	72.140**
Neighbors	43(86)	06(12)	01(2)	38(76)	06(12)	06(12)	102.620**
Gram pradhan	–	15(30)	35(70)	02(4)	32(64)	16(32)	44.420**
Progressive farmers	–	04(8)	46(92)	02(4)	15(30)	33(66)	98.180**
Local leaders	–	26(52)	24(48)	–	19(38)	31(62)	1.000

Figures in parentheses indicate percentage.

** Significant at 1 per cent level of significance (p<0.01).

Table 17.4: Mass Media Ownership and its Frequency of use of the Sampled Households

Mass Media	Female Headed Households (n=50)					
	Ownership		Frequency of use			
	Yes	No	Daily	Weekly	Monthly	As per Need
Radio	18 (36.00)	32 (64.00)	12 (66.67)	6 (33.33)	–	–
Newspaper	–	–	–	–	–	–
Magazine	–	–	–	–	–	–
T.V.	5 (10.00)	45 (90.00)	5 (100.00)			
Mobile phone	36 (72.00)	14 (28.00)	–	–	–	36 (100.00)
Male Headed Households (n=50)						
Radio	24 (48.00)	26 (52.00)	20 (83.33)	4 (16.67)	–	–
Newspaper	2 (4.00)	48 (96.00)	2 (100.00)	–	–	–
Magazine	–	–	–	–	–	–
T.V.	15 (30.00)	35 (70.00)	15 (100.00)	–	–	–
Mobile phone	41 (82.00)	9 (18.00)		–	–	41(100.00)

Figures in parentheses indicate percentage.

Conclusion

Women were found to be the main bread earner in female headed households, thus priority needs to be given for improving their socio-economic status. Rearing one to two cattle or buffalo and five to six goats were the major livestock resource for women and played a central role as a source of food, income and critical inputs for livelihood. Majority of females, heading the households were depended on single animals either cattle, buffalo or goats whereas male headed households reared more animals in different combinations. Male and female respondents, heading their households engaged in small scale dairying differed significantly in institutional and non institutional information seeking sources thus interventions and trainings must be focused based on their several characteristics. Extension approach should be need based with problem solving dimensions and participatory in nature. Women rearing dairy animals offer a beneficial entry point in shaping major policy decisions in view of their unique potential of promoting gender aspects and alleviating poverty.

REFERENCES

Duku, S., Price, L. L., Tobi, H. and Zijpp, V.A., (2011), Influence of Male or Female Headship on the Keeping and Care of Small Ruminants: The Case of the Transitional zone of Ghana. *Livestock Research for Rural Development*, 23(11).

FAO. (2010-11), The State of Food and Agriculture: Women in Agriculture: Closing the Gender Gap. Food and Agriculture Organization of the United Nations, Rome, Italy.

Khin Mar Oo. (2005), Knowledge and Adoption of Improved dairy Management Practices by Women Dairy Farmers in Dharwad District. M.Sc Thesis, University of Agriculture Science, Dharwad.

Rao, S.V.N., Ramkumar, S., Waldie, K. (2003), Dairy Farming by Landless Women in the Southern States of India. In: Morrenhof, J., Ahuja, V. and Tripathy, A. (eds), Livestock Services and the Poor: Papers, Proceedings and Presentations of the International Workshop, Bhubaneswar, India, pp. 73-86.

Rathod, P. K., Nikam T. R., Sariput, L., Vajreshwari, S. and Hatey A. (2011), Participation of Rural Women in Dairy Farming in Karnataka. *Indian Research Journal of Extension Education*, 11 (2): 31-36.

Rezvanfar, A., Moradnezhai, H., and Vahedi, M. (2007), Information needs of Farm Women Related to Dairy Farming and Home Management in Ilam State of Iran. *Livestock Research for Rural Development*, 19(8).

Subba, I. (2010), Role of Women in Dairying in the Mountainous Region of Sikkim M.V.Sc. Thesis, Indian Veterinary Research Institute, Izatnagar Bareilly.

UBOS (2007), Uganda National Household Survey 2005-06. Agricultural Module. Uganda Bureau of Statistics, Kampala.

18

Situational Analysis of Children in Mysore City – India

Some Preliminary Annotations

— Nanjunda — P.T Dinesha
— V.G. Sidda Raju — Ramesh

Preventing and addressing violence, abuse, and exploitation is part of achieving the MDGs. Even though Government has brought various programmer still children are in more disasters situation. They facing various social legal and economical problems. Children have been subjected to various exploitations continuously. Poverty and exclusion contribute more in this regard. Child Protection demands inter-sectoral cooperation at the national and state and lower levels. Creating a protective environment for children means partnering with local Government, civil society, and NGOs. This paper is based on the field work conducted in Mysore districts and it deals about the various problems facing by the children in Mysore districts – India 'Child Protection' refers to protection from violence, exploitation, abuse and neglect. Violations of the child's right to protection, in addition to being human rights violations, are also massive, under-recognised and under-reported barriers to child survival and development. The need to protect some children is certainly greater than others due to their specific socio-economic and political circumstances and geographical location. These are the children who are more vulnerable in terms of the harm/danger/risk to their right to survival/ development/participation. They are children in difficult circumstances and include: The Government's approach to child protection so far has addressed largely those children who have already missed the protective net and fallen into difficult circumstances. Unfortunately the current coverage falls short of reaching the most vulnerable because the interventions through the existing schemes do not cover all the categories of children in difficult circumstances. Even where the interventions exist, for instance, institutional care for children in difficult circumstances, there is much room for improving the infrastructure and expanding the outreach. The quality of services needs up-gradation and regional imbalances need to be addressed. This paper deals about current status of the children in Mysore districts.

Research Methodology

Objective

To study about various problems facing by the children in Mysore districts.

Study Area

This study was conducted in Mysore city-Karnataka.

Data Sampling

Data have been collected on the following type of children's: Orphaned or abandoned and destitute children, Street and working children, Child beggars, Children in conflict with law ,Children in contact with law ,Child marriage, Trafficked children, Child prostitutes, Children of prisoners, Children affected by disasters, Child abuse, Victims of various crimes, HIV infected children, Disabled children etc., from various Government offices.

(a) Primary Data

- Interviews and discussions with members of the various Government dept/bodies/committees.
- Interviews with children and families affected by the issues – samples.
- Case studies.
- Consultations.

(b) Secondary Data

Data collected from various Government documents and other reports.

Consultations

(a) *District Level one day Consultation:* All key functionaries and stakeholders at district level met including depts., CWC, JJB, SJPU members, ZP/TP/GP representatives, CBO reps, youth/children's group rep, other district committee members, DLSA, NGOs, research/academic reps working on children's issues.

Data Analysis

Suitable software (SPSS) have been used to analyze the field data.

About Mysore District

Mysore district lies in the Southern Plateau and it is in the southern most part of Karnataka State. Physiographically, the region in which the district is found may be classified as partly maidan (plain) and partly semi-malnad (hilly land). The district forms the outhern part of the Deccan Peninsula with Tamil Nadu on the southeast, the Kodagu district on the west, Mandya district on the north, Hassan district on the northwest and Bangalore district on the northeast.

Demography

According to the Census of India 2001, the total population of Mysore district was 2.64 million, out of which 1.34 million were males and 1.29 million females. In 1991, the total population of Mysore district was 2.28 million out of which 1.16 million were males and rest females. Between 1981 and 2001, the size of population has increased but the rate of growth has declined. According to the 2001 Census, the sex ratio of Mysore district was 964 as compared to that of Karnataka at 965; and this shows that the district sex ratio was a little less than the State average. The sex ratio for the age group of 0-6 years was 962 in 2001 while the State average for this age group was 949. There has been a Gradual increase in literacy rates among both female and male populations over the past two decades from 1981 to 2001. The literacy rates of male and female populations in 2001 census have increased when compared to 1991 and 1981 censuses. In 1991 census, the literacy rate of the district was 48.32 per cent; and there was a dramatic increase in the next decade, to 63.48 per cent; that is, more than 15 per cent rise in the previous ten years.

Result and Discussion

1. *Drop Outs Children in Primary Schools in Mysore District (in numbers)*

SC Boys	SC Girls	ST Boys	ST Girls	OBC Boys	OBC Girls
7	10	15	22	19	21

Impression: In Primary Schools, ST Girl's drop-out rate is higher and SC Boys drop-out is the lowest.

2. *Reasons for Drops out in Mysore Districts (Boys) (in numbers)*

Parents are not interested	25
Poverty	33
Health	9
Child not interested in the study	11
Repeated failures	8
Corporal punishments	2
Disability	4
Migration	6
Socio-cultural reasons	1
Others	1

Impression: Most of the drop-out among boys is due to Poverty and the least contributing factor is socio-cultural reasons.

3. *Various Crimes against Children in Mysore District (in numbers).*

Kidnapping		Child Trafficking		Child Abuse		Prostitution		Forced Child Begging	
Boys	Girls	Boys	Girls	Boys	Girls	Boys	Girls	Boys	Girls
43	27	5	18	3	21	0	43	18	23

Impression: Kidnapping of Boys and Girl child prostitution is in higher rate. Next the lowest occurred crime is male child abuse.

4. *Total Number of Cases Registered at Juvenile Justice Board in Mysore Taluk (in numbers)*

Boys	Girls
53	5

Impression: 91 per cent of cases of boys and 9 per cent cases of girls were registered at Juvenile Justice Board.

5. *Children in Conflict with Law in Mysore (in numbers)*

10-14 Years	15-18 Years
46	116

Impression: Majority of the boy children in the age group of 15-18 are in conflict with law than of 10-14 years.

6. *Children in Conflict with Law in Mysore District (Gender-wise)*

Boys	Girls
159	3

Impression: More boys are involved in conflict with law than girls.

7. *Major Issues of Children in Mysore District (in numbers)*

Poverty	33
Running away	7
Orphans	4
Uncontrollable children	4
Single parent/poor children	21
Escaped from home	13
Child begging	23
Child abuse	1

Impression: Major issues of the boys are Poverty and least one is Child Abuse.

8. *Children Found Working in Hazardous Sector in Mysore City (in numbers)*

Boys	Girls
132	10

Impression: Majority of the Boys are found to be working in the hazardous sector.

9. *Situational Analysis of Street Children (Type of Child) in Mysore District*

Disabled	HIV/AIDS Affected	HIV/AIDS Infected	Orphans	Escaped from Home	Others
22	18	21	185	33	207

Impression: The street children belonging to others are most and HIV/ AIDS affected children are least.

10. *Number of Children Went Missing in Mysore District*

Below 18 Years (Girls)	Below 18 Years (Boys)
25	24

Impression: There is no much difference in child missing cases between boys and girls below 18 year.

11. *Child Marriage Issue in Mysore District*

Number of Marriages Stopped after Departmental Intervention	Could not be Stopped
6	1

Impression: Departmental intervention and awareness creation should be enhanced.

12. *Children Required Special Needs in Mysore District (Gender and Community-wise)*

SC Boys	SC Girls	ST Boys	ST Girls	OBC Boys	OBC Girls	Minority Boys	Minority Girls	Other Boys	Other Girls
190	114	100	49	265	182	7	2	52	26

Impression: Majority of the OBC Boys and least Minority Girls require the Special Needs.

Suggestive Conclusion

It is found that there must be close coordination among Juvenile Justice Board – Railway? Special Juvenile Police, District Rehabilitation Committee, Ministry of Women?? Police, State Monitoring Committee and Child Development Department to tackle child trafficking and children conflict with law. Also child protection units(CPU) should arrange specialized medical treatment and care, for the children infected with HIV and nutrient supplements along with the pediatric ART. There is a dearth of comprehensive statistics on child trafficking and other children issues. Absence of a tracking system makes it difficult to assess the real situation and plan for it. It is need to focus on this area. Improve the professional level of social welfare staff responsible for the initial reception of children of prisoners through professional development: issue guidelines and conduct trainings on child friendly assistance procedures based on national and international experience, the treatment of traumatised children, as well as on guardianship, adoption, fostering procedures, etc.

Establishing standards procedure for the initial identification and handling of child victims of trafficking, to be implemented by public and private social care institutions, other child protection structures, and criminal justice and law enforcement authorities, based on the best interest of the child. Next, Develop and provide training and awareness programmes directed at law enforcement and other services providers (Fire, EMS, Social Services, school systems, etc.,) on recognition of and response to trafficking/ street children is must. Conducting training for local law enforcement, prosecutors and judges on model programmes for interdiction, investigations, prosecution, and prevention on child abuse is also must. Developing programmes targeting juveniles at high risk for victimization and exploitation, with the goal being to intervene, redirect and support runaway, throwaway and exploited children who are at risk of trafficking, or who are being exploited is need of the hour.

CPU should create teams of researchers, journalists, social service groups, advocacy groups, and law enforcement to develop 'on-the-ground' and 'real time' information relating to strategies employed by traffickers, numbers of victims being trafficked, and to develop comprehensive understanding of using children for inter-related to labour trafficking, drug trafficking, and other organized criminal enterprises. In order to ensure effective service delivery to children in need, regular training and capacity building of all service providers (Government and Non-Government) at various intervals including at the time of induction and subsequently through refresher courses is a necessary requirement. A protective environment for children requires an effective monitoring system that records the incidence and nature of child protection abuses and allows for developing informed and strategic responses. Lack of data adversely affects planning of appropriate access and nature of services required for children. There Should carryout need-based research and documentation activities at district-level for assessing the number of children in difficult circumstance and creating district-specific databases to monitor trends and patterns of children in difficult circumstances.

REFERENCES

Anil Aggrawal. India, Age of consent http://members.tripod.com/~Prof_Anil_Aggrawal/index.htm

Ali, Masud, Ali, M, Sarkar, R. (1997): *Misplaced Childhood: A Short Study on the Street Child Prostitutes in Dhaka City.* Incidin, Dhaka.

Manihara, (2002), A Study of Street Children in India, Source Webmaster@skcv.com.

Reports

Sexually Abused and Sexually Exploited Children and Youth in South Asia: A Qualitative Assessment of their Health Needs and Available Services, United Nations Publication. Economic and Social Commission for Asia and the Pacific. United Nations Publication, 1999.

Child Rights World wide-prostitution – Official Definition of United Nations, 1994.

19

Poverty, Human Trafficking and Social Exclusion
Space for New Discourses

— Mahdeviah V N
— Dr. Roopa Suresh

Till very recently the term 'trafficking' was not precisely defined in international law despite its inclusion in a numbers of international legal agreements. Human trafficking has been defined as the commercial trade of human beings, who are subjected to involuntary acts such as begging, prostitution or forced labour. Human trafficking takes place both within the border and beyond borders. Countries in South Asia region act as source, transit and destination countries Poverty and lack of education make the women, particularly in the rural areas, vulnerable to the problem. Due to the lucrative nature of the prostitution business in the urban areas, socially and economically deprived women find no other options but to take it as a profession. To combat human trafficking, several short-term and long-term measures are needed to be taken up at all levels. There is an urgent need to create awareness among the public about human trafficking. Media can play a very effective role here. Poverty alleviation measures too will help in combating it in the long run. This article gives a solid background for future discourses.

Introduction

Trafficking is a lucrative industry. It is now the fastest growing criminal industry in the world. Globally, it is tied with the illegal arms trade, as the second largest criminal activity, following the drug trade. Human trafficking usually affects women and children. The total annual revenue for trafficking in persons is estimated to be between USD$5 billion and $9 billion. The Council of Europe states, "People trafficking has reached epidemic proportions over the past decade, with a global annual market of about $42.5 billion". The United Nation estimates nearly 2.5 million people from 127 different countries are being trafficked around the world.

Human Trafficking

Human trafficking threatens human security and human development of any country. It has an economic angle as the majority of women and men who are trafficked are economically vulnerable. It has a health angle, as trafficked women and children are most at risk of HIV infection and other sexually transmitted diseases. It is also a social and a gender problem, as unequal power relations in society makes them more vulnerable to human trafficking. Lastly, it is a human rights issue, as its victims are stripped of their rights and lack any access to redress for the crimes committed against them. As an organized crime, globally, human trafficking is an estimated US$ 32 billion illegal industry and third to illegal drugs and arms smuggling.

The word 'trafficking' includes the word 'traffic', which we often equate with transportation or travel. However, while the words look and sound alike, they do not hold the same meaning. Human trafficking does not require the physical movement of a person (but must entail the exploitation of the person for labour or commercial sex). Additionally, victims of human trafficking are not permitted to leave upon arrival at their destination. They are held against their will through acts of coercion and forced to work or provide services to the trafficker or others. The work or services may include anything from bonded or forced labour to commercialized sexual exploitation. The arrangement may be structured as a work contract, but with no or low payment or on terms which are highly exploitative. Sometimes the arrangement is structured as debt bondage, with the victim not being permitted or able to pay off the debt. Poverty is the primary factor in human trafficking. Most girls are not outright kidnapped, at least not in the sense that they are taken from their homes in the dead of night. They are often promised a modeling job or simply selling vegetables to provide for their families, then locked up in a brothel until they die of AIDS (Sarah, 2006).

All over Europe, Trafficking In human beings is affecting peoples' lives. Anywhere between 700,000 to four million people worldwide are estimated to have fallen victim to this practice in recent years. Such a statistic clearly indicates the severity of the problem. Exploitation is not limited to the sex industry. It also occurs in domestic labour, agriculture, construction, and sweatshops. There are endless stories of individual misery and sorrow, while ruthless criminal gangs earn millions of euros from this trade. Insufficient attention is being paid to these new forms of slavery. This is why the Netherlands has decided to make trafficking in human beings one of its main priorities during its OSCE chairmanship. But what can actually be done to tackle this problem?

Types of Human Trafficking

- *Sex Trafficking:* victims are generally found in dire circumstances and easily targeted by traffickers. Individuals, circumstances, and situations vulnerable to traffickers include homeless individuals, runaway teens, displaced home-makers, refugees, and drug adductors. While it may seem like trafficked people are the most vulnerable and powerless minorities in a region, victims are consistently exploited from any ethnic and social background. The fact that sex trafficking is a direct product of poverty is a widely recognized truth by humanitarian organizations, governments and academic researchers. The United States Agency for International Development (USAID) says: "Trafficking is inextricably linked to poverty. Wherever privation and economic hardship prevail, there will be those destitute and desperate enough to enter into the fraudulent employment schemes that are the most common intake systems in the world of traffic. The threat of HIV/AIDS among prostituted women has not slowed down the sex trafficking and prostitution trades, rather it has increased the sex trafficking of younger girls. That is, girls who will be perceived by clients to be 'virgins' and therefore uninfected by the virus are becoming an increasingly popular commodity to trafficking syndicates.

Prostitution and related activities – including pimping and patronizing or maintaining brothels – fuel the growth of modern-day slavery by providing a façade behind which traffickers for sexual exploitation operate. Where prostitution is legalized or tolerated, there is a greater demand for human trafficking victims and nearly always an increase in the number of women and childrent rafficked into commercial sex slavery. Of the estimated 600,000 to 800,000 people trafficked across international borders annually, 80 per cent of victims are female, and up to 50 per cent are minors. Hundreds of thousands of these women and children are used in prostitution each year.

- *Bonded Labour*: or debt bondage, is probably the least known form of labour trafficking today, and yet it is the most widely used method of enslaving people. Victims become bonded labourers when their labour is demanded as a means of repayment for a loan or service in which its terms and conditions have not been defined or in which the value of the victims' services as reasonably assessed is not applied toward the liquidation of the debt. The value of their work is greater than the original sum of money 'borrowed'.
- *Forced Labour:* is a situation in which victims are forced to work against their own will, under the threat of violence or some other form of punishment, their freedom is restricted and a degree of ownership is exerted. Men are at risk of being trafficked for unskilled work, which globally generates $31bn according to the International Labour Organization. Forms of forced labour can include domestic servitude; agricultural labour; factory labour, food service and other service and begging.

Traffickers, also known as pimps or madams, exploit vulnerabilities and lack of opportunities, while offering promises of marriage, employment, education, and/or an overall better life. However, in the end, traffickers force the victims to become prostitutes or work in the sex industry. Various work in the sex industry includes prostitution, dancing in strip clubs, performing in pornographic films and pornography, and other forms of involuntary servitude.

- *Child Labour:* is a form of work that is likely to be hazardous to the health and/or physical, mental, spiritual, moral or social development of children and can interfere with their education. The International Labour Organization estimates worldwide that there are 246 million exploited children aged between 5 and 17 involved in debt bondage, forced recruitment for armed conflict, prostitution, pornography, the illegal drug trade, the illegal arms trade and other illicit activities around the world.

According to a recent survey women are bought and sold with impunity and trafficked at will to other countries from different parts of India. These girls and women are sourced from Dindigal, Madurai, Tiruchirapalli, and Chengalpattu in Tamil Nadu, Gaya, Kishanganj, Patna, Katihar, Purnea, Araria and Madhubani from Bihar, Murshidabad and 24 Parganas in West Bengal, Maharajgunj from UP, Dholpur, Alwar, Tonk from Rajasthan, Mangalore, and Gulbarga and Raichur from Karnataka. These women and girls are supplied to Thailand, Kenya, South Africa and Middle East countries like Bahrin, Dubai, Oman, Britain, South Korea and Philippines.

Trafficking in Children

Trafficking of Children

The adoption process, legal and illegal, when abused can sometimes result in cases of trafficking of babies and pregnant women between the West and the developing world. In David M. Smolin's papers on child trafficking and adoption scandals between India and the United States, he presents the systemic vulnerabilities in the inter-country adoption system that makes adoption scandals predictable. Thousands of children from Asia, Africa, and South America are sold into the global sex trade every year. Often they are kidnapped or orphaned, and sometimes they are actually sold by their own families. In the U.S. Department of Justice 07-08 study, more than 30 per cent of the total number of trafficking cases for that year were children coerced into the sex industry.

General Reasons for Trafficking

Factors conducive to trafficking:

1. Poverty and unemployment.
2. Illiteracy.

3. Feminization of poverty.
4. Migration.
5. Demand on cheap.
6. Unprotected labour and services etc.

Socio-cultural Reasons

1. Acts of violence committed by men against women and other social evils in the family are compelling factors in cases where women ask for a divorce or are forced to leave their homes and manage on their own where there is more chance of being misused by the others.
2. The prevailing widespread acceptance of prostitution and the sex trade must of course be regarded as a symptom of this attitude
3. Other factors that tend to make people dependent and vulnerable are ethnic or social discrimination.
4. Western lifestyles and consumption patterns are paraded in the media and commodity markets.

Legal Reasons

The lack of adequate legislation, properly functioning administrative machinery and an effective judiciary are the most obvious causes of human trafficking in this category.

Affirmative Actions

Law Enforcement and Prevention

International co-operation in the legal field has grown markedly against the trafficking in persons, especially children. There are age old treaties on the issue of trafficking. These include the International Agreement for the suppression of White Slave Traffic (1904), the International convention for the suppression of White Slave Traffic (1910), the International convention for the suppression of traffic in women and children (1921), the International convention for the suppression of Traffic in women in full age (1933) and the convention on the suppression of trafficking and exploitation of the prostitution of others (1949). However, early treaties were not gender sensitive enough and were not broad enough to cover the range of the trafficking situations. A variety of treaties tackles the issue of trafficking with increasing emphasis on a human rights perspective from the angle of protection of the victims. These include:

1. The Convention on the Elimination of All Forms of Discrimination against Women (1979).
2. The Convention on the Rights of the Child (1989).
3. The International Convention on the Protection of Rights of All Migrant Workers and Their Families (1990).
4. The Hague Convention on the Protection of Children and Co-operation in Respect of Inter Country Adoptions (1993).

5. The Inter-nation Labour Organization's Convention No. 182 Concerning the Prohibition and Immediate Action for the Elimination of the Worst Forms of Child Labour (1999).
6. The Optional Protocol to the CRC on the Sale of Children, Child Prostitution and Child Pornography (2000).

Actions taken to combat human trafficking vary from government to government. Some have introduced legislation specifically aimed at making human trafficking illegal. Governments can also develop systems of co-operation between different nations' law enforcement agencies and with non-government organizations (NGOs). Criticisms include failure of governments in not properly identifying and protecting trafficking victims, immigration policies which potentially re-victimize trafficking victims, or insufficient action in helping prevent vulnerable people from becoming trafficking victims. A particular criticism has been the reluctance of some Government to tackle trafficking for purposes other than sex. Another action governments can take is raising awareness of this issue. This can take three forms. *Firstly*, in raising awareness amongst potential victims, particularly in countries where human traffickers are active. *Secondly*, raising awareness amongst police, social welfare workers and immigration officers to equip them to deal appropriately with the problem. UNESCO, UNIFEM, AED like international NGOs are working against human trafficking in Mysore dist., in asocating with various NGOs Koettl, 200).

The central government and state governments continued to demonstrate efforts to combat sex trafficking of women and children, though convictions and punishments of sex traffickers were infrequent according to the report. The central government's National Crime Records Bureau data, compiled from state and union territory governments, on actions taken against sex trafficking offenses in 2007. The 2007 data indicated that 4,087 cases were registered (investigations started) which likely includes sex trafficking cases referred to courts for prosecution as well as cases investigated and closed without such referrals.

The Ministry of Women and Child Development remained the central government's coordinator of anti-trafficking policies and programmes, though its ability to enhance interagency co-ordination and accelerate anti-trafficking efforts across the bureaucracy remained weak. The Ministry of Women and Child Development continued to give grants under its Ujjawala programme for the prevention, rescue, rehabilitation, and reintegration of sex trafficking victims. The ministry approved funding for at least 53 state projects under this programme, benefiting more than 1,700 victims. Since August 2008, the ministry provided the states of Karnataka, Maharashtra, Manipur, and Nagaland almost $243,000 for 18 projects at 12 rehabilitation centres. Andhra Pradesh established a fund specifically for victim rehabilitation, giving victims rescued from sexual exploitation $200 in temporary relief (Nandita, 2008).

Poverty and Human Trafficking

A long-speculated theory in the anti-human trafficking community, poverty's link to international human trafficking patterns was previously supported only by anecdotal evidence. Poverty is a root cause of international human trafficking, according to analysis conducted by the Institute for Trafficked, Exploited and Missing Persons (ITEMP). This conclusive information was released by ITEMP to raise awareness of the link between poverty and modern day slavery in conjunction with Human Trafficking Awareness.

For the first time, ITEMP can statistically demonstrate poverty's connection to international human trafficking. By comparing gross domestic product information with source/destination information provided in the State Department's 2009 Trafficking in Persons report, ITEMP personnel discovered a strong correlation between a country's per capita GDP and their odds of being a source or destination country for international human trafficking.

Not only is blaming poverty alone for human trafficking disheartening, it's also misleading and inaccurate. There may be a correlation between the two phenomena, and poverty almost certainly increases an individual's vulnerability to trafficking, but so many other factors come into play too. To name but 5: the approach taken by law enforcement authorities to the issue; the legislative measures taken by national governments; global gender inequalities; the level of access to education; falling in love with the wrong guy... Most of these things can be shaped and influenced, and it's up to us to do so. What we do know is that poverty drives sex trafficking, and that sex trafficking as the delivery system for prostitution means that each day scores of young, poor women and girls will turn to sex trafficking and prostitution as a means to provide for themselves, and for their families, because they have no other choice. The hope is that funds earmarked for fighting poverty will eventually fight sex trafficking, too, putting an end to this exploitative practice by offering viable economic options for poverty-stricken trafficking (Noor, 2009).

Social Exclusion and Human Trafficking

Social exclusion is a complex and multidimensional concept having social, cultural, political and economic ramifications. These dimensions are interwoven. The relations of social exclusion can be differentiated in quite a few ways. One can talk of systemic or constitutive exclusion which is inbuilt in hierarchical social system. It excludes certain communities from contact and access to social resources through social arrangements, normative value systems and customs. The exclusion based on caste is one example. Patriarchy is another example. Social exclusion not only generates tension, violence and disruption but also perpetuates inequality and deprivation in Society. Overcoming 'exclusion' constitutes the most elementary pre-requisite for the building of a democratic society. Social exclusion refers to lack of participation in society and emphasizes the multi-dimensional, multi-layered, and dynamic nature of the problem. Definitions of the concept emanate from diverse ideological perspectives.

Financial exclusion is one of the major causes leading to peoples becoming victims of trafficking. Faced with few options to help provide for their families these women and children become vulnerable to the sex trade. Often the victims are lured into the trade by the false promise of a job. Evidence suggests that children in need of special protection belong to communities suffering from disadvantage and social exclusion such as scheduled casts and tribes.

Trafficked persons often come from countries and communities marked by poverty and social exclusion. It is important to take into account gender aspects. Women and girls often have less access to education, jobs or social services than men. Gender-based discrimination is not only a problem in patriarchal societies, but also in countries experiencing rapid political, economic and social transition which is due to social exclusion. Traffickers have benefited from situations where women seek a better life abroad, yet lack the means and/or valid documents to travel and work abroad. Similarly, many men are forced to emigrate and sell their labour force. Others agree to sell their organs only to find out that their hope to make money was betrayed (Sanlaap, 1997).

Conclusion

Victims of trafficking can claim for compensation within the civil action or within the criminal proceeding sunder the internal law of Poland. It is also possible to combine a civil claim with criminal proceedings in so called adhesive procedure. Despite of existing legal framework there is still a small number of cases where the trafficked persons received compensation. It is due to the lack of experience and knowledge how to proceed. Even though marvelous efforts have already been made at both national and international levels, the response systems to combat human trafficking are still not adequate for a range of reasons. Many challenges still remain to be addressed in order to close existing gaps and loopholes, such as data collection, legislation, training and capacity building among law enforcement authorities, and better prevention and protection of vulnerable groups at risk of human trafficking. The World Bank Group could contribute to the fight against human trafficking by scaling up its interventions in the following areas.

REFERENCES

Krishnan, Sunita and Jose Verticattil, 2001, A Situation Report: Trafficking for Commercial Sexual Exploitation, India., *Journal of Social Develoopment*, Vol. 3, No. 2.

Koettl, Johannes 2009. "Human Trafficking, Modern Day Slavery, and Economic Exploitation". *Social Protection Discussion Paper*. Washington, DC. The World Bank. Report.

Noor Adam Essack, 2009 View Point: Poverty, Drug Trafficking and Social Exclusion, *Journla of Social Defense,* Vol. 2 No. 5.

Nandita Baruah, 2008, Trafficking in Women and Children In South Asia – A Regional Perspective: *Journal of Exclusion,* Vol. 2 No. 3.

SANLAAP, 1997, A Study on Child Prostitution in West Bengal: The Velvet Blouse, Kolkatta.

Sarah M. Gonzales,2006, Poverty and Sex Trafficking:, Web Article.

Reports

- The Juvenile Justice (Care and Protection of Children) Act, 2000.
- The Immoral Traffic (Prevention) Act, 1956.
- Government of India, 1991, Central Social Welfare Board report on Trafficking, Delhi.
- HAQ, Centre for Child Rights, 2001, Child Trafficking in India.
- ILO and the United Nations Children's Fund (2009). *Training Manual to Fight Trafficking in Children for Labour, Sexual and Other Forms of Exploitation*. Geneva: ILO.
- UNODC (2009). *Global Report on Trafficking in Persons*. Vienna: UNODC. http://www.unodc.org/documents/Global_R eport_on_TIP.pdf

20

Local Self Government and Rural Development in India

— C. S. Chandrika
— Prof. Midatala Rani

ABSTRACT

'People are the real wealth or riches of a nation. A nation that facilitates for the maximum number of people who are happy, is the richest nation ever', quotes Mahatma Gandhi. With India being one of the largest democracies of the world, the process of nation building, with such parameters of richness is indeed challenging. Decentralisation of power is one of the ways that India chose to face such a challenge efficiently and effectively since independence. The essence of such decentralisation of power in India is the 'Local Self Government or the Panchayat Raj System (PRS)'. In the history of PRS, April 24th, 1993 can be considered a remarkable day. The 73rd Amendment of the Constitution was implemented on this day, introducing three tier PRS to give constitutional status to Panchayat Raj Institutions (PRIs). This article sheds administrative techniques in the process of nation building and development works.

Introduction

Panchayaths have been the backbone of the Indian villages since the beginning of record history. Gandhiji the father of the nation, in 1946 had aptly remarked that the Indian Independence must begin at the bottom and every village ought to be a Republic or pachayath having powers. [Jawaharlal Guptha, 2013] The same sentiment was also echoed Jawahjaral Neharu, 'India is poor because the villages of India poor, India will be rich if the villages of India are rich'. Panchayath should be given greater power; for we want the villagers to have a greater measure of real swaraj [self government] in their own. [Ravi Goel, 2012]. Including Ghandhiji and all political thinkers dreams have been transferred into reality by instituting local self government to ensure people's participation in rural development. Local self government is an important instrument of rural development and of promoting and nurturing democracy at the grassroots. Gandhiji asserted that unless panchayaths were invested with adequate powers villages cannot have a real 'Swaraj', article 40 in Para IV of the constitution of India was introduced at Ghandhiji's insistence. The article state that, "the state shall take steps to organize village panchayaths and endow them with such powers authority as may be necessary to enable them to function as units of self government". To achieve the goal of a welfare state. India being a democratic country established local self government system for the overall development of the country, why because local self government have been proclaimed as the vehicles of political transformation in rural India.

Objectives

The main objectives of the article are as follows:

1. To identify the rural development steps which are to be adapted to the villages through local self government.
2. To know the strengthening of local self government as a part of national reconstruction.

Concept of Rural Development

Development is a process of growth in the direction of modernity, especially towards nation – building and socio-economic progress. [Thomos William, Christopher, 2011]. It has many dimensional views, explored by different scholars in different times. The basic purpose of development is to enlarge people's choices. Rural development is not in action plan, however, it is a continuous and ever moving process. Rural development informs a novel society, which has the quality of collection as its primary goal. A village is the focal point of the Government, which holds the responsibility of creating such an atmosphere. However, in this context, it is essential to understand the concept of rural development.

Rural development is a process of studying the social, economical, cultural and political dimensions of grassroots people in a scientific way. Also, comprehending the co-relative reasons for the problems therein and finding suitable solutions for the same. In this context, *Uma Lele* defines, 'Rural development as improving the living standards of the mass of low income population residing in rural areas and making the process of their development self-sustaining'.

Facts of Rural Development

Primarily, the structure of rural development has three dimensions.

1. Rural development, in a way, tries to involve everyone in the process of development.

2. It is a process involving in rural development, by the utilisation of better and scientific and technological tools.
3. Its aim is to implement high standard of living among the rural people.

Apart from the above dimensions, United Nations Economic and Social Commission for Asia and the Pacific (*ESCAP*) defines rural development is:

1. To attract the labour class people to the national main stream activities through economic opportunities.
2. To generate awareness about the creative power in the rural people.
3. To check the rural and urban migration.
4. To promote the participation of rural women and children in all the activities related to rural development.
5. Improving the living conditions of rural life by creating harmony between environment and development.
6. Overall development of all the dimensions of creative power of the immense human resources.

With this background, rural development is exploring the idea that involvement of community in a systematic way towards overall development of the society. However, it is desirable to understand the opinions of Nobel laureate Indian Economist, Amarthya Sen, on human development ideologies, since the focal point of development is the human being.

Sen's theories enrich the ideology of development. During the process of economic development, because of an increase in unemployment and poverty, the process of human development once again became significant and it was propagated that human development and human welfare was the final goal of development. At this juncture, Sen contributed significance to the aim of increasing the human potential. According to him, the primary aim of human welfare was to increase the independent choices with regard to high living conditions, health, awareness, attainment of self-respect and increase the potentialities of the people for the effective participation in the community life. Further, he expressed, the overall social living standards should rather be measured by the net measures of the potentialities of its people, than gross national product and the availability of specific goods. The United Nations Development Programme (UNDP) included this rationale of Sen in its very first, 'Human Development Report' (1990). It has defined development as 'a process of expanding the people's choices' and called for the process of human development to focus on people. That means, it was said that, development should aim for the increase in the potentialities of the people in such a way that they are capable of leading a long and healthy life. Moreover, the propagators of developmental attitudes stated that the human development process should be supported by giving more importance to the quality of development.

It is fact that all these aspects are good indicators to guide the lives of the rural people towards development perspective. However, an effective and systematic implementation of all these plans is essential. The responsibility of the same lies with the local Government. However, the process of rural development facing several obstacles in connection to development of community at large. The implementation of plans is not an easy task in a gigantic nation like India. Many problems arise in the initial stages of the implementation of developmental programmes, because the political system in India, has given importance to power decentralisation. In this system, the plans weaken in the process of reaching down from the Central Government to the State Government.

The process of rural development has weakened in three primary stages of development, which are listed here below:

- Absence of systematic and comprehensive developmental plans.
- Weak and ineffective plans to provide for personal or individual stages of regional necessities.
- The presence of corruption in the implementation of systematic plans – the key factor noted that the primary reason for the rural development to remain unprogressive is due to the lack of punishments to the officers, in the case of delay or failure in the implementation of these plans.

Due to these underlined factors, it is very significant fact that, rural development has become mirage in Indian village square. Thus, the existing local self-government is the solution to carry rural development plans.

Indicators of Rural Development and Local Self Government

Development is not possible without man, as it is a process that should occur continuously because of human effort. If the resources in India are utilised appropriately, development will be an achieved effort, because development does not mean that a nation is poor; instead, it means that a particular nation has not utilised its resources properly. It provides a positive notion that any nation can move towards progress through the partially utilised or unutilised resources, immensely found inside its boundaries.

The local self-government is the key player to achieve the rural development schemes. This type of government is the media to reach individuals and meet their aspirations. Certainly, the 'emergence of advanced India', lays in this ideology.

(i) Role of Local Government in Checking Developmental Imbalances

The imbalances in the development can be seen everywhere in a country like India. As stated above, development indicates 'to increase the opportunities of choices for people'. It is not practically possible to remove all the existing imbalances in the matters like basic facilities and investments for developmental amenities. Moreover, it is essential to have a corruption free plan to remove the disparities in irregular usage and distribution of wealth. This is a continuous process. Very balanced development is still a mirage in the rural areas. It is important to note that even with the achievement of balance with regard to services and facilities, the backwardness in development might still persist based on those parameters of development, from which this achievement is considered. Thus, the constructive and systematic operation strengthens local Government. Hence, more the imbalances in development, the backwardness will be more. It is significant that the Government should maintain balance in the demand and provision of developmental facilities for people. Moreover, the Government should involve in obtaining maximum achievement to remove the poverty co-efficient like diseases, death, infant mortality and other such elements in the lives of people, particularly, below the poverty line.

Mehboob-ul-Haq opines 'the problem of development should be termed as the selective assault on poverty'. For this, the Government should achieve balanced development in agricultural modernization, employment opportunities, health, education, hygiene and level of livelihood along with the improvements in choices for the people. Also, government should take care off the rate of population explosion. For instance, in one perspective, the rate of population explosion is higher in northern parts of Karnataka, compared to that of Southern parts of the State. Thus, the resources utilised in this part, irrespective of its nature, has a negative effect on the rate of development. Quoting fundamental problems, hurdles and poverty related issues in rural areas, which is a cliché in development, Letton Stin observes 'the encouraging elements like income, production, employment, investment are necessary to move from backwardness towards progress. This affirms the attempts for development'. To achieve all this, it is essential for the 'just and rational distribution of plans' in the local bodies.

(ii) Progress with Social Justice

Lawful share is not yet provided in solving the problems of every citizen of India. The process of wealth distribution, which is partial and headed by corruption, has led to dissatisfactory cries among people. Though development is a process undertaken by a nation to improve the level of life of its people, the primary objective of development is to increase the opportunities of choices among people.

The Expert Committee of the United Nations Organization, clarifying its stand on the process of development states that the process of development not only includes the physical needs of a being but also the improvement in the social status of people's life. It has clarified that, development is not just financial development; rather development includes the changes in the social, cultural, statistical and financial areas. Overall, it is the progress of the social system. If any one nation or area is to be developed, it is essential to understand how that area or the Government therein has involved itself in this process. Therefore, sub administrative unit of the Government is primarily responsible for development.

Even though rural development has gained the top spot in this view, the real fact is that it is not able to respond to all the stimulations rising out of various projects. Moreover, anyone, without the aid of any statistical data can comprehend the level of poverty in the rural areas. Thus, it is essential that the local government should increase the grant being released in this context. In Indian context, the Universal Development Programme should become a revolution of people. People should prepare their own project and participate in the same. Along with these, it is also essential to achieve the development of the backward and minority classes of the society.

(iii) Administrative Potentiality

For achieving the administrative potential, it is essential that the staff of the local governments is well educated and well trained. Moreover, the administrative potential is dependent on human resources and the methods of maintaining the same. In addition, developmental administration is essential to increase the administrative potential. According to the dictionary of Public Administration, in order to increase, improve the administrative potential, techniques, actions and methods have to be drafted. Local Government should improve the efficiency and effectiveness of the governing body. The results should be fruitful with the implementation of the developmental administration.

(iv) Right to Information and Transparency

Transparency in the Village, Taluk and District level administration is very essential to check the misuse of funds. The information regarding the grants released for every Village/Gram Panchayat, Guidelines of the Plan etc., should be available to all the people including those below the poverty line. Right to Information is the 'Right' in which every citizen to obtain information regarding all the activities of the Government. Accountability of the Government is one of the significant factors that gains attention to community development. There should be transparency regarding all the activities of the Government. If do not have the right to obtain essential and honest information regarding the matter on which people express their opinion, then the Right to Freedom of Speech and Expression becomes meaningless. Hence, the Right to Information is embedded in the Freedom of Speech, and the participation of people in administration becomes meaningful only when complete information regarding a particular issue is provided to them.

In the modern democracy, the term accountability has an expansive meaning. Accountability of the government does not mean that the government is accountable only to the policies implemented. The nature of its operations is also a part of accountability. Such accountability is possible only with the availability of information. Openness and transparency regarding the operations of public institutes is essential for clean administration. Due to this cause, it is properly said, 'sunlight is the best treatment for allergies'. The practical usage of Right to Information makes the administration more accountable for people. This aids in rational and constructive criticisms regarding the administration. Thus, it limits the extent of corruption and ultimately highlights the morals of democracy. Based on these experiments, the Government of India introduced Right to Information Act in 2005.

(v) Role of Civil Society

'Civil Society' is a term that extensively used politically, administratively and ethically in recent times. The primary aim of government formation is the good being of the civilians. In the arena of the civil society, a person can fulfill his desires, develop his personality, attain social unity and his progress and comprehend the importance of dependence on others. All these factors prepare a person to participate in the field of politics. In this context, the participation of people is essential for the success of the local Government. As this people-centered government is based on the philosophy of people's autonomy and the central focus of the power is people themselves. Hence, the local government administration is ultimately the responsibility of the people themselves. This system converts the representative democracy into cooperative democracy. This is a contribution towards transparency in administration.

Conclusion

The local government will 'direct the rights and duties of the local authorities and the natural and voluntary participation of the local citizens under Panchayat Raj Act 1993. Such a system has identified itself as a magnificent political institute. The local government has specified the conformity of citizenship to the people. Local administrative bodies are the weapons used against poverty. This system should take up effective operations for the betterment of health and security of the people. To connect this, World Health Organization has instructed the governments to take up stringent measures concerning health, hygiene, environmental changes, global temperature and other serious issues. Moreover, local governments need to achieve overall development by giving primary importance to the proper utilisation of resources. In India, the local bodies are the bottom level organizations and explore techniques of administrative maintenance. In the backlight of all such issues, the developmental works local government operations have provided commendable results.

REFERENCES

Durga Das Basu, 2011, 'Introduction to the Constitution of India' – Wadhwa Publication.

Goel Ravi, 2012 'Local Self Government' – New Delhi; Sonali Publication.

Geoege Mathew. 2002, 'Panchayath Raj: From Legislation to Movement. Concept' – New Delhi; Concept Publishing Company.

Jawarlal Gupta, 2013, 'Panchayath Raj and Rural Development' – Wisdom Publication.

Khan M Adhil, 2007, 'Rural Reconstruction' – New Delhi; Anmol Publication.

Kanna. B.S. 1991, 'Rural Development in South Asia' – New Delhi; Deepa and Deepa Publication.

Kanna. B.S. 1994, 'Panchayath Raj in India. Rural Local Self Government' – New Delhi; Deepa and Deepa Publication.

Krishnamurthy. H. R., Virappa Gowda, 2011, 'Development Economics' Sapna Publishing.

Mishra. S.N., 1996, 'Panchayat Raj in Action' – New Delhi; Mittal Publication.

William. A.T., A.J. Christopher, 2011 'Rural Development – Concept and Recent Approaches' – New Delhi; Rawath Publication.

Reports

1. Decentralisation and Local Democracy in the World – 2008 First Global Report – A Co – Publication of the World Bank and United Cities and Local Governments.
2. Karnataka Human Development Report – 2008.
3. Indian Rural Development Report – 1999.
4. Nanjudappa committee Report – 2002.

21

Impact of Corruption on Rural India and Role of E-Governance in Prevention of Corruption

— RANGASWAMY D
— RAMESH

The impact of corruption on the poor and on poverty reduction processes has now been reasonably and widely debate issue in India. The effect of corruption on the poor can be gauged through both its direct impact (through, for example, increasing the cost of public services, lowering their quality and often all together restricting poor people's access to such essential services as water, health and education) and the indirect impact (through, for example, diverting public resources away from social sectors and the poor, and through limiting development, growth and poverty reduction).

The State and Central governments have moved quickly into various anticorruption measures against this menace. Millions of Rupees has been spent to address these issues year after year in India with little impact and the gravity of corruption and its clutch over India as well as the world is very high.[1] Various tools and techniques have been evolved against this social evil, yet the magnitude of corruption is continuously increasing.

Amongst many tools being developed to fight against corruption, lately there has been much focus on E-Government by using Information and Communication Technology (ICT) to open up Government process and enable greater public access to information.[2] In this paper, I have made a prompt attempt to explore the current developments regarding E-Government and best practices in the Government for the implementation of Information and Communication Technologies in combating corruption. This paper also examines the relevance and recent evolution of e-governance in government services and promoting strategies of organizations and inhabitants in the fight against corruption.

Keywords: E-Governance, Rural India, Corruption.

Introduction

India is a big democratic Country. It is well known for its Constitutional text. The Social economic and political justice enshrined under the Constitution is the basic structure of the Indian Constitution.[3]

In order to achieve this noble goal, the Constitution has clearly articulated ways and means. Various policies and programmes have been designed with the aim of achieving these noble goals which has been one of the primary objectives of planned development in India. Special attention has been paid by the Government in order to provide the rural people with better prospects for economic development, social transformation, increased participation in administration, better enforcement of land reforms and greater access to credit.

But the fact is that the 20th century democracy meets new challenges while fulfilling these Constitutional goals and expectation of rural India. One of such challenges is society's increasing demand for more qualitative and efficient work of democratic institutions.[4] Corruption is a very complex phenomenon which is shaking the basis of working of democratic institutions in achieving the Constitutional goal. The State and Central governments have moved quickly into various anticorruption measures against this menace. E-Governance or using of Information and Communication Technology in administration is innovative and recent one among them.

Conceptual Analysis

There is no universal definition for the concept of Corruption. There is ambiguity and controversy on defining and understanding the concept of corruption which result in a number of competing approaches to define and understanding the corruption. Definitions of corruption focus on one of several aspects of the phenomenon. Various approaches to corruption can be placed into five groups. These are public-interest-centerd, market-centerd, public-office-centered, public-opinion-centered and legalistic.

Proponents of the public-interest-centered approach believe that corruption is in some way injurious to or destructive of public interest.[5] Market-centered enthusiasts suggest that norms governing public office have shifted from a mandatory pricing model to a free-market model, thereby considerably changing the nature of corruption.[6] Public-office-centered protagonists stress the fact that misuse by incumbents of public office for private gain is corruption.[7] Those who believe in public-opinion-centered definitions of corruption emphasize the perspectives of public opinion about the conduct of politicians, government and probity of public servants.[8] Others have suggested looking at corruption purely in terms of legal criteria in view of the problems inherent in determining rules and norms which govern public interest, behaviour and authority.[9]

Nye has proposed the most frequently employed one, draw in upon formal-legal norms for identifying abuse: "Corruption is behaviour which deviates from the formal duties of a public role (elective or appointive) because of private-regarding (personal, close family, private clique) wealth or status gains: or (which) violates rules against the exercise of certain types of private-regarding influence".[10] By analyzing various definitions of corruption and exiting literature on corruption, by the Corruption we can say that it is the use of public position for private gain.

Although the term 'E-Governance' has gained currency in recent years, there is no standard definition of this term. Different governments and organizations define this term to suit their own aims and objectives.

According to the World Bank

'E-Government' refers to the use by government agencies of information technologies such as Wide Area Networks, the internet, and mobile computing that have the ability to transform relations with citizens, businesses, and other arms of government. These technologies can serve a variety of different ends: better delivery of government services to citizens, improved interactions with business and industry, citizen empowerment through access to information, or more efficient government management. The resulting benefits can be less corruption, increased transparency, greater convenience, revenue growth, and/or cost reductions.[11]

According to UNESCO

"Governance refers to the exercise of political, economic and administrative authority in the management of a country's affairs, including citizens' articulation of their interests and exercise of their legal rights and obligations. E-Governance may be understood as the performance of this governance via the electronic medium in order to facilitate an efficient, speedy and transparent process of disseminating information to the public, and other agencies, and for performing government administration activities."[12]

According to Council of Europe

The Council of Europe has taken e-Governance to mean: "the use of electronic technologies in three areas of public action:

1. Relations between the public authorities and civil society.
2. Functioning of the public authorities at all stages of the democratic process (electronic democracy).
3. The provision of public services (electronic public services)".[13]

The common theme behind all these definitions is that E-Governance or Electronic Governance involves the use of Information and Communication Technologies in public administration combined with organizational change and new skills in order to improve public services and democratic processes and strengthen support to public policies. It aims to enhance access to and delivery of government services to benefit of citizens and strengthen the Governments drive toward effective Governance and increased transparency and accountability in management of country's social and economic resources for overall development of the nation.

Impact of Corruption on Rural India

India is a developing nation with rapid population growth and modernization, India is experiencing drastic problems in the areas of education, health, unemployment, and law and order. The vast majority of India's population remains illiterate and impoverished. In order to address these problems, stable governmental and committed institutions must be formed and maintained. All efforts to do so are reliant on the transparency of these institutions. Unfortunately, the corruption is rapidly increasing in the Governmental activities and institutional functioning.

Practice of corruption and existence of corrupt official in the society is undemocratic culture. It is menace to the democratic form of governance. It is a serious threat for the proper functioning of the government and implementation of laws. Social services like free and compulsory education, grant of scholarship and strengthen the condition of health, sanitation, water supply and housing are also expected to play major role in ensuring greater equalities of opportunities to different section of the population and greater mobility.

Entry of corruption in to these basic services is serious obstacle for foundation of democracy and certainly it leads the state towards disrepute and disregard. In a civilized society corruption is a disease like cancer, which if not detected in time, sure, the polity of country will lead to disastrous consequences. Unlike new emphasis on social sector there is still lack of efforts and want of sufficient resource in reforming and strengthening of transparency and accountability in India.

- *Health:* In spite of spending significant per cent of the state budget on health, the poor have benefited very little because of this cancerous corruption. The pathetic condition is that the Doctors and medicines are not available in government hospital and Primary Health Centres (PHCs) on which there is large dependence of the poor for health service. They have to pay bribe at various stages starting from entry into hospital to their discharge. Corruption is playing pivotal role in allowing substandard medicines to market, non control of essential drugs, issuing license to the manufacturer. Those who are paying bribes are getting royal treatments by the authorities in the hospital, and those refusing to bribe are being harassed. Ultimately and unfortunately beneficiaries of all these activities are last man of the main stream who targeted by the Constitution for the promotion of health and wealth of these people.

- *Education:* "Corruption is the major drain on the effective use of resources and should be drastically curbed".[14] A cursory review of the literature shows that there are very few documents available dealing in comprehensive and systematic with the various aspects of the corruption that exist in the field of education. Yet it is clear that the fight against corruption in the specific sphere of education should be regarded as major issue as it affects not only the volume of the services, including their efficiency, equity in education and public confidence in educational system.[15] High rate of teacher absenteeism, private tutoring practices, cheating in examinations, these are various facets of corruption in education which highly affecting the concept of social justice in India.[16]
- *Housing:* Despite the allocation of considerable funds by central and state governments, the housing problem for poor is deteriorating in India for the number of reasons. Among such miserable reasons corruption is one which prime cause beyond the housing problems in India. According to Abraham George, the founder of George foundation, an NGO focused on poverty alleviation in south India, "The adequate housing is integral part to poverty reduction and social justice". Even though government has introduced so many programmes for allotment of plats and loan for construction of the houses, most poor people do not have the ability to apply for these benefits without assistance of the middle man or the intervention of government officials. Such intervention is expensive for beneficiary because it invites kickbacks, commissions and bribes.
- *Poverty:* One more intensive crisis which India facing in accessing social justice is poverty. It indicates the condition of a person in which a person is fails to maintain living standards adequate for his physical and mental efficiency. Statistics clearly indicates that the number of poverty alleviation programmes have been launched by governments. On the other hand index of development categorically shows the deep fallen of such programmes in execution. The reason for the existence of this situation in India is that, at every level of alleviation programmes, corruption interfering and diverting Government funds to the pocket of corrupt officials and thereby it is reducing the per capita income of the individual.

Funds coming in the name of poverty alleviation are swallowed by people in the administration. For example the much-touted Orissa Tribal Development Project (OTDP)[17] at the starvation-prone Kashipur blocks is the best instance for such programme. The union government had given nearly Rs. 60 crore brought from international fund for agriculture development exclusively to the block for all round development of the tribals over a period of nine years from 1998-97.

But at the end of the project, it has been discovered that the number of families living below poverty line (BPL) in the block has increased from 15,471 in 1992 to 24,582 by 1997. How did it happen? The reason is simple, as elaborated in an official inquiry report. "The project has created a large number of contractors and suppliers who have made easy money without doing any work and have become a powerful group of vested interests. No significant intervention in terms of increase in income and sustainable agricultural productivity has been achieved" the report by Dr. Hrushikesh Panda, former KBK (Koraput, Balangir, Kalahandi) deputy Chief Administrator, said. There is no trace of a single plant claimed to have been planted under the programme. Payments were made against non-existent works, while roads were built from 'no where to no where'.

- *NREGA:* As the Central Government gears up to implement NREGA across all the districts in the country, instances of corruption and irregularities in implementing the scheme are tumbling out. The projects of the NREGA are feeding well to the sarpanch, middlemen and concerned block level officials. Though the wage seekers are not getting 100 days of work in a year, the sarpanch gets more than hundred days of work every day and those who never work in any project, find their place in the list of the unskilled labourers who have been provided 100 days employment in a financial year.

A government-sponsored study on NREGA has found large-scale corruption and irregularities in the implementation of the programme in several states with authorities in some areas 'misappropriating' central funds and 'threatening' workers to keep their mouth shut. The study has found that in many cases, workers performed one day's job but their attendance was put for 33 days.

Information Technology and Prevention of Corruption

Bhoomi (Land Records)

It is a self sustainable E-governance project for the computerized delivery of 20 million rural land records to the 6.7 million farmers through 177 government owned kiosks in the State of Karnataka. Boomi has reduced the arbitrariness of public officials by introducing provisions for recording a mutation request online. Farmers can now access the data base and are empowered to follow up.[18]

Survey conducted by Public Affairs Centre Bangalore in July 2002, quoted by World Bank[19], Bhatnagar *et al.*,[20] and UNDP[21] disclose that 79 per cent users found availing services under Bhoomi through kiosks operators to be simple; 74 per cent could get error free records and 93 per cent of detected errors could be rectified instantly; 72 per cent got records in very first visit, only 3 per cent had to pay bribes as against 66 per cent earlier and average bribe per user reduced from Rs. 152.46 earlier to Rs. 3.09.

E-Governance of Stamp and Registration in Maharashtra

The Department of Registration and Stamps has a vast expanse in the state of Maharashtra and is the 2nd highest revenue earning department of the state, has 412 offices managed by 2500 employees.

In a bold IT initiative taken by the department, all the 360 sub registrar offices, 31 district level offices, 9 division levels and the Head Quarter at Pune have been computerised and automated. The project is called SARITA (Stamps and Registration Information Technology based Administration) which encompasses the entire state of Maharashtra and is operational since January 2001. Till date close to 2.2 million documents have been registered across the state and revenue handled is Rs. 5000 crores. Approximately 8 million people are direct beneficiaries of SARITA betterment of quality of service given to millions.

Quoting report of Caseley's survey in 2005, World Bank[22] confirms significant reduction in corruption in registration of documents in Maharashtra – 93.5 per cent respondents did not pay 'extra' fees, only six per cent had paid the bribes. Cent per cent respondents claimed that registration was done within 30 days and most of them did not take help of any tout, showing a significant turnaround from corrupt practices.

Gujarat Computerised Interstate Check Posts (CICP)

In late 1999, to improve the situation at check posts, the transport department of Gujarat redesigned the processes at its check posts. Large yards were created at the check posts and processes of inspection and estimation were mechanized by deploying electronic weighbridges, video cameras and computers. Such modernized check posts called the Computerized Interstate Check Posts (CICP) were created at all the 10-interstate sites. This technology is expected to plug the leakage and significantly increase revenues from the check post for the state government.

Referring to earlier survey of Indian Institute of Management, Ahmadabad (IIMA) and its own study in February 2005, World Bank[23] mentions that this project has experienced bumpy road map. Initially introduction of new procedures and technology led to increased revenue but with the transfer of reform champion and quick successive changes of four transport commissioners within 18 months, check post inspectors *i.e.* Corruption entrepreneurs got opportunity to subvert the system on the pretext of machines not working properly and old practices of corruption unravelled. However, the State could ill-afford the huge loss in revenue the reform had shown and therefore, the new stable leadership subsequently rectified the subversion. Report quotes that the revenue increased from Rs. 56 crore in 1998-99 to Rs. 291 crore in 2003-04.

E-Governance in Hyderabad Metropolitan Water Supply and Sewage Board (HMWSSB)

The E-Governance experiment in Andhra Pradesh is a bold attempt to use Information and Communications Technologies (ICT) to improve governance processes. The experiment is motivated by the desire to transform the state as captured by the vision statement.

Since inception in 1998, Hyderabad Metropolitan Water Supply and Sewage Board has been the model of back end 'E-readiness' in the Government of Andhra Pradesh. With the active support of Government and media, reform champion took various bold steps in improving service delivery. This included setting up of Single Window Cell (SWC) to receive applications for new water/sewage connections and process them in a time-bound manner(against earlier system wherein customer 'chases no objections' with 14 offices, each being potential corruption points), providing 24x7 telephone helpline called Metro Customer Care (MCC) for receiving complaints and coordinating expeditious actions, launching Customer Redressal Efficiency System(CRES) software for monitoring performance data against laid down standards under Citizens Charter and therefore, holding frontline and middle level accountable for service quality and compliance.

Davis J[24] estimates that these measures decreased payment of average bribe of US$22 earlier to US$ one, which is not bribe but token of appreciation. Caseley J[25] concludes that the initiative succeeded in curbing corruption by triangulating accountability relationship between citizens, senior managers and frontline workers. Studies have shown the significant improvement in transparency and accountability, media participation and substantial reduction in discretionary powers of board employees, which led to reduction in corruption.[26]

Suggestive Conclusion

Corruption is an intractable problem. It is like diabetes, can only be controlled, but not totally eliminated. It may not be possible to root out corruption completely at all levels but it is possible to control it within tolerable limits. Honest and dedicated persons in public life, control over electoral expenses could be the most important prescriptions to combat corruption. Corruption has a corrosive impact on our rural India. It worsens programmes and policies of the Government in achieving the Constitutional goals and degrades our image in international arena.

Institutional and legal frame work for addressing the problem of corruption in India is well developed. However according to Transparency International and Global Integrity, institutional setup is suffering from lack of coordination between the different actors and efficiency is often reducing due to conflicting mandates.

Under these circumstances it is very expedient that E-Governance can boost the strength of anticorruption techniques in India. There is a serious lack of awareness among the lower classes of society regarding technological growth in the area of E-Governance. This ignorance would result in not reaping the optimum benefits expected in combating corruption through E-Technology. There is a need for government and other nongovernmental organizations to take up the task of spreading the knowledge regarding E-governance projects in the villages. Moreover, without participation of citizens, e-governance projects are not likely to be successful. Public participation in both policy making and governmental decisions by using technology is continuously missing in India. Government need to take cautious steps to ensure better reach and access to information to the society, otherwise disparities in access will only increase problems of corruption in spite of existence of e-governance.

FOOTNOTES

1. Recently Article 21 of the Indian Constitution has been interpreted to incorporate the right to health in right to life and hence this right having now acquired a constitutional status through judicial activism. Article 21 of the constitution guarantees right to life and this court has interpreted the guarantee to cover a life with normal amenities assuring good living which include medical attention, life free from diseases and longitivity up to normal expectations" (Supra no. 20). It is also "...the constitutional obligation of the state to provide adequate medical services to the people. Whatever is necessary for this purpose has to be done (AIR 1996 SC 2426).
2. When the study was conducted, the West Bengal was led by the left government under the leadership of Buddhadeb Bhattacharya. The CPI (M) was defeated in the year 2011 Assembly Elections by the Trinamool Congress.
3. Anti Retro Viral Therapy is the life saving medicine for AIDS patients. When an infected body starts showing symptoms, ART medicine becomes a part of the daily life of people.
4. However, with the persistent effort of the Kolkata Network of Positive people, these two district hospitals only recently have started treating HIV positive people.
5. The state government has recently proposed to set up one more ART centre in Siliguri.
6. Particularly in a society like in India where majority of the infection is led through heterosexuality contact.
7. In Kolkata, a hospital refused to touch the body of a young AIDS patient who died later. In Indore, a pregnant woman died outside a government hospital without treatment. In Lucknow, a renal failure patient (HIV positive) had to wait for 16 hours before activists could get him a hospital bed (The Times of India, 2007).
8. The state of Karnataka as well as West Bengal have succeeded in co-opting a few dedicated and responsible counsellors for providing proper counselling to HIV positive people.

REFERENCES

1. "India's Rural Poor: Why Housing Isn't Enough to Create Sustainable Communities – WSJ.com". Business News and Financial News – *The Wall Street Journal* – WSJ.com http://online.wsj.com/article/SB12469771466980 6043.html, retrieved on 30th December 2010.
2. Bhagava, Vinay, "Curing the Cancer of Corruption". Global Issues for Global Citizens, Washington DC: *The World Bank*, 2006. pp. 341-370.
3. Bhatnagar and R Chawla, "Online Delivery of Land Titles to Rural Farmers in Karnataka, India", A Case Study Presented in Scaling up Poverty Reduction: A Global Learning Process and Conference Held in Shanghai on May 25-27, 2004.
4. Caseley J "Public Sector Reform and Corruption: CARD Facade in Andhra Pradesh", Economic and Political Weekly, 13th March 2004.
5. Caseley J, "Multiple Accountability Relationships and Improved Service Delivery Performance in Hyderabad City, South India", *International Review of Administrative Sciences*, Vol. 72, No. 4, 2006.
6. Caseley J, "Multiple Accountability Relationships and Improved Service Delivery Performance in Hyderabad City, South India", *International Review of Administrative Sciences*, Vol. 72, No. 4, 2006.
7. Eigen, Peter. "Message from Transparency International". Corruption and Integrity Improvement Initiatives in Developing Countries. Paris: United Nations Development Programme, 1998, pp. 1-4.
8. French, Hilary. "Reshaping Global Governance", in Linda Starke (ed.), State of the World 2002: A World watch Institute Report on Progress toward a Sustainable Society, New York: W. W. Norton, 2002. pp. 174-98.
9. Joseph S. Nye, "Corruption and Political Development: A Cost-Benefit Analysis", *American Political Science Review* 61 (June 1967).
10. Kersly R H, Brooms Legal Maxims, 10th Edition, Universal Book Traders New Delhi, 1993.
11. Kurer, Oskar. "Why Do Voters Support Corrupt Politicians", in Arvind K. Jain, (ed.) *The Political Economy of Corruption*. London: Routledge, 2001. p. 63-86.
12. Leys, C. "What is the Problem about Corruption?" in A.J. Heidenheimer (ed.), *Political Corruption: Readings in Comparative Perspective*, New York: Holt, Rinehart and Winston, 1970.
13. Mehra, Malini. "India Starts to Take on Climate Change", State of the World 2009: A Worldwatch Institute Report on Progress Toward A Sustainable Society. (ed.), Linda Starke. New York: W. W. Norton, 2009. pp. 80-84.
14. Midathala Rani, "E-Governance initiatives in Karnataka", *Journal of the Indian Association of Social Science Institution*, (IASSI), Vol. 26, July-Sep 2007.
15. Rogow, A.A. and H.D. Laswell, "The Definition of Corruption" in A.J. Heidenheimer (ed.), Political Corruption: Readings in Comparative Analysis, New York: Holt, Rinehart and Winstan, 1970.
16. Scott, J. C. Comparative Political Corruptio,. Englewood Cliffs, N.J. Princeton Hall, Inc., 1972.

17. Theobald, R., Corruption Development and Underdevelopment, London: Macmillan, 1990.
18. Tilman, R.O. "Black Market Bureaucracy" in A.J. Heidenheimer (ed.) *Political Corruption: Readings in Comparative Analysis*, New York: Holt, Renehart and Winston, 1970.
19. UNDP, E-Governance, Essentials, No. 15, April 2004.
20. World Bank, Reforming Public Services in India: Drawing Lessons from Success, New Delhi, Sage Publications India, 2006.

Index

U

V

W

Y

Z